D1571371

LIVING IN MY
FAMILY

A Series of Distinctively Christian Support-Group Curriculum Guides

Making Wise Choices
Facing My Feelings
Living in My Family
Growing Through Changes

Illustrations by Jared D. Lee Studio, Inc.
Cover design by Barry Ridge Graphic Design
Photography and art direction by Coleen Davis
Text designed and edited by SETTINGPACE
Project direction by Linda Ford

The Standard Publishing Company, Cincinnati, Ohio
A division of Standex International Corporation
Text © 1997 by Linda Kondracki Sibley
Illustrations © 1997 by The Standard Publishing Company
All rights reserved
Printed in the United States of America

04   03   02   01   00   99   98   97   5   4   3   2   1

ISBN 0-7847-0642-5

LIVING IN MY
FAMILY

by Linda Kondracki Sibley

STANDARD PUBLISHING
Cincinnati, Ohio

Guidelines for Using Reproducible Pages

You may make copies of the sessions, activity pages, and forms in this book for your Confident Kids ministry. Please observe the following guidelines:

- Authorized copies may be made by the original purchaser or by someone in the same Confident Kids organization.

- Copies must be used for a noncommercial purpose within your Confident Kids program or to promote your Confident Kids program.

- It is illegal for you to make copies for other ministry programs or for Confident Kids programs in other ministries or churches.

- If you or your organization is not the original purchaser of this material, it is illegal for you to copy these Confident Kids materials.

These guidelines allow you to provide copies of all materials needed by the staff of your Confident Kids program while protecting copyrights for both author and publisher.

The Standard Publishing Company continues its commitment to offering reproducible products at affordable prices.

Living in My Family

Topic Overview xix

Getting Started 1

About Confident Kids 3

Why a Support Group for Children? 3
What Is Confident Kids? 3
What's in This Manual? 4
Can I Use This Series in Settings Other Than a Support Group? 4
Understanding How Confident Kids Works 4
Limitations of Confident Kids 5

How to Start a Confident Kids Program 7

Step #1: Build a Strong Foundation 7
Step #2: Recruit Families and Set Up the Groups 11
Step #3: Wrap Up the Unit 12

Using the Session Plans 13

Kids Sessions 13
Parent Sessions 15

Welcome to Confident Kids! 19

    Outline 21
    Opening 22
    Getting Acquainted 23
    Bible Time 25
    Snacks 25
    Family Shield Activity 26

Preschool Sessions 27

**Tips for Working with Preschoolers
in a Support-Group Setting** 28

Preschool Session 1: All About My Family 31

    Session Plan 31
    Opening Play Centers 32
    Circle Time 32
    Small Groups 33
    Bible Time and Closing Prayer Huddle 34
    Snack and Quiet Games/Stories 35
    Circle Time Skit: "I Want a Different Family!" . . 36
    Bible Story Skit: "Introducing Adam and Eve" 37
    My Family Is Special 38

Preschool Session 2: What's a Family For, Anyway? 39

    Session Plan 39
    Opening Play Centers 40
    Circle Time 41
    Small Groups 41
    Bible Time and Closing Prayer Huddle 42

Snack and Quiet Games/Stories 42
Circle Time Skit: "The Runaway" 43
Bible Story Skit: "Adam Isn't Lonely Anymore" 45

Preschool Session 3: Changes Can Upset My Family 47

Session Plan 47
Opening Play Centers 48
Circle Time 48
Small Groups 49
Bible Time and Closing Prayer Huddle 49
Snack and Quiet Games/Stories 50
Circle Time Skit: "The New Baby" 51
Bible Story Skit: "Adam and Eve Make a Big Change" 52
Sometimes I Feel Sad or Mad or Lonely 53

Preschool Session 4: Actions Can Hurt—Or Help—My Family . . . 55

Session Plan 55
Opening Play Centers 56
Circle Time 56
Small Groups 57
Bible Time and Closing Prayer Huddle 58
Snack and Quiet Games/Stories 58
Circle Time Skit: "The Cereal Bowl" 59
Bible Story Skit: "Adam and Eve Have a New Baby!" 61

Preschool Session 5: Words Can Hurt—Or Help—My Family . . . 63

Session Plan 63
Opening Play Centers 64
Circle Time 64
Small Groups 65
Bible Time and Closing Prayer Huddle 66
Snack and Quiet Games/Stories 66
Circle Time Skit: "Sticks and Stones" 67

Bible Story Skit: "Eve Learns to Say Words That Help" 68
Words Can Help; Words Can Hurt 69

Preschool Session 6: "I Care About You!" 71

Session Plan 71
Opening Play Centers 72
Circle Time 72
Small Groups 73
Bible Time and Closing Prayer Huddle 73
Snack and Quiet Games/Stories 74
Circle Time Skit: "The Affirmation" 75
Bible Story Skit: "Adam and Eve Learn to Affirm" 76
Affirmation Cards 78

Preschool Session 7: I Can Belong to God's Family, Too 79

Session Plan 79
Opening Play Centers 80
Circle Time 80
Small Groups 81
Bible Time and Closing Prayer Huddle 81
Snack and Quiet Games/Stories 82
Note 82
Circle Time Skit: "Coming to Jesus" 83
Bible Story Skit: "Adam and Eve Tell a Story" 85
Family Night Invitation 87
Coming to Jesus Coloring Sheet 88

Elementary Sessions 89

Tips for Working With Elementary Kids in a Support-Group Setting   90

Elementary Session 1: There Are No Perfect Families! 93

Outline 93
Opening 94
Small Groups 95
Bible Time 96
Snack 97
Opening Skit: "What's Wrong With My Family?" 98
Bible Story Skit: "Introducing the First Family" 99
Family Mobile 101

Elementary Session 2: What's a Family For, Anyway? 103

Outline 103
Opening 104
Small Groups 105
Bible Time 106
Snack 106
Opening Skit: "The Runaway" 107
Bible Story Skit: "Adam Isn't Lonely Anymore!" 109

Elementary Session 3: Changes Can Upset My Family 111

Outline 111
Opening 112
Small Groups 112
Bible Time 114
Snack 114
Opening Skit: "The Divorce" 115
Bible Story Skit: "A Big Change for Adam and Eve" 117
Humpty Dumpty 119

Elementary Session 4: Actions Can Help—Or Hurt—My Family . . . **123**

Outline 123
Opening 124
Small Groups 125
Bible Time 126
Snack 126
Opening Skit: "The Cereal Bowl" 127
Bible Story Skit: "Adam and Eve Have a Baby" 129
Actions Cards 131
Feelings Cards 132

Elementary Session 5: Words Can Help—Or Hurt—My Family **133**

Outline 133
Opening 134
Small Groups 135
Bible Time 137
Snack 137
Opening Skit: "Sticks and Stones" 138
Bible Story Skit: "Eve Learns to Use Words That Help" 139
Talking Together in My Family 141

Elementary Session 6: "I Care About You!" **143**

Outline 143
Opening 144
Small Groups 145
Bible Time 146
Snack 146
Opening Skit: "The Conference" 147
Bible Story Skit: "Adam and Eve Learn to Affirm" 150
Affirmation Badges 152

Elementary Session 7: I Can Belong to God's Family, Too! 153

Outline 153
Opening 154
Small Groups 154
Bible Time 156
Snack 156
Opening Skit: "The New Family" 157
Bible Story Skit: "Adam and Eve Present
                'The Parable of the Lost Son'" 159
The Parable of the Lost Son 161
Family Night Invitation 163
Adoption Invitation 164

Preteen Sessions 167

Tips for Working With Preteens
in a Support-Group Setting 168

Preteen Session 1: There Are No Perfect Families! . . 171

Outline 171
Opening 172
Small Groups 173
Bible Focus 174
Snack 175
Focus on Session Theme Skit: "That's It! I'm Moving to
                Joe's House!" 176
Bible Focus Skit: "Lifestyles of the Biblically Famous!—I" . . . 177

Preteen Session 2: What's a Family For, Anyway? 179

Outline 179
Opening 180
Small Groups 181
Bible Focus 182
Snack 182
Bible Focus Skit: "Lifestyles of the Biblically Famous!"—II . . . 183
Family Introductions 185
Finish This Sentence 186

Preteen Session 3: Changes Can Upset My Family 187

Outline 187
Opening 188
Small Groups 189
Bible Focus 190
Snack 191
Focus on Session Theme Skit: "The Divorce" 192
Bible Focus Skit: "Lifestyles of the Biblically Famous!"—III . . . 194
Handling Changes in My Family 197

Preteen Session 4: Actions Can Help—Or Hurt—My Family. 199

Outline 199
Opening 200
Small Groups 201
Bible Focus 202
Snack 202
Bible Focus Skit: "Life in My Family"—Mini-Skit I 203
Bible Focus Skit: "Life in My Family"—Mini-Skit II 205
Bible Focus Skit: "Lifestyles of the Biblically Famous!"—IV . . . 208
Actions and Feelings in My Family 211
My Growth Goal 212

Preteen Session 5: Words Can Help—Or Hurt—My Family . . 213

Outline 213
Opening 214
Small Groups 215
Bible Focus 216
Snack 217
Focus on Session Theme Skit: "Talking Together in
My Family" Scenarios 218
Bible Focus Skit: "Lifestyles of the Biblically Famous!"—V . . . 222
"Can We Talk?" 224

Preteen Session 6: "I Care About You!" 225

Outline 225
Opening 226
Small Groups 227
Bible Focus 228
Snack 228
Focus on Session Theme Skit: "When I Grow Up" 229
Bible Focus Skit: "Lifestyles of the Biblically Famous!"—VI . . . 231
Create-a-Family 233
What a Family! 236

Preteen Session 7: I Can Belong to God's Family, Too . . . 237

Outline 237
Opening 238
Small Groups 239
Bible Focus 240
Snack 241
Focus on Session Theme Skit: "The New Family" 242
Family Night Invitation 244
Agree/Disagree Cards 245

Prayer Scroll 246
The Parable of the Lost Son 247

PARENT SESSIONS 249

TIPS FOR WORKING WITH PARENTS IN A SUPPORT-GROUP SETTING 250

PARENT SESSION 1: THERE ARE NO PERFECT FAMILIES 253

Outline 253
Getting Started 254
Teaching Time 254
Making It Personal 257
Building on God's Word 257
Reflections: "Get Real About Your Family" 258
Building on God's Word: Romans 8:1, 2 260

PARENT SESSION 2: WHAT'S A FAMILY FOR, ANYWAY? 261

Outline 261
Getting Started 262
Teaching Time 262
Making It Personal 264
Building on God's Word 264
Traits of a Healthy Family 266
Reflections: "My Family—For Better or for Worse" 267
Building on God's Word: 2 Corinthians 6:18 269

PARENT SESSION 3: CHANGES CAN UPSET MY FAMILY 271

Outline 271
Getting Started 272
Teaching Time 272

Making It Personal 274

Building on God's Word 275

Reflections: "Responding to Change" Scenarios 276

Reflections: "Weathering the Storms of Life" 280

Building on God's Word: Romans 8:38, 39 282

PARENT SESSION 4: MY ACTIONS CAN HELP—OR HURT—MY FAMILY 285

Outline 285

Getting Started 286

Teaching Time 286

Making It Personal 288

Building on God's Word 288

Reflections: "It Started to Be Such a Nice Day!" (Skit) 289

Reflections: "Increasing the Good Feelings in My Family" . . . 292

Building on God's Word: Galatians 5:14-26 294

PARENT SESSION 5: MY WORDS CAN HELP—OR HURT—MY FAMILY 295

Outline 295

Getting Started 296

Teaching Time 296

Making It Personal 299

Building on God's Word 300

Reflections: "Let's Talk About It!" 301

Building on God's Word: Ephesians 4:29 303

Talking Together in My Family 304

PARENT SESSION 6: "I CARE ABOUT YOU!" 305

Outline 305

Getting Started 306

Teaching Time 306

Making It Personal 309

Building on God's Word 310

Reflections: "Affirmations in My Life" 311
Building on God's Word: John 3:16, 17 313

PARENT SESSION 7: I CAN BELONG TO GOD'S FAMILY, TOO 315

Outline 315
Getting Started 316
Teaching Time 316
Making It Personal 319
Building on God's Word 319
Reflections: "Responding to God's Invitation" 320
Building on God's Word: 2 Corinthians 6:18; Romans 6:23 . . 322
Reflections: "The New Family" (Skit) 323

FAMILY NIGHT (SESSION 8) 325

Outline 325
Gathering Activity 326
Family Games 326
Split Session 327
Closing Program 327
Snacks and Evaluations 327
"The Parable of the Lost Son" 329
Unit Verse Cards 331

PARENT INFORMATION HANDOUTS 333

GETTING INFORMATION TO THE PARENTS 335

HANDOUTS 337

Welcome to Confident Kids! 337
Let's Learn Healthy Living Skills! 339
Living in My Family Topic Overview 341

Session Summary 1 343
Session Summary 2 345
Session Summary 3 347
Session Summary 4 349
Session Summary 5 351
Session Summary 6 353
Session Summary 7 355

APPENDIX A: FORMS 357

FACILITATOR APPLICATION FORM 359

FAMILY ENROLLMENT FORM 361

PARENT PHONE INTERVIEW 363

CHILDREN'S EVALUATION FORM 365

PARENT'S EVALUATION FORM 367

POSTCARDS 369

AFFIRMATION BALLOONS 371

UNIT CERTIFICATE 373

APPENDIX B: RESOURCES 375

Living in My Family
Topic Overview

Unit Slogan

There Are No Perfect Families!

Key Verses
2 Corinthians 6:18, Romans 8: 38, 39, and Ephesians 4:29

"I will be your father, and you will be my sons and daughters, says the Lord All-Powerful." *(ICB)*

Yes, I am sure that nothing can separate us from the love God has for us. Not death, not life, not angels, not ruling spirits, nothing now, nothing in the future, no powers, nothing above us, nothing below us, or anything else in the whole world will ever be able to separate us from the love of God that is in Christ Jesus our Lord. *(ICB)*

When you talk, do not say harmful things. But say what people need—words that will help others become stronger. Then what you say will help those who listen to you. *(ICB)*

Bible Lessons

The first family, Adam and Eve (Genesis 1–4) and The Prodigal Son (Luke 15:11-24)

Key Concepts

- Every family is special and unique, and every family has weaknesses and problems!
- Changes in family life disrupt our sense of security and force us to adapt.
- There will always be times when our family won't—or can't—meet all our needs.
- Good communication skills are the primary building blocks of a strong family.
- Families grow when all members take responsibility to act and speak in ways that help—not hurt—the family unit.
- Belonging to God's family gives us the strength and security we need to face whatever life brings our way.

Session Titles

1   There Are No Perfect Families!

2   What's a Family For, Anyway?

3   Changes Can Upset My Family

4   My Actions Can Help—Or Hurt—My Family

5   My Words Can Help—Or Hurt—My Family

6   "I Care About You!"

7   I Can Belong to God's Family, Too!

8   Family Night

Living in My Family

From the beginning of time, God's design has been for people to live in families. But in our world today, the family is often a confusing and even hurtful place, especially for children. Divorce, absent parents, adjusting to blended families, abusive relationships, and kids left home alone have become family norms in many of our communities. Even intact families suffer the effects of trying to survive in our increasingly fast-paced, morally decaying world. It is unlikely that family life has ever been more challenging than it is at this time in our history.

For children, the center of the universe is their family. It is not only their primary source of belonging and caring, but also the place where they learn who they are and what it means to live in the world. To the degree that the family functions in healthy ways, children grow up feeling valued, secure, and empowered to take their place in the world. When families experience high amounts of stress, however, the likelihood of children growing up feeling valued and secure is dangerously threatened. In fact the opposite can easily be true: If the family cannot find a sense of balance and relief from the stress, the children may grow up feeling hopeless and ill-equipped to lead a healthy, fulfilling life.

In this unit, we will address what it means to live in and be part of a family. Our goal is to help both you and your children realize that living in families is not always easy and that in order to be successful, family members must learn how to work together. We also want you and your children to see that all families change, make mistakes and sometimes fail to meet each others' needs. But it is also true that your ties to your family are the most powerful bonds you will ever have and it is possible for everyone in your family to learn to work together to make it the best place possible for all the members!

GETTING STARTED

* ABOUT CONFIDENT KIDS

* STARTING A CONFIDENT KIDS PROGRAM

* USING THE SESSION PLANS

As you read this section, you will want to review the forms and information in Appendices A and B.

ABOUT CONFIDENT KIDS

WHY A SUPPORT GROUP FOR CHILDREN?

Because times have changed. The emotional needs of children growing up in America today are greater than ever before. Growing up with divorce, stepparents and stepsiblings, drugs and alcohol, gangs, community violence, absent parents—and more—is taking its toll. Children often spend less than one hour per week in church, so children's workers simply do not have time to teach Bible stories, memory verses, missions, and music *and* be responsive to the deepest emotional needs of so many of today's kids! As a result, many of us live with the feeling that we aren't helping the kids who need us most.

WHAT IS CONFIDENT KIDS?

Have you ever thought, *"Wouldn't it be great if we had a place to give focused time and attention to struggling kids? A place where we could support and encourage them, pray with them, and teach them skills to cope with their life circumstances? And wouldn't it truly be a dream come true if we could help their parents, too?"* Well, Confident Kids is that place!

Confident Kids is a Bible-based support-group program that helps families with children ages 4–12 deal with the stresses of living in today's world. Since 1989, Confident Kids has been used by churches and other Christian organizations to offer hope, help, and healing to struggling families. The heart of the program is the Confident Kids curriculum:

- **Facing My Feelings**

  Using the theme "All my feelings are OK," children learn how to name their feelings, how to express them in healthy and appropriate ways, and how to use their feelings to know when it's time to ask for help.

- **Living in My Family**

  Using the theme "There are no perfect families," children are encouraged to see the family as their primary place of belonging and practice a variety of family-living skills.

- **Growing Through Changes**

  Using the theme "Nothing stays the same forever," children learn to deal with change by grieving the losses that occur when things change. They learn to identify and manage the six stages of grief: denial, anger, bargaining, depression, acceptance, and hope.

- **Making Wise Choices**

  Using the theme "I always, always have choices," children learn the difference between wise and unwise choices, practice six steps for making wise choices, and decide how to find wise adults who can help them choose when needed.

WHAT'S IN THIS MANUAL?

This manual contains all the materials you need to conduct one of the four Confident Kids units. This includes the basic information you need to start a Confident Kids support-group program in your area, and the necessary curriculum material.

- **Age-graded session plans**

  Each of the unit's eight sessions has a complete session plan for the following age groups: preschool (ages 4 years through kindergarten), elementary (grades 1 through 4), preteen (grades 5 and 6), and parents.

- **Session summaries for parents**

  These materials tell parents what their children are learning each week and provide suggestions for reinforcing the session themes at home each week.

- **Resources**

  Game and activity ideas as well as media resources are given.

CAN I USE THIS SERIES IN SETTINGS OTHER THAN A SUPPORT GROUP?

Yes! Although designed as a support-group curriculum for high-stress families, Confident Kids' life skills emphasis makes it a valuable teaching tool in a variety of settings. Here are some of the ways you can use the Confident Kids series:

- **A life skills educational curriculum for all kids**

  Use Confident Kids in Sunday morning classes, vacation Bible schools, weeknight youth programs, and camp or retreat settings.

- **A family life enrichment program for families with preschool and elementary age children**

  Because everyone studies the same life skills curriculum and parents learn how to reinforce the concepts at home, Confident Kids can dramatically impact entire families.

- **A community outreach/evangelism tool**

  Churches that begin a Confident Kids program can be helpful with neighborhood families who may never come to their church for any reason other than seeking help for their struggling children.

- **Single-parent ministry**

  Confident Kids helps children with divorce recovery, as a follow-up after divorce recovery, and in retreat settings for single parents and their kids.

- **A supplement to classroom curriculum**

  School teachers can add a life skills component to their curriculum by using segments of the Confident Kids curriculum in their classrooms.

UNDERSTANDING HOW CONFIDENT KIDS WORKS

PROGRAM GOALS

The Confident Kids program seeks to:

- Teach children the skills necessary to understand, talk about, and cope with their life circumstances in healthy and positive ways
- Encourage children to talk about their experiences in a loving, safe environment

- Build self-esteem and a sense of trust through relationships with caring adults (program facilitators)
- Influence homes by teaching parents the same skills being taught to their children
- Guide children and parents into a relationship with God and teach them to value prayer and Scripture as resources

THE POWER SOURCE: SCRIPTURAL FOUNDATIONS

Confident Kids seeks to help kids who may withdraw from God find Him a personal friend and source of strength. The session plans include carefully selected Bible stories, memory verses, and small group prayer times to communicate four Scriptural truths.

- **God is a loving caregiver who is always present and gives us support in difficult times.**

  Joshua 1:9; Romans 8:38, 39; 1 Peter 5:7

- **Jesus knows what it means to suffer and feel pain and therefore can help us when we experience suffering and pain.**

  Hebrews 2:18, and the Easter events and themes (which help kids connect with Jesus' suffering and difficult choices)

- **When we pray honestly about what we are feeling, God helps us find comfort and peace.**

  Philippians 4:6, 7

- **God intends a hopeful, purposeful future for us, no matter how painful the present may seem.**

  Jeremiah 29:11

LIMITATIONS OF CONFIDENT KIDS

Like all programs, Confident Kids has limitations:

- **Support groups are not therapy groups**

  Support groups at any age level never replace professional help. In cases where children or parents are significantly damaged by their life circumstances, a referral to other appropriate sources of help must be made.

- Confident Kids **cannot "cure" all the problems of children!**

  Confident Kids is just one program. It is not a cure-all for helping kids grow up healthy in the midst of our confusing world. It is important for both leaders and parents to maintain reasonable expectations as to the results of participating in the support-group experience (i.e., participating in Confident Kids does not guarantee kids will not have struggles in their teen years)!

Three Program Elements
The Keys to Success

Successful support groups for children blend three program elements:

Life Skills Education

Since high-stress children are at risk for developing unhealthy and destructive coping skills, Confident Kids begins by teaching children healthy ways to deal with life's pain and stress.

A Support-Group Setting

The life skills curriculum is taught in a caring, supportive setting. This environment helps make it easier for the kids to develop trust and talk about their lives.

Concurrent Parent Group

By taking parents and the kids through the same material, the entire family is helped. Parents also receive support from meeting other parents who are dealing with the same or similar issues.

Life Skills Education
- Feelings
- Family
- Changes
- Choices

Concurrent Parent Group
- Life skills education
- Safe, supportive environment
- Impacts the family

A Support-Group Setting
- Small groups
- Safe, supportive environment to talk
- Trained facilitators

How to Start a Confident Kids Program

STEP #1: BUILD A STRONG FOUNDATION

DETERMINE THE TARGET AUDIENCE

Whom do you want to come to your Confident Kids groups? High-stress families in your church? In your community? Both? Single-parent families? Know the people you want to help. The target audience you select will influence the way you organize the program.

RECRUIT LEADERS

Perhaps the most difficult part of any ongoing children's ministry is recruiting and maintaining qualified leaders. Many churches are concerned that beginning a support group for children will further drain their already overtapped leadership pool. However, experience has taught us that Confident Kids often attracts new leaders. Follow these guidelines as you recruit.

Successful Confident Kids leaders exhibit the following characteristics:

- A deep love for children
- A high degree of responsibility and dependability
- Some experience in working with children in group or class settings
- A concern for hurting children
- A level of understanding and sensitivity to hurting children that is crucial to the Confident Kids program. This sensitivity is prevalent in leaders who experienced a painful childhood.

In addition, successful leaders must be committed to the following three principles:

- **Consistently "being there" emotionally and physically**

  Leaders must be totally committed to being at Confident Kids each week, both physically and emotionally. This is crucial because many of the children have been hurt by adults they trusted.

- **Being nonjudgmental**

  Leaders must realize that children may reveal family secrets or behave in certain ways that go against their personal value systems. Although leaders do not have to condone these issues, they must realize that unconditional love and acceptance are important to the healing process.

- **Confidentiality**

  All leaders must realize they will be called upon to use wisdom and discretion as the kids reveal details of their lives. In most cases, the leaders must be able to keep what children or parents say in the group setting confidential, with a few notable exceptions. See "Handling Sensitive Issues" (page 9) for more information on this vital subject.

THE LEADERSHIP TEAM

The Program Administrator

This person oversees the entire program. Ideally, this is a paid staff member or someone with easy access to the administrative resources of the organization (i.e., office equipment, publicity vehicles, room allocation schedules, knowledge of potential volunteers, etc.). The responsibilities of the program administrator include:

- Introducing the program to the sponsoring organization
- Securing the time and place for the meetings
- Recruiting and training the facilitators
- Arranging child care for younger siblings
- Publicity
- Registration
- Securing all needed supplies
- Maintaining records
- Evaluation and follow-up

Parent Group Facilitator

It is helpful if the parent group facilitator has had some experience teaching or leading parenting groups, but not required. This person's responsibilities include:

- Knowing the Confident Kids curriculum thoroughly
- Conducting the group, using the Confident Kids parent group guide
- Attending all facilitator training sessions and meetings
- Being involved in parent conferences and/or referrals, when necessary

Small Group Facilitators

The small group facilitators work directly with the kids. Each facilitator is assigned three to five children (usually four), and then grouped with two or three other facilitators and their kids to form a room. Using the Confident Kids curriculum, these facilitators conduct the meetings each week.

LEADERSHIP TRAINING

Facilitator training generally takes place in three stages:

Orientation

The first step in the training process is a "no-obligation" orientation. This gives both the potential leaders and the program administrator a chance to explore whether this ministry will be a good match for both. This meeting generally is conducted as follows:

- **Get-acquainted time**

  Participants share their backgrounds and why they are interested in a ministry like Confident Kids.

- **Overview of the Confident Kids program**

  Includes program goals, qualifications of leaders, and a look at the curriculum and meeting format.

- **Explanation of the details of the facilitator commitment**

  Expectations and the importance of follow through once commitment is made are discussed.

- **Distribution of facilitator applications**

  Appendix A ("Forms") contains a sample facilitator application. For legal reasons, it is important to have an application on file for every facilitator. Prospective participants can fill out applications at home, and return them before the basic training session, should they decide to continue.

Basic Training

Once the team is in place, training begins. Confident Kids leaders are trained in:

- **Small group facilitation**

  Skills are needed in listening and responding, keeping the group on track, and recognizing behaviors that indicate a need for professional help. Your church or organization's policy for handling sensitive issues should be discussed as well.

- **Classroom management**

  Maintaining discipline and control, providing smooth transitions between program segments, and having well-prepared lessons are important to the success of Confident Kids.

- **Teamwork**

  Facilitators work together to plan sessions, discipline consistently, solve problems, and pray.

On-the-Job Training

Training does not stop once the sessions begin. Leaders will continue to learn if they meet briefly immediately following each session. Use this time to:

- **Debrief the meeting**

  What happened? Was there anything you didn't know how to handle? Was anything said by a child that concerned you?

- **Plan for the next meeting**

  Take time to prepare for the next session.

- **Pray**

  Prayer should be a priority.

- **Write postcards**

  Kids love to get mail! Sending a postcard each week helps the kids and facilitators bond. Taking time to write them at this meeting ensures every child will receive a card.

Getting Help With Training

Program administrators can get help with the Confident Kids training process from several sources:

Training Seminars. Learn from the creators of the Confident Kids program and those who have used it. The Confident Kids national office offers two-day program administrator training seminars several times a year in various parts of the country as well as four-day leadership institutes. See Appendix B ("Resources") for contact information.

Training Series on Tape. The Confident Kids office also makes available six-hour training programs in audio- or videocassette formats. Program administrators can use these as a self-study program, or to train their facilitators.

Nearby Churches That Have Completed a Confident Kids Unit. If another church in your area has offered a Confident Kids program, ask their leaders for help with your training, or send a key leader or two to participate in their program to gain some firsthand experience.

Local Professionals. Therapists, social workers, children's pastors, and teachers can train leaders.

SET POLICY FOR HANDLING SENSITIVE ISSUES

Most of the time, Confident Kids groups are straight-forward and predictable. However, from time to time children or parents may reveal sensitive matters. Decisions about how these matters will be handled must be made *before you begin* a support-group program so you will not be caught off guard, should the occasion arise in your program. Many churches now have *written* policies for handling sensitive issues. If your church does not have written policies, encourage your church leaders to establish some before beginning any Confident Kids unit. See Appendix B ("Resources") for resources that can help you with this task.

Handling Confidentiality

Our Confidentiality Agreement With the Kids. In the children's groups, confidentiality is the first rule placed on the "group rules" posters. The facilitators will explain to the children that Confident Kids is meant to be a safe place where they can talk about whatever they want to talk about, and in order to feel safe, everyone needs to know that what they say in group will stay in group. This will be explained further to mean that when they leave the group, they cannot tell anyone else about personal, private things another child has shared in the group. They can talk about whatever else they want. The kids will also be told that the confidentiality agreement extends to the facilitators. The facilitators will not tell anyone what the kids share with them without their permission, and *this includes their parents*. We cannot be helpful to the kids if they believe we will repeat everything they say in the group to their parents.

Our Agreement With the Parents About Getting Information to Them About Their Kids. Although we respect and will hold to the confidentiality agreement with their kids, parents need to know that we will find a way to get information that concerns us to them. This is usually not difficult to do; remember, the key phrase is "without their permission." Most often, when we ask the kids if we can talk to their parents about a particular issue, they are very happy to have us do so; some kids are even relieved. Even when they do not give us permission, we can usually find a way to get information to parents without violating confidentiality, such as making observations of behavior we see. Parents can be assured that it is not our intent to hide things from them. Rather we want to make it as easy as possible for the kids to find help.

Children's Understanding of Confidentiality. The distinction between what is acceptable to talk about outside the group, and what is to be kept confidential is very blurred at the elementary age level. Therefore, parents need to be prepared that their children may come home and say that they were told that they could not tell Mom or Dad anything that happened in the group. In fact, this is the very issue that started Confident Kids parent groups! We want every parent to know that we value confidentiality so much we will not compromise it.

Exceptions to Confidentiality. There are two exceptions to the confidentiality rule:

- **Confidentiality among the** Confident Kids **leaders**

  If we are to be as helpful as possible to all participants, Confident Kids facilitators must be free to share information about what happens in the groups each week. Facilitators can then be given guidance as to the best way to deal with the issues

their group members discussed. This sharing also allows the program administrator to note any information that seems out of the ordinary.

- **Reports of abusive behaviors**

  Any reports of abusive behavior against the kids must—by law in most states—be reported to authorities.

Making Referrals

When families have problems that go beyond the scope of the support-group program, refer them to other sources for help. If your church does not have an approved list of counselors or agencies, build one of your own. Look for the following.

- Counselors and counseling agencies that include one or more counselors on their staff who specialize in working with children and/or family therapy *and* include a sliding scale fee structure
- Lawyers and legal aid services to assist parents with legal issues
- Community resources for specialized issues such as chemical dependency treatment, ADHD diagnosis and treatment, shelters for women and children, etc.
- Local meetings of Alcoholics Anonymous, Al-Anon, and other twelve-step groups
- Other professionals who specialize in issues common to families in your community

Reporting Abuse

In most states, church workers are required by law to report any reports of suspected abuse. Be sure you know in advance the signs to look for and the proper procedures for making reports.

Preventing Legal Problems

It is not likely that your church will encounter any legal difficulties from your Confident Kids program. However, you can safeguard against this possibility by giving attention to the following three issues:

- **Have parents sign a release form**

  The purpose of this form is to make it clear to parents that they are attending a support group only, and not a therapy group. Most courts will recognize that support groups are peer-led groups, and do not incur the same legal liabilities as professionally-led therapy groups.

  A sample enrollment/release form is included in Appendix A ("Forms").

- **Know when and how to report abusive behaviors**

  Never act alone in reporting abuse. Make this decision in consultation with your Confident Kids program administrator, and any other program supervisors (e.g., pastors, counselors). The main point to emphasize here is the need to know the proper procedure to follow in your church or organization *before* the issue actually comes up. *Don't wait until you are in a crisis situation to ask these questions!*

- **Screen your Confident Kids facilitators carefully**

  This is a very important responsibility of the program administrator. It is mentioned here for emphasis. For more information, see Appendix B ("Resources").

STEP #2: RECRUIT FAMILIES AND SET UP THE GROUPS

PUBLICIZE YOUR PROGRAM

Publicize your program in as many of the following as seem appropriate:

- Place announcements in church bulletins and newsletters, school newsletters, etc.
- Distribute informational brochures to selected audiences (i.e., families with elementary-age children, single parents, families living within a five-mile radius of the sponsoring organization)
- Invite teachers and counselors to make referrals to the program
- Place articles and advertisements in your local newspaper(s)

All publicity materials should include the purpose of the program and a clear statement of registration procedures.

REGISTER FAMILIES

Advance registration is necessary to control the size of the groups, gather information about each family, and ensure that parents understand the goals of the group and the commitment that is necessary.

Advance registration is handled through a phone interview. See Appendix A ("Forms") for a sample parent phone interview guide sheet.

Following the phone interview, send a release form to the parent and ask him or her to sign it and return it to you. For legal reasons, it is wise to keep these signed release forms on file for approximately two years.

Appendix A ("Forms") contains a sample parent release form.

SET UP THE CHILDREN'S GROUPS

In a support-group program, how children are grouped and the size of the groups is crucial. In Confident Kids, a "small group" comprises one facilitator and no more than five children. The "large group" is no more than three or four small groups in one room (e.g., nine to fifteen children with three facilitators, or twelve to sixteen children with four facilitators). You can have many rooms running at one time, but never place more than sixteen children in a room.

Children are assigned to a small group and remain in that group for eight weeks. When assigning children to small groups, follow these guidelines:

- Do not place siblings or other family members in the same small group

- Age-grade the groups as closely as possible
- Use same-sex groups, as long as doing so does not violate the first two guidelines

Don't Forget the Parent Group

As stated earlier, an important part of the Confident Kids program is to involve parents in a parent group, unless they are involved in another support group or parenting class meeting at the same time. In general, parents are quite willing to attend the parent group, especially when it is presented to them as an important part of the program. Normally, only one parent group is offered, with all parents meeting together. It is helpful to provide child care for younger children, since many who come to the parent group are single parents.

Welcome Everyone to the First Session

The first meeting is crucial! Since most children attending will have been enrolled by a parent, the kids may be apprehensive and possibly even resistant. The primary goal of the first meeting is to put children at ease and help them begin bonding to the group. We recommend you use the "Welcome to Confident Kids" session (page 19). In this session, all age groups meet together and are introduced to the Confident Kids program.

Step #3: Wrap Up the Unit

Family Night

The last meeting of each session, Family Night, brings everyone together for a closing program and party. Many relationships are built during the seven weeks, and saying good-bye is important. Be sure any parents who may not have participated in the parent group are invited to this session.

Schedule Additional Units

It is likely that at the end of each eight-week unit, your groups will want to continue meeting. If this is the case, you can offer one of the other Confident Kids topics. Start by inviting current parents to enroll their children for another unit. Then add new families to fill any spaces left by those who may choose not to return. Churches that have used Confident Kids for a long period of time simply cycle through all four of the books, adding families at the beginning of each unit as space allows.

USING THE SESSION PLANS

KIDS SESSIONS

MATERIALS NEEDED FOR THE GROUP MEETINGS

Each session plan contains a list of materials needed for that session. This is only a listing of the materials *unique* to that session, such as activity sheets, posters, craft materials, etc. In addition, each room should be stocked with the following basic supplies:

- Pencils, fine-tip markers, and broad-tip markers
- Scissors and staplers
- Glue or glue sticks
- Masking and clear adhesive tape
- Assortment of construction paper and poster board

- *Optional:* A costume/props box for role plays and skits
- *Optional:* An audio- or video-cassette recorder/player
- *Optional:* Games
- Snack tin(s)

SESSION PLAN COMPONENTS

Each session lasts 90 minutes and includes the following segments.

Getting Started (Large Group)—25 Minutes

Gathering Activity. The gathering activity is usually a game or a craft designed to involve the kids as soon as they arrive, to begin the meeting in a positive and fun way. Facilitators should be available to greet the kids warmly and immediately direct them to this activity.

Group Rules. Some children have never been given clear expectations of appropriate behavior. It is important to establish what is expected of them in Confident Kids almost immediately. This is done through the use of group rules. Most facilitators find it best to have the children help establish these rules. The following four rules should always be included:

---

1. What is said in group, stays in group (confidentiality)

2. No name-calling or putdowns (respect one another)

3. The "right to pass" (although participation is desired, every child must feel free not to participate if the activity or discussion feels threatening or hurtful)

4. Let the leaders lead (children need to know that the adults are in control, and that they are to be respected)

Once the list of rules has been established, discuss with the group what will happen when the rules are not followed. Most groups have successfully used a simple time-out system. Consistent disruptions result in a consultation with a parent. If a satisfactory change is not made, the child is removed from the group permanently.

Introduction to the Session Theme. The lesson theme is introduced each week through a skit or activity to which the kids can easily relate. In most cases, the story will end with a question or issue designed to stimulate discussion of the session theme. Immediately following the skit, the kids are dismissed to their small groups where this discussion takes place.

Small Groups—35 Minutes

The small group experience is the heart of the Confident Kids program. It is here that the dynamic of teaching life skills in a support-group setting emerges in a powerful way. The small group time comprises these elements:

- **Discussion of the opening skit/activity**

  Each session plan contains questions to debrief the opening skit or activity the kids have just watched.

- **Teaching**

  The life skill being taught is presented.

- **Reinforcement activity**

  A role play, activity sheet, or other involvement activity is used to reinforce the teaching, and help kids to apply it to their own lives.

- **Prayer**

  Prayer is a vital part of Confident Kids. It is during this time that many kids share their most personal concerns, and facilitators can encourage children who are disappointed that God has not answered their prayers in the past (e.g., "I prayed and prayed my parents wouldn't get a divorce, and they did anyway, so what's the point?"). Facilitators can optimize this time by using a prayer journal or some other means to keep a record of kids' requests and answers.

Bible Time (Large Group)—25 Minutes

Regathering. The transition from the small groups to the Bible time should be handled well. Since not all of the small groups will end at exactly the same moment, use music or a short game to draw the kids back into the larger group. Assign one facilitator to lead this time. Use songs or games your kids know and like, or see Appendix B ("Resources") for ideas. *Note:* A tape of songs that correspond to the Confident Kids curriculum for preschoolers through grade four is available from the Confident Kids office. (See Appendix B for ordering information.)

Bible Story/Skit. The Bible stories in all Confident Kids sessions are presented in the form of a skit or puppet show. Careful thought and preparation of these skits will increase the effectiveness of the Bible teaching. (See "Tips for Successful Meetings" below.)

Key Verse. Each unit has two or three key verses, which can be taught using a variety of memory verse games. (See Appendix B.)

Closing Prayer Huddle. This method of closing each meeting brings a sense of ritual to the group, which helps to develop a sense of belonging. Instructions for the prayer huddle are included in each session plan.

Snacks—5 Minutes

Snacks are an important part of Confident Kids meetings. The kids love bringing the treats as well as eating them! Bringing treats in a special Confident Kids snack tin provides a reminder and keeps the snack simple. Of course, in areas where families cannot afford to send treats, they can be provided each week.

TIPS FOR SUCCESSFUL MEETINGS

Years of experience have revealed some pitfalls you can avoid as you run a program like Confident Kids. You can benefit from others' mistakes by carefully observing the following guidelines:

- **Maintain the ratio of one adult per four children**

  Small groups are a key element to the success of your program. Don't let anything compromise this standard! If you have three leaders, twelve children is ideal. Take no more than fifteen. It is better to hold families on waiting lists for the start of another unit than to take too many kids into your program.

- **Enforce the group rules consistently**

  New facilitators who are eager to work with high-stress, hurting kids are often reluctant to deal with kids' inappropriate behavior. Since high-stress kids often act out their feelings in disruptive ways, all facilitators must work together to see that the group rules are enforced from the very first meeting. The adults must maintain control of the room, or the kids will never let down their defenses and trust the group experience.

- **Give attention to transitions**

  Be sure all facilitators are well prepared. Most of the difficulties encountered in Confident Kids groups happen during transition times when the facilitators are trying to gather materials or practice skits instead of leading the kids smoothly from one activity to another.

- **Insist on after-group staff meetings**

  Getting all Confident Kids leaders together after each meeting to debrief, share information, plan for the next meeting, and pray together is important. Even though everyone may be tired and want to go home, do not skip this vital communication link! See "Step #1: Build a Strong Foundation" (page 7) for more information about the after-meetings.

- **Send postcards every week**

  Anything we can do to let the kids know we are thinking about them is valuable. The simple exercise of having facilitators write postcards to the kids in their small group every week says volumes to the kids. These can be written out in the after-

meeting before facilitators go home, and mailed a few days later by the program administrator. That way, every child is sure to receive a card.

PARENT SESSIONS

The parent group sessions follow their own format. Each session follows the same basic outline.

GETTING STARTED—20 MINUTES

In this time, you will need to accomplish the following:

Check-In

This is merely a time of conversation to relax group members and give everyone a chance to visit.

Group Rules

As with all support groups, the parent group has several rules, which are designed to keep the group emotionally safe for all participants. The three rules for parent groups are:

- **Confidentiality**

  Confidentiality is foundational to the Confident Kids program. It is also new to many parents, and therefore needs some careful explanation in the group at the beginning of each unit. See page 9 for more information.

- **No advice giving**

  This rule keeps parents from telling other parents what they "should" do to solve their problems, which is not helpful to anyone. Tell parents that they are not to use phrases such as: "What you should do is—" or "Why don't you just—" or "If I were you, I'd—". It *is* helpful when parents share with each other from their own experiences. Encourage parents to use phrases such as: "When we faced that in our family, we found _____ to be helpful." Or, "We have the same problem in our family, and we found _____ to be not helpful." Or, "Here are some resources we found that helped us with _____."

- **The right to pass**

  To feel emotionally safe, parents need to know they will never be put on the spot to share something they feel uncomfortable sharing. Let parents know that when you go around the circle and ask for responses to questions, they may simply say, "I pass," and you will move on to the next person.

Review Session Summary for Parents

Each week you will review with the parents a handout containing an outline of the lesson material the kids will be covering in their groups, with a suggested activity to do at home. These handouts begin on page 329. You need not spend much time on this summary; the purpose is merely to give parents a concise picture of what their kids are doing in their groups each week.

TEACHING TIME—20 MINUTES

This segment is an expansion of the children's material for parents. This material has been written to accomplish two goals:

1. To help the parents better understand what we are teaching their children and how to apply it at home
2. To guide the parents in their own personal growth

The material in the teaching section contains lecture material, plus a few skits, activities, and discussion questions.

MAKING IT PERSONAL—35 MINUTES

The Confident Kids parent group is a support group, not a parenting class. Therefore, we try to give the parents

opportunity to personalize the material being presented each week. This is accomplished through a personal reflection sheet, which parents fill out during the session and discuss during an open sharing time. These sheets help parents make connections with how they were raised as children (family-of-origin issues) and how they are functioning as parents today. We believe that these insights help break cycles of destructive behavior patterns that parents may unknowingly be following.

Some parent group leaders like to collect the reflection sheets at the end of each session, providing a personal link between them and the parents. This also gives the parents the experience of having an interested person "listen" to their personal issues. Other parent group leaders feel it is best to keep these sheets completely private, and encourage parents to use them during the week at home, to think through the issues at a deeper level.

BUILDING ON GOD'S WORD—15 MINUTES

Each session ends with a time for Scripture emphasis and prayer. A second take-home sheet, "Building on God's Word," is included with each session for this purpose. It is not necessary to teach directly from this sheet, unless you want to. It is more important to encourage parents to use this sheet at home as an aid to spending some quiet time with God during the week. Devote most of this time to focusing on prayer requests and emphasizing the power of prayer.

PREPARING TO LEAD A SESSION

Your effectiveness will be greatly increased by following these steps:

- **Read the children's curriculum before preparing your session.**

  Remember that the parent group is an expansion of the same material the kids are learning. The goal is for the *whole family* to feel they have experienced the same program. You will be better prepared to coordinate the total experience for the parents if you are well acquainted with what the kids are doing in their groups.

- **Take time to make the material your own.**

  There is nothing magical about the session plan; it is simply a tool. Therefore take time to personalize it. You will be effective as a parent group leader only to the extent you feel personally connected to the material you are presenting. Add personal examples and illustrations, expand on the material from your area of expertise and past experience, and add activities or approaches you feel are appropriate to your group of parents. Obviously, the session plan does not know you or your parents; it is *you* as the parent group leader who must add life to your session!

- **Choose which parts of the session seem to be most effective for your style and your setting.**

  You will probably not be able to do everything the session plan calls for each week. You will need to make some choices about what you will do. For example, if you are a good teacher, you may want to spend more time teaching. Or, if you feel the parents are benefiting more from the personal reflection time, keep your teaching time short and spend more time doing that. In the beginning, remain flexible and don't become frustrated if you don't get through everything. It takes time to discover the best format for you and your group!

- **Pray.**

  The families in your group will grow and change as God's Spirit moves in their hearts and lives. Therefore, you can facilitate the most powerful change of all by holding them up to God during the weeks of this unit!

WELCOME TO CONFIDENT KIDS!

If this is your first Confident Kids unit and all the participants are new to the program, consider adding this optional introductory session to your schedule.

Introducing all the family members together to Confident Kids helps them relax and feel more comfortable. This session is only necessary when *all* the families are new. Once at least some of your participants have experienced a Confident Kids unit, this session is no longer necessary.

GOALS

- Reduce participants' anxiety by establishing a warm, caring, and fun environment
- Introduce the Confident Kids program and purpose of the group
- Develop the group rules
- Use Joshua 1:9 to assure children of God's presence and care for them

NEEDED

- Family Shield activity sheet (one per family)
- Ball of yarn
- Blank poster boards (one for each room)
- "Welcome to Confident Kids" letter (one per family)
- Theme verse (Joshua 1:9) posters
- Snacks

WELCOME TO CONFIDENT KIDS
OUTLINE

Opening (40 Minutes)

    Family Shields

    Group Game and Introductions

    Introduction of the Confident Kids Program

    Dismissal to Individual Rooms

Getting Acquainted (25 Minutes)

    The Reporter Game and Parent Group

    Group Rules

    Small Groups

Bible Time (15 Minutes)

    Confident Kids Theme Verse

    Prayer Huddle

Snack (10 Minutes)

WELCOME TO CONFIDENT KIDS

"God Be With You"

Joshua 1:9

OPENING (40 MINUTES)

FAMILY SHIELDS

As children and parents arrive, have Family Shield activity sheets (page 26) and markers available. Say:

> As a family, work together to complete your shields by filling in the quarters of the shields as follows:
>
> 1. Draw a picture of your family.
> 2. Draw or write about a favorite family activity.
> 3. Draw or write about something you would like to change about your family.
> 4. Draw or write the best thing about your family!

When completed, ask them to bring their shields and move to the group area for the next part of the program.

GROUP GAME AND INTRODUCTIONS

Play the "Spider Web" game, or use any game that the parents and kids can play together. If you have preschoolers present, ask parents to help them play along.

Spider Web

You will need a ball of yarn for this activity. Have everyone stand in a circle. One person begins by holding onto the strand of yarn in one hand. Then he says his name before throwing the ball to a person somewhere else in the circle (without letting go of the strand). Whoever catches the ball is next, and repeats the process, also holding onto the yarn. As group members continue to throw the ball back and forth, the middle of the circle will transform into a "spider web." After everyone has had a turn, tell the group that they must now do something with their web (e.g., lay it on the floor, get into the middle of it, undo it). It's fun to see what they choose to do!

After the game, ask everyone to sit in a circle. Use the Family Shields as a way for families to introduce themselves.

INTRODUCTION TO Confident Kids

The program administrator (or another leader) should make the following presentation to help the group understand what Confident Kids is all about:

> Welcome to Confident Kids. This is a group especially for kids. It is your group and we want you to feel comfortable here! (Ask the following questions)
>
> Why do you think we named the group Confident Kids?
>
> What does it mean to be confident?
>
> What do you think we will be doing in this group?
>
> There are many special things about being a kid and growing up. When life is going well, you are exploring new things and spending time with people who will help you become all you can be. It is a time for you to be loved and cared for and to learn what things make you special and unique.
>
> But sometimes life is not what we want it to be, and even kids feel hurt and disappointed. Sometimes things change when we don't want them to, sometimes people hurt us without knowing it, and sometimes we don't feel like anyone could love us or we are good at doing anything. Those kinds of things happen to everyone from time to time. You are in this group because we care about you and want to

help you learn how to handle those kinds of things—now—while you're still a kid.

> In Confident Kids, we will play games, do activities, have snacks, watch and act in skits, learn from the Bible, and pray together. While we are having fun doing those things, we'll also have lots of time to talk about things that we really want to talk about. That's all I want to say right now, except that we are on an adventure, and we're really glad you are with us!

DISMISSAL TO INDIVIDUAL ROOMS

At this time, send everyone to their respective rooms, with their facilitators. Participants will spend the rest of the session there, coming back together for snacks at the end of the session.

PARENT GROUP

Parents will spend their time introducing themselves, going over their group rules (below), and discussing the "Welcome to Confident Kids" letter (page 337). Build in enough time to answer any questions parents may have.

GETTING ACQUAINTED (25 MINUTES)

THE REPORTER GAME

Preschool

If you have a preschool room (kids age 4 years through kindergarten), use a variation of the reporter game. Use a microphone and act as a reporter. Interview each child by asking one or two questions such as:

> How many brothers and sisters do you have?

Do you have any pets?

What is your favorite _____ ?

Do you go to preschool? kindergarten?

Note: You can add interest by using a real tape recorder and playing the tape back for the kids to hear.

Grades 1–6

Divide the groups into pairs, being sure that brothers and sisters and kids that know each other are separated. Tell the kids that they are newspaper reporters and their assignment is to find out as much as possible about the other person in their pair. Encourage them to find out unusual things like famous relatives, unusual hobbies, awards won in the past, etc. Give them five minutes to talk to each other. Then reconvene the circle and ask each child to share one interesting fact they learned about their partners.

GROUP RULES

Establishing the group rules is an important part of this meeting. As you discuss the rules, write them down on a blank piece of poster board. (*Note:* In the preschool groups, prepare a rules poster in advance, using pictures and simple words to depict the rules.) A facilitator begins by saying:

This is our group, and we are going to be together for the next few weeks. All groups—like families, school classes, and even groups of friends—have rules.

What do rules do for us? *(Help us get along better, have fun, and stay safe)*

What would life be like if we didn't have any rules? *(Refer to what it would be like to play games, drive on roads, etc. if there were no rules)*

So, today we will spend some time making a list of rules that will make our

group a good place to be. I'll start us off with one rule that is important to me—confidentiality. *(Write on board)* **What do you think that word means?** *(Allow for responses)* **It means that when the others in your group share something that is really personal—maybe something about their family or how they are feeling inside—you agree not to tell those personal stories to anyone else outside of this room. Confidentiality goes for the leaders, too. When you share with us, we will not tell your stories to anyone else *without your permission.***

Exception! There is one exception to confidentiality. If we find out you are being hurt by someone, particularly an adult, we will not keep that confidential. We will tell someone, and get you some help. We will never let you stay in a place where you are unsafe.

At this point, invite the kids to help you add rules to the poster. Keep this moving and keep it serious! Don't let the kids make fun of the rules. Let them know you take them very seriously, and expect them to as well. Periodically, the facilitators add rules. Be sure these are included:

—No put-downs or name-calling
—Leaders lead (kids follow directions and participate)
—The right to pass (no one has to do or say anything that make them uncomfortable)

When you have six or seven good rules, move on to talking about what will happen when the rules are not followed. This will have been determined in advance and communicated to facilitators during the training process (page 8). Communicate this to the kids now. Then display your group rules poster in a prominent place and be absolutely sure that every facilitator works together to maintain the rules consistently!

SMALL GROUPS

Divide the kids into their small groups to get acquainted with their facilitator for a few minutes. During this short time, the facilitator should introduce himself by telling a few personal things the kids would enjoy knowing, and ending with a short prayer for each child in the group.

BIBLE TIME (15 MINUTES)

REGATHERING

Gather everyone back together into the larger group for the remainder of the session.

Confident Kids THEME VERSE

Before the meeting, print the Confident Kids theme verse (Joshua 1:9) on two posters: one for preschoolers and one for first through sixth graders. The preschool verse should use pictures instead of words. Use the versions listed below. Say:

> Each week in Confident Kids, we are going to talk about how God helps us become confident kids. We will learn that no one has to face difficult things in their lives alone. We can find lots of people to help us. We're also going to learn that the best source of help we have is God! We have a theme verse that tells us about this. Let's say it together:

Preschool: "So don't be afraid. The Lord your God will be with you everywhere you go" (*ICB*).

Grades 1–6: "Have I not commanded you? Be strong and courageous. Do not be terrified; do not be discouraged, for the Lord your God will be with you wherever you go" (*NIV*).

Conclude with a short personal example of how God's presence has helped you be strong and courageous when facing difficult things in your life.

PRAYER HUDDLE

Teach the kids the traditional Confident Kids closing. Gather everyone into a tight circle and instruct them to "stack" their hands on top of each other in the middle of the circle. As they stand in this position, a facilitator says a short closing prayer. At the end, everyone yells out, "Amen!" as they raise their hands out of the stack and over their heads.

SNACKS (10 MINUTES)

Make this first meeting special by providing a nice refreshment table for families to enjoy. You might get a decorated cake, with the words "Welcome to Confident Kids!" or have make-your-own sundaes. This will make the kids feel welcome and comfortable with the program.

Draw a picture of your family

Draw or write about a
favorite family activity

Draw something you would like to
change about your family

Draw the best thing about your family

FAMILY SHIELD

Preschool Sessions

Tips for Working With Preschoolers
in a Support-Group Setting   28

All About My Family   31

What's a Family For, Anyway?   39

Changes Can Upset My Family   47

Actions Can Hurt—Or Help—My Family 55

Words Can Hurt—Or Help—My Family   63

"I Care About You!"   71

I Can Belong to God's Family, Too   79

Tips for Working With Preschoolers in a Support-Group Setting

What to Expect From Preschoolers in Confident Kids Groups

Preschoolers are at a much different developmental level than elementary age kids, and function in and respond to the support-group experience uniquely. Here are a few key points about preschoolers to help you plan for your group:

- **Preschoolers hurt deeply but have few developmental skills to deal with emotional pain.**

  A preschooler cannot reason, "I feel guilty and abandoned because my parents are getting a divorce. I need to grieve this great loss in my life." Rather, she is confused by the intense pain she feels and responds by acting out. Since she cannot verbalize what is really going on, adults may miss the connection between a child's feelings and her behavior. In Confident Kids, we understand this connection and help preschoolers deal with their emotional pain by helping them name their feelings, release them through play and story activities, and by teaching them to ask for help when they need it.

- **Preschoolers express themselves best through play and pretending.**

  Preschoolers have limited verbal skills. Therefore, they are helped more through play centers, puppet role plays, and art activities than through dialogue and discussion. The most strategic time you have with your preschoolers may be in the opening play centers!

- **Preschoolers are concrete thinkers and have difficulty with the abstract concepts in the Confident Kids material.**

  Feelings, grief, and evaluating the results of choices are abstract concepts. Although the session plans make these concepts as concrete as possible, you may have to simplify them even further. Don't be alarmed if the children do not understand everything perfectly.

- **Preschoolers cannot think in terms of cause-and-effect relationships and complex processes.**

  This means your preschoolers will not be able to understand the deeper complexities that make up family life. For instance, a preschooler will not be able to reason that Dad is yelling at her because he had a bad day at work and not because he is mad at her. Nor will preschoolers be able to relate concepts from week to week. Therefore, consider each week's concept an entity in and of itself. Pay particular attention to any feelings about living in their families that arise during the meeting.

- **Preschoolers have trouble participating in group discussions.**

  To get the kids to focus on the questions, go around the circle and ask each child a question. Be prepared to help them respond by suggesting possible answers.

- **Preschoolers remember and respond to only one direction at a time.**

  Make your directions clear and simple and stay focused on one task at a time. For example, don't tell preschoolers to finish their coloring sheets, clean up, get their snack, and then sit on the story rug for the Bible story—and expect them to get it all accomplished!

Activity Centers Maximize the Confident Kids Experience

Since preschoolers express themselves best through play and pretending, one of the most strategic times of the Confident Kids meeting is the opening activity centers. In each session plan you will find suggestions for opening centers that are related to the theme. However, any of the following centers allow children the opportunity to express their feelings through play:

- **Home Living Center**

  Have items available to "play house."

- **Doll House Center**

  Display a doll house complete with furniture and a family of dolls the kids can manipulate.

- **Stuffed Animal Center**

  This center can be effective when supervised and kids use the animals for cuddling and storytelling. Do not allow rough play with the stuffed animals.

- **Book Center**

  Display books that talk about feelings, family relationships, and problem solving. Preschoolers are particularly interested in animal and fantasy stories.

- **Puppet Box**

  Have a variety of puppets that can be used to act out scenarios or problem-solving situations.

- **Dress-Up Corner**

  A big box of old clothes, shoes, jewelry, hats, costumes, and a floor-length mirror will help kids express themselves through pretending and role playing.

- **Art Corner**

  Offer different art mediums throughout the unit.

Facilitators can make the activity centers places of healing by guiding the conversation and listening for key expressions from the kids. For example, if you are working in a puppet center, you could engage the kids in conversation by having a puppet pretend to have a problem typical of preschoolers. Kids can talk to the puppet about the problem, or take another puppet and have that "friend" talk to your puppet about his problem. In the art center, a facilitator can guide kids with simple suggestions such as: "What do you think happy looks like? Can you draw it? How about sad?" Listening to the children's responses and observing their behavior during these times will reveal a great deal about the kids and their experiences.

Skits and Bible Stories Are Key Learning Times

Another key time for preschoolers is story time. The preschool Confident Kids curriculum, like the elementary curriculum, offers both an opening skit and an ending Bible story. *Unlike the older kids, however, preschoolers respond best if you do not use facilitators as actors.* This confuses children at this age. Use one of the following ideas instead.

- **Recruit a drama team to do the skits and Bible stories.**

  Whatever format you use to tell the story, having someone else do it frees you from a large piece of the preparation. You can use live actors as long as the kids do not know them as their facilitators.

- **Use puppets to tell the story.**

  Puppets take some practice and equipment, but it is well worth the effort, as the kids respond unusually well to them. You might consider recruiting a puppet team whose only responsibility is to prepare and present the skits each week.

- **Prerecord the skits on videotape.**

  Videotaped skits allow you the freedom to be creative with the skits and give the kids the familiar experience of watching a "movie" on video. Again, recruiting a team to produce the tapes would be ideal. High schoolers may really enjoy this "high-tech storytelling."

- **Involve the kids in the action.**

  Kids love to pretend, and can be recruited to act as a crowd, an army, or animals. Look for ways to get them to participate in the stories.

- **Use purchased visual aids or videos to tell the Bible stories.**

  Pictures, flannelgraph figures, objects, and animated videos are excellent ways to help the kids focus on the story. If you have an artist available to you, develop your own visual aids.

Have Basic Materials on Hand for All Sessions

Each session plan in the curriculum lists supplies unique to that session. However, before you begin any unit, be sure to set up your room with the following basic supplies. Adding the optional materials will further enhance the group's experience.

- **Basic Supplies**

  Confident Kids postcards and stamps
  Crayons, markers, pencils
  Colored drawing paper
  Tape, glue sticks, stapler
  Blunt scissors
  Paper towels and other supplies for clean up
  Paper cups and napkins for snack time
  Extra snacks (in case someone forgets to return the snack tin)

- **Optional Supplies**

  Roll of butcher paper
  Glitter, lace doilies, scraps of fabric and ribbon
  Paints and painting supplies
  Old magazines with lots of pictures
  Cassette tapes of songs for preschoolers
  A variety of stickers
  Preschool games and craft books to supplement the curriculum, if needed

Goals

- Get acquainted with each other and establish a warm, caring environment for the group
- Help children identify one unique trait about their families
- Introduce Adam and Eve as the unit Bible story characters

Needed

- Places around the room for kids to play safely
- Many pictures of people of all ages, either individuals or in families
- Group rules poster
- Happy/sad face masks
- *Optional:* Feelings faces poster
- Story puppets, dolls, or costumes and props for skit, plus a video segment from a favorite preschool TV show, or a recording of its theme music
- Copies of "My Family Is Special" activity
- Prayer notebook or prayer boxes
- Items for regathering, if any
- Costumes, props, or pictures for Bible story (depending on how you choose to tell it)
- Bible
- Snacks or drinks
- Items for quiet games
- Storybook
- Other:_____

All About My Family
Preschool Session 1 Plan

Fill in the name of the person responsible for each activity and post this sheet in the room.

Time: _____

    Greeter

    Center #1: Free Play

    Center #2: Family Montages

Arrival and Play Centers (20 Minutes)

_____

_____

_____

Time: _____

    Introduction of New Kids

    Group Rules and "How Are You Today?"

    "In My Family" Game

    "I Want a Different Family!"

Circle Time (15 Minutes)

_____

_____

_____

_____

Time: _____

    Talk About It

    "Family Pictures"

    Prayer Time

Small Groups (25 Minutes)

_____

_____

_____

Time: _____

    Regathering

    "Introducing Adam and Eve"

    Memory Verse

    Closing Prayer Huddle

Bible Time and Closing Prayer Huddle (15 Minutes)

_____

_____

_____

_____

Time: _____

    Snack

    Quiet Games/Stories

Snack and Quiet Games/Stories (15 Minutes)

_____

_____

All About My Family

Preschool Session 1

Opening Play Centers (20 Minutes)

Center #1: Free Play

Each week you can offer a free-play area where children can play safely. Provide a home living area or dollhouse, blocks, modeling clay, puzzles, books, a sand table, etc. One or two facilitators should be available to supervise this time by encouraging kids to move freely between this area and Center 2. Make sure all the kids are participating.

Center #2: Family Montages

As kids arrive, have a table set up with pictures of people of all ages (either alone or in family groups) that you have cut out of magazines, newspapers, coloring books, etc. Include pictures of pets, as well. Have the kids choose and paste pictures to a sheet of paper to form "families." As they work, talk with them about families:

> **Joey, who is in your family picture?** *(A mommy, daddy, and baby)* **Are these others aunts and uncles?**

The point here is to talk about the many kinds of families, not necessarily their own.

Circle Time (15 Minutes)

Introduction of New Kids

If you have done a Confident Kids unit before, you will likely have both returning kids and new kids in the group. Welcome the new ones by calling each one to the front of the room. Ask the child to say his name and his favorite flavor of ice cream (or ask some other "ice breaker"). When the child is finished, lead the group in yelling, "Welcome, *(child's name)*!" and give each child a round of applause.

Group Rules

In advance, prepare a poster with the group rules on it, depicted in pictures and simple words. Display the poster and explain how the group rules work. Be sure all of the children understand the rules and the time-out system. (See pages 15 for more information.) Use these rules with preschoolers:

1. We won't tell each other's secrets (be sure to explain this carefully)
2. Only one person talks at a time and everyone else listens
3. We will not hurt each other (e.g., no hitting, kicking, name-calling)
4. Listen to the teachers and follow directions carefully
5. You don't have to take a turn if you don't want to (i.e., it's OK to pass)

"How Are You Today?"

Ask the kids to think about how they are feeling today. Can they think of a feeling word to describe it? If you like, make happy/sad face masks out of two paper plates and dowel sticks. Draw a happy face on one plate and a sad face on the other. Fasten the plates to the dowels so you can hold up either a happy face or a sad face in front of your own. Invite kids to use the masks to tell you how they are feeling today. Pass them around the circle and let everyone have a turn. *Optional:* If you have a feelings faces poster, invite kids to come forward and point to the face that describes how they are feeling today.

"I Want a Different Family!"

Introduce the story by playing a game.

In this Confident Kids unit, we will be talking about families. Everyone's family is different. Let's see how different all of our families are.

Then ask the following questions to each child in the circle, one at a time. If the answer is yes, have them stand up. If it is no, have them stay seated.

- Do you have a mommy *and* a daddy living in your house?
- Do you have a baby brother or sister living in your house?
- Do you have a pet living at your house? *(If yes, have kids tell about their pet)*
- Do you have a big brother or sister at your house?
- Do you have any cousins that you like to visit?

All of our families are different. But one thing is the same: Sometimes living in our families is lots of fun, and sometimes it isn't so much fun. Let's watch a story about a boy who wished he could live in a different family than his own!

Use puppets, dolls, or a drama team to present the skit (see "Tips for Working With Preschoolers" on page 28 for ideas on story presentation). The story script is on page 36.

Small Groups (25 Minutes)

Talk About It

Use the following questions to discuss the story:

Have you ever felt like Joey? *(Let kids respond)* **What happened that made you want to live in another family?** *(Offer suggestions: Mommy yelled at you; you got into a fight with a brother or sister)*

 Confident Kids © 1997 Linda Kondracki Sibley. Permission granted to photocopy. The Standard Publishing Co.

Do you know a family you would rather live in than your own? *(Let kids respond)*

In the next few weeks, we are going to talk about what it means to live in our families. Even though your family may have things about it that you don't like very much, your family is your family, and for you it is a special place. Let's find out about each other's families and what makes each of them special.

Use the following activity as a way to talk about the uniqueness of each family.

"Family Pictures" Activity

Distribute copies of the "My Family Is Special" coloring sheets (page 38). Ask children to draw a picture of everyone who lives in their house, including pets. Help each child to think of one thing that makes their family special (they will need lots of help thinking of things). If kids are unable to draw, offer to draw stick figures for them and let them color the rest of the sheet. As you talk with the kids during this time, be alert for information that will help you understand their families better.

Prayer Time

Each week you will spend the last few minutes of your small group time in prayer. The purpose of this time is to teach the kids how God's presence and power help them face the circumstances in their lives. To make this tangible, keep a prayer notebook or set up two boxes, one labeled *Requests* and the other *Answers*. Ask for prayer requests from the kids and either record them in the notebook or write them on slips of paper and place them in the *Requests* box. Review past requests each week and talk about how God has responded to each one. When an answer has been given, write it in the notebook, or move the slip to the *Answers* box.

Bible Time and Closing Prayer Huddle (15 Minutes)

Regathering

Assign one facilitator each week to lead the kids in music as they come from their small groups to the Bible story area. You may prefer to use a favorite game or activity instead (see Appendix B, "Resources," for ideas). This facilitator will have to finish his small group time a few minutes early to be ready to gather the kids as they come from their groups.

"Introducing Adam and Eve"

As with the opening skit, you will have to decide how to present the Bible stories each week. Preschoolers will follow the story better if you add pictures or flannel-graph figures to your presentation. (Check with the children's department supervisor at your church, or ask for these items in your local Christian bookstore.) See "Tips for Working With Preschoolers" (page 28) for ideas. The Bible story script is on page 37.

Memory Verse

This week's memory verse is 2 Corinthians 6:18 (*ICB*, condensed):

> **"I will be your father, says the Lord All-Powerful."**

Introduce the verse by holding up your Bible and saying the verse to them, explaining how wonderful it is that our All-Powerful God tells us He will be our heavenly Father! Be sure kids understand that God is different than our earthly fathers, who make mistakes and sometimes disappoint us. God is our heavenly Father, and we can always count on Him to care for us. Then have the kids say the verse with you several times.

Closing Prayer Huddle

Each week the meetings will close in the same way. Gather all the kids into a tight circle and instruct them to stack their hands on top of each other in the middle of the circle. As they stand in this position, have them recite the following prayer together:

Dear God, thank You for giving me my family! Amen!

Have them raise their hands out of the stack and over their heads as they yell out "Amen!"

Snack and Quiet Games/Stories (15 Minutes)

End each session with a snack. After the snack, have activities ready to fill any time left before parents arrive to collect their children. A storybook, short video, or coloring page would work well. The kids may enjoy coloring a picture of Adam and Eve.

Circle Time

Characters

- Joey and his mom

Needed

- Toys strewn around
- A video segment from a favorite preschool TV show, or a recording of the show's theme music

"I Want a Different Family!"

Joey	*(Enters)* Oh, boy! It's time for my favorite show, *[Name of show]*. I'll just sit right here in my favorite chair and turn the sound up real loud! *(Play tape)*
Mom	*(Enters, after the tape has played for a minute or so)* Joey, would you please turn the TV down? *(Looks around)* And how many times do I have to tell you to pick up your toys? Do it right now, please!
Joey	Oh, Mom, wait until this show is over! It's my favorite!
Mom	No more waiting! Turn off the TV and pick up your toys right now. And when your daddy gets home, he'll have something to say to you!
Joey	Humph! This family is the pits. Mom is so bossy! "Wait until my daddy comes home"—right! My daddy never comes home! He just works and works and then goes to more meetings. And my brother beats up on me all the time. I want a different family! Maybe I'll go to Billy's house and live with him. I'll bet his mom never makes him turn off the TV and pick up his toys! *(Exits looking sad and angry)*

Bible Story

From

- Genesis 1 and 2

Characters

- Adam and Eve

Needed

- Pictures, flannelgraph figures, or a video of the creation story

"Introducing Adam and Eve"

Adam and Eve enter, talking excitedly about how glad they are to be here, and how anxious they are to meet all the kids.

Adam	Do you know who we are? We are the very first family that God ever created. You can read about us in the first chapters of God's book, the Bible. What are our names? *(Let kids guess. Then use a teaching aid to briefly tell the events of Genesis 1 and 2, emphasizing Adam's loneliness until God created Eve)*
Eve	And so we became the very first family! Our family was a lot like yours. We had some very good times and some very bad times. I think my favorite time was learning the names of all the animals.
Adam	I had so much fun teaching all those names to Eve. She especially liked elephant and crocodile and hippopotamus. Some days we just laughed and laughed!
Eve	My favorites were the platypus and the rhinoceros; they sound so silly and fun. What are your favorite animal names? *(Let kids respond)*
Adam	We're going to be with you every week for the next few weeks to tell you about what life was like in our family.
Eve	We'll also tell you the best part of all—that God was always with us, taking care of us. He was our heavenly Father, and He's your heavenly Father, too.
Adam	That's all the time we have today. But we'll be back next week! Good-bye!

They exit.

My Family Is Special

Goals

- List things families do for us
- Emphasize that each child is an important part of his family, even though he may not always feel loved or special
- Help the children identify points of strength and weakness about their families
- Use the story of Adam and Eve to assure kids of God's desire for families to be good places in which to grow up

Needed

- Places around the room for kids to play safely
- A spinner with six sections or a pair of dice
- Group rules poster
- Happy/sad face masks
- *Optional:* Feelings faces poster
- Story puppets, dolls, or costumes and props for skit
- Pictures depicting elements of what families do for us, mounted on cardboard
- Blank, precut puzzles or blank pieces of lightweight cardboard
- Prayer notebook or boxes
- Items for regathering, if any
- Costumes, props, or pictures for Bible story
- Memory verse poster
- Snacks or drinks
- Items for quiet games
- Storybook
- Other: _____

What's a Family For, Anyway?

Preschool Session 2 Plan

Fill in the name of the person responsible for each activity and post this sheet in the room.

Time: _____

Greeter

Center #1: Free Play

Center #2: "Question and Answer" Game

Arrival and Play Centers (20 Minutes)

_____

_____

_____

Time: _____

Group Rules and "How Are You Today?"

"The Runaway"

Circle Time (15 Minutes)

_____

_____

Time: _____

Talk About It

"My Family" Puzzles

Prayer Time

Small Groups (25 Minutes)

_____

_____

_____

Time: _____

Regathering

"Adam Isn't Lonely Anymore"

Memory Verse

Closing Prayer Huddle

Bible Time and Closing Prayer Huddle (15 Minutes)

_____

_____

_____

_____

Time: _____

Snack

Quiet Games/Stories

Snack and Quiet Games/Stories (15 Minutes)

_____

_____

What's a Family For, Anyway?

Preschool Session 2

Center #1: Free Play

As you did last week, offer a free-play area where children can play safely. Provide a home living area or dollhouse, blocks, modeling clay, puzzles, books, a sand table, etc. One or two facilitators should be available to supervise this time by encouraging kids to move freely between this area and Center 2. Make sure all the kids are participating.

Center #2: "Question and Answer" Game

Have available a spinner with six sections on it, or one die. As kids come to this center, talk with them about the strengths and weaknesses of their families:

> **Everyone has some things that they really like about their families (strengths) and things they don't like at all (weaknesses). This game will help you find out some of those things about your family.**

To play the game, let kids take turns spinning the spinner or throwing a die. Then have them answer the question that corresponds with their number. *Note:* Preschoolers may have some trouble thinking of things to say. Be prepared to offer lots of suggestions:

1. What does your family have the most fun doing together? *(Ordering pizza, playing games, going on vacation, etc.)*
2. What do you like or not like about your bedroom?
3. What is your favorite dinner that your mom or dad cooks for you?
4. Can you think of something that you wish were different about your family? *(Wish Mom would not yell so much, wish we had a dog, wish we lived in a different house, etc.)*

5. Tell us about one (or two) family members who do not live in your house. *(Dad or mom, grandparents, aunts and uncles, cousins)*
6. Tell about a game your family plays—or you wish your family would play.

Circle Time (15 Minutes)

Group Rules

Welcome everyone to the group and use your poster to review the group rules.

"How Are You Today?"

As in the previous session, use the happy/sad face masks (or the feelings faces poster) to invite kids to tell you how they are feeling today.

"The Runaway"

Introduce the story (script is on page 43):

> In this Confident Kids unit, we are learning about our families. Everyone's family is different. Sometimes living in our families is lots of fun, and sometimes it isn't so much fun. Let's watch a story about a little girl who was not feeling very good about her family.

Small Groups (25 Minutes)

Talk About It

Use the following questions to discuss the story:

Why was Suzy running away from home? *(She thought no one cared about her)*

What did Suzy's sister say that helped her feel better? *(We're a family and we need you)*

Have you ever felt like no one cared about you in your family? *(Let kids respond)*

What do you think it would be like to run away and live in the park? *(Great, scary, lonely, etc.)*

God made us to live with other people in families instead of in the park all by ourselves. That's because our families do special things for us. Let's name some of them.

Show a set of pictures you gathered in advance, depicting various things families do for us. As you show each picture, ask the kids to name what need it represents. Possibilities include provide shelter (house) to keep us safe and warm, provide food and clothes, someone to love us (hug us, talk to us), someone to care for us when we're sick, other people to have fun with, etc.

"My Family" Puzzles

Show the kids a puzzle.

> **Puzzles are made up of many different pieces that all fit together.**

Remove a piece and say:

> **But look what happens if I take one piece away. The puzzle is not complete, is it?** *(Replace the piece)* **We need all the pieces to make the whole puzzle.**

Now show them a sample puzzle that you prepared in advance with a picture of your family on it, and tell them about your family. Then say:

Your family is like a puzzle; it is made up of several parts—people. And every person is important to your family—especially you! *(Remove a piece of the puzzle)* **Without you, your family would not be complete. And there is no one anywhere in the whole world who could ever take your place. That's how special you are to your family.**

Give each child a precut puzzle, or a piece of light-weight cardboard on which you have lettered "My Family" across the top. Have them draw a picture of their family on it, and then decorate it any way they choose. If kids cannot draw, help them by drawing stick figures for them, then let them color the rest. When they are finished, help them separate the pieces (or cut it apart if you are using the cardboard), and then re-assemble it. If time allows, the kids can exchange and assemble each other's puzzles.

Prayer Time

Use your prayer journal or prayer boxes to help you follow-up on last week's requests. Add some new ones this week and pray for each child in your group.

Bible Time and Closing Prayer Huddle (15 Minutes)

Regathering

Handle this transition time as you did last week, by having one facilitator lead the kids in songs or a favorite game or activity.

"Adam Isn't Lonely Anymore"

Incorporate the same visual aids from last week into today's skit, reviewing the creation of Eve as a companion for Adam. The script is on page 45.

Memory Verse

In advance, make a poster to represent this week's memory verse (2 Corinthians 6:18, *ICB*, condensed) in pictures. Use the poster to have the kids "read" the verse, reminding them of God's special promise to be our heavenly Father.

> **"I will be your father, says the Lord All-Powerful."**

Closing Prayer Huddle

Close the meeting with the huddle, as you did last week. Use this prayer:

> **Dear God, thank You for giving me my family! Amen!**

Snack and Quiet Games/Stories (15 Minutes)

Have ready a storybook, short video, or coloring page to use after the snack and before parents arrive. The kids may enjoy coloring a picture of Adam and Eve.

Circle Time

Characters

- Suzy, a policeman, and Suzy's big sister

Needed

- A backpack or small bag
- Something to serve as a park bench

The Runaway

Suzy enters dejectedly, wanders around, and sighs heavily. She finally sits on a "park bench."

Suzy	*(Sighs)* It's nice here in the park.
Policeman	*(Walks up to Suzy, who looks startled and begins to move away)* Wait a minute little girl! Its getting kind of late for you to be in the park by yourself. What are you doing here?
Suzy	Well—I—uh, I guess I'm running away.
Policeman	I see. *(Sits down next to her)* Are you planning to live here in the park?
Suzy	Yes! I like it here.
Policeman	And where are you going to sleep tonight? Don't you think you'll get cold here on this bench?
Suzy	Uh—
Policeman	And how about supper—do you have any food?
Suzy	I have a peanut butter sandwich in my bag.
Policeman	Wouldn't a nice hot supper at your house be better?
Suzy	No! Anything is better than living at my house. Nobody wants me there.
Policeman	Why do you say that?
Suzy	My daddy moved away and I think it's because he doesn't like me. And now my mom has to work and when she comes home she yells a lot and says she's too tired to talk to me.
Policeman	I see. So, you think your mom and dad don't like you a whole lot right now. Got any brothers and sisters?

Suzy	Yeah. They're older than me. They pick on me all the time.
Policeman	Well, it hurts when things aren't the way we want them to be.
Big Sister	*(Enters, sees Suzy, and gives her a hug)* Oh, Suzy! There you are! What are you doing here? Mom and Davey and I were so worried about you! You can't run away, we need you! Who would I pick on if you weren't there? Look, Suzy, we're a family, and we need each other. We need you! Let's go home!

They exit.

From

- Genesis 2:18–25

Characters

- Adam and Eve

Needed

- Pictures, flannelgraph figures, or a video about the creation of Eve

Adam Isn't Lonely Anymore

Adam and Eve enter, talking excitedly about returning.

Adam	Well, we're back! Today—
Eve	Wait a minute! Do you think they remember who we are?
Adam	Sure they do! *(Looks at kids)* You *do* remember us, don't you? *(Let kids guess; they may need help)*
Eve	You remembered!
Adam	As I started to say, today I really liked hearing Suzy's story. Remember what she was feeling when she ran away to the park? *(Kids will probably respond "sad")* I think she was feeling sad and lonely. That's not a comfortable feeling! I know, because when God created me, there weren't any other people around at all. I felt very lonely.

Use visual aids to review the story of how God provided animals to be companions for Adam, but they weren't adequate. So God created Eve to be his wife, and created the first family.

Eve	Ta-da! And here I am! Together, we made a family and we took care of each other and had fun together. And God knew that putting people together into families was the best way for us to live—way back then and today! *(Adam starts to wander offstage)* Hey! Where are you going?
Adam	Me? Oh, I'm going home to feed the aardvark. You know how he is when we don't feed him on time!
Eve	Oh, my, we better go! Last week he ate our bedspread and a bar of soap! He was breathing bubbles for two days! We'll be back next week. In the meantime, don't forget—your family is a special place God has given you!

They exit, saying: "Good-bye!" "Let's hurry!" etc.

Goals

- List some changes that can upset our families
- Describe the feelings that result when changes happen in our families
- Identify several healthy things to do when we feel sad, mad, or lonely
- Use the story of Adam and Eve to illustrate the difficulty of facing change

Needed

- Places around the room for kids to play safely
- Modeling clay and a variety of accessories to use with it
- Group rules poster
- Happy/sad face masks
- *Optional:* Feelings faces poster
- Story puppets, dolls, or costumes and props for skit
- Copies of "Sometimes I Feel Sad or Mad or Lonely" activity
- Prayer notebook or prayer boxes
- Items for regathering, if any
- Costumes, props, or pictures for Bible story
- Memory verse
- Snacks or drinks
- Items for quiet games
- Storybook
- Other:_____

Changes Can Upset My Family
Preschool Session 3 Plan

Fill in the name of the person responsible for each activity and post this sheet in the room.

Time: _____

    Greeter

    Center #1: Free Play

    Center #2: Modeling Clay

Arrival and Play Centers (20 Minutes)

_____

_____

_____

Time: _____

    Group Rules and "How Are You Today?"

    "The New Baby"

Circle Time (15 Minutes)

_____

_____

Time: _____

    Talk About It

    "Sometimes I Feel Sad or Mad or Lonely"

    Prayer Time

Small Groups (25 Minutes)

_____

_____

_____

Time: _____

    Regathering

    "Adam and Eve Make a Big Change"

    Memory Verse

    Closing Prayer Huddle

Bible Time and Closing Prayer Huddle (15 Minutes)

_____

_____

_____

_____

Time: _____

    Snack

    Quiet Games/Stories

Snack and Quiet Games/Stories (15 Minutes)

_____

_____

Changes Can Upset My Family

Preschool Session 3

Opening Play Centers (20 Minutes)

Center #1: Free Play

As before, offer a free-play center where children can play safely.

Center #2: Modeling Clay

As kids arrive, direct them to a table where you have set up modeling clay and a variety of accessories to use with it (e.g., cookie cutters, rolling pins, molds). As the kids play, talk with them about changes (the theme of today's session).

> **Change is when something is one way, and then it is another.**

Then help the kids see the changes they are making with the modeling clay. For example:

> **Jamey, you changed your modeling clay from a cookie to a round ball.**

> **Joseph changed his modeling clay into a monster.**

Circle Time (15 Minutes)

Group Rules

Welcome everyone to the group and use your poster to review the group rules.

"How Are You Today?"

As in last session, use the happy/sad face masks (or the feelings faces poster) to invite kids to tell you how they are feeling today.

"The New Baby"

Introduce the story (script is on page 51):

> In this Confident Kids unit, we are learning about our families. And sometimes things change in our families. Do you remember what change is? *(Change is when something was one way and now it is different)*

Have the kids experience change by having them change position (sit, stand, hop on one foot, stand on head, etc.). You can also refer to the modeling clay activity they did earlier, using some modeling clay to demonstrate a change. Then say:

> Now let's watch a story about a girl who had a big change happen in her family.

Small Groups (25 Minutes)

Talk About It

Use the following questions to discuss the story:

> In the story, something had changed in the family. What was it? *(A new baby joined the family)*

> What do you think the little girl was feeling when the change happened? *(Sad, mad, and lonely)*

> Did you ever have a new baby at your house? *(Let kids respond)* Did you ever feel like Jessie did, and wish the baby would go away? *(Let kids respond)*

> Sometimes things change in our families. Some changes are easy and some are hard. Can you think of a time when something changed in your family? *(Give lots of examples: a new baby, a working*

mom, a divorce, a move, etc.) **How did you feel when that change happened?** *(Help kids see that when difficult changes happen, we may feel sad, mad, or lonely)* **There are lots of things we can do when changes happen and we feel sad, mad, or lonely. Some things will help us feel better, and some will make us feel worse. Let's see if we can find out what those things are.**

"Sometimes I Feel Sad or Mad or Lonely" Activity

Distribute copies of the "Sometimes I Feel Sad or Mad or Lonely" activity sheet (page 53). Look at each picture, and talk about it as a way to handle our feelings. Ask:

> Is this something you could do when you feel sad? mad? lonely? Will *(Name the action in the picture)* help you feel better or worse?

Help kids distinguish between healthy and unhealthy, or helpful and hurtful, ways to express their feelings. Have them cross out the unhealthy actions. *("Get into a fight" and "Bite somebody")* Let kids color the sheets as you talk together.

Prayer Time

Conduct your prayer time as in weeks past.

Bible Time and Closing Prayer Huddle (15 Minutes)

Regathering

As in weeks past, have one facilitator lead the kids in songs or a favorite game or activity.

"Adam and Eve Make a Big Change"

Present the Bible story (script is on page 52). *Note:* You may want to use visual aids to help tell the story of Adam and Eve being sent out of the garden.

Memory Verse

Introduce a new verse (Romans 8:38, *ICB*, paraphrased):

> **I am sure that nothing can ever stop God from loving me!**

Say:

> **Sometimes when hurtful changes happen in our families, we may think that God has stopped loving us or taking care of us. But the Bible tells us that absolutely nothing that happens to us can ever keep God from loving us!**

Then teach the verse by making up a few motions to go with the words. Have the kids repeat the verse with the motions several times.

Closing Prayer Huddle

Close the meeting as in weeks past. Use this prayer:

> **Dear God, thank You for giving me my family! Amen!**

Snack and Quiet Games/Stories (15 Minutes)

Have ready a storybook, short video, or coloring page to use after the snack and before parents arrive. The kids may enjoy coloring a picture of Adam and Eve.

Circle Time

Characters

- Jessie and her mom

Needed

- A doll and crib or a box with a blanket or other appropriate prop to represent the new baby
- A recording of a baby crying

The New Baby

Jessie enters and looks in the crib.

Jessie Humpf! You're finally sleeping. Maybe now Mom will read to me, like she used to before you came along! *(Looks offstage and yells)* Mom! Where are you? *(Baby starts to cry)*

Mom *(Enters in a hurry)* Jessie, why did you do that? You woke the baby! *(Looks in cradle)* There, there, my little one! Don't cry! Go back to sleep. *(Crying fades)*

Jessie Will you read me a story?

Mom Now? I'm in the middle of doing laundry, and in a minute I'm going to start dinner. Later, OK? By the way, the next time you want me, don't yell in the baby's ear! *(Exits)*

Jessie *(Looks in cradle)* It's all your fault! Everything around here was just great until you came along! Now everything's different. Mom never has time to do anything with me anymore. *(In a taunting voice)* "Not now, Jessie, I have to feed the baby! Play with that later, Jessie, the noise will wake the baby!" And when daddy comes home, he runs to pick you up before he even says "Hi" to me! How long are you going to live here anyway? If you went away, maybe we could all get back to the way things used to be!

Mom *(Enters)* Jessie, I heard what you just said. I'm sorry I've not spent much time with you since the baby was born. Let's make a deal, OK? After dinner tonight we'll play a game, OK?

Jessie *(Brightens)* OK, Mom! Can I go play with Jake before dinner?

Bible Story

From

- Genesis 3:1–7

Characters

- Adam and Eve

Needed

- Pictures, flannelgraph figures, or a video of Adam and Eve leaving the garden
- *Optional:* A stuffed or rubber snake

Adam and Eve Make a Big Change

Adam enters carrying the snake and greets the kids. Eve enters behind him, obviously upset about the snake.

Eve	Did you have to bring that thing? You know I can't stand snakes! And neither can anyone else here! Right, kids?
Adam	I know snakes aren't your favorite, but when I heard the kids were talking about changes in families today, I just had to bring it! After all, it was a snake that started the first—and biggest—change in our family!
Eve	True. Let's tell the kids about it. *(Relate the incidents of Genesis 3:1–7, using a visual aid to tell about Adam and Eve leaving the garden)*
Adam	Well, that changed everything.
Eve	We tried to hide from God—
Adam	But we couldn't.
Eve	We had to leave our beautiful home in the garden—
Adam	And we felt sad and mad and lonely!
Eve	But even though everything changed, one thing always stayed the same! God never stopped loving us!
Adam	Even when we felt sad and mad and lonely, we always knew God was there taking care of us, just like He's taking care of you!
Eve	We'd better go so you can learn a verse from the Bible to remind you that God always takes care of you, even when things change in your family and you feel sad and mad and lonely.

Both say good-bye as they exit.

Sometimes I Feel Sad or Mad or Lonely

Ask for a hug

Bite somebody

Tell God when you feel sad, mad, or lonely

Talk to Mom or Dad

Ouch!
Hey!
Get into a fight

Draw pictures of how you feel

Goals

- Identify pleasant (happy) and unpleasant (angry or sad) feelings we have in our families
- Role-play actions that can increase positive feelings in our families
- Hear how jealousy between Cain and Abel affected their family

Needed

- Places around the room for kids to play safely
- Paper plates on which you have drawn a variety of feelings faces (one on each plate)
- Group rules poster
- Happy/sad face masks
- *Optional:* Feelings faces poster
- Story puppets, dolls, or costumes and props for skit
- Lunch-size paper bags
- *Optional:* Fabric "clothes," ribbons, etc. for decorating the puppets
- Prayer notebook or prayer boxes
- Items for regathering, if any
- Costumes, props, or pictures for Bible story
- Memory verse
- Snacks or drinks
- Items for quiet games
- Storybook
- Other:_____

Actions Can Hurt—Or Help—My Family

Preschool Session 4 Plan

Fill in the name of the person responsible for each activity and post this sheet in the room.

Time: _____

Greeter

Center #1: Free Play

Center #2: Feelings "Follow the Leader"

Arrival and Play Centers (20 Minutes)

_____

_____

Time: _____

Group Rules and "How Are You Today?"

"The Cereal Bowl"

Circle Time (15 Minutes)

_____

_____

Time: _____

Talk About It

Paper Bag Puppet Role Plays

Prayer Time

Small Groups (25 Minutes)

_____

_____

_____

Time: _____

Regathering

"Adam and Eve Have a New Baby!"

Memory Verse

Closing Prayer Huddle

Bible Time and Closing Prayer Huddle (15 Minutes)

_____

_____

_____

_____

Time: _____

Snack

Quiet Games/Stories

Snack and Quiet Games/Stories (15 Minutes)

_____

_____

Actions Can Hurt— Or Help—My Family

Preschool Session 4

Opening Play Centers (20 Minutes)

Center #1: Free Play

As before, offer a free-play center where children can play safely.

Center #2: Feelings "Follow the Leader"

For this activity, you will need paper plates on which you have drawn a variety of feelings faces (e.g., happy, sad, mad, shy, sleepy, surprised, loved). As kids arrive, tell them you are going to play "Follow the Leader." Start by doing some simple things, like hopping on one foot, twirling in a circle, etc. Let kids choose actions. As you play, mix in the feelings plates by choosing one and holding it in front of your face. Help kids name the feeling represented, and then lead them in using their whole bodies to display what that feeling looks like. For example, "angry" kids may make an angry face, tighten up their bodies, clench their fists, etc. "Happy" children may jump up and down, etc. Continue playing until you are out of time.

Circle Time (15 Minutes)

Group Rules

Welcome everyone to the group and use your poster to review the group rules.

"How Are You Today?"

As in the last session, use the happy/sad face masks (or the feelings faces poster) to invite kids to tell you how they are feeling today.

"The Cereal Bowl"

Introduce the story (script is on page 59):

> In Confident Kids, we are learning about our families. Everyone's family is different. Sometimes living in our families is lots of fun and we feel happy, and sometimes it isn't so much fun and we feel sad or angry. Let's watch a story about a little boy who was feeling angry and sad about his family.

Small Groups (25 Minutes)

Talk About It

Use the following questions to discuss the story:

> Why did Skip throw his cereal bowl at his brother? *(He called him a runt)*
>
> Was he feeling happy or angry when he threw the cereal bowl? *(Angry)*
>
> Do you think saying he was sorry to his brother will help make him feel better? *(Yes)*
>
> Have you ever gotten into a fight with your brother or sister? *(Let kids respond)* Did you feel happy when you were fighting, or angry and sad? *(Let kids respond)*
>
> When we live in a family there will always be things that happen that make us feel angry and sad. Sometimes other people in your family will do things that make you feel angry and sad, and sometimes you will do things that will make others feel angry and sad.

Everyone's family has those things happen. But we can make choices in our families to do things that will make ourselves and others feel happy and loved, rather than angry and sad. Let's discover some of those things.

Paper Bag Puppet Role Plays

Before the session, prepare a paper bag puppet for each child by drawing a face on it. Have the kids add clothes and hair with crayons or markers. *Optional:* Have available fabric scraps for clothes, pieces of yarn for hair, ribbons, etc. to glue on the puppets.

Read one of the story starters to the kids, and have them use their puppets to do the actions in the story. Do two versions—one that shows actions that would bring angry and sad feelings to the family, and then one that would bring happy feelings. The object is to help the kids see how they can choose actions that will improve their family life. *Note:* Manipulating the puppets is enough for preschoolers to do. You can have the kids help you think of ideas, but you will need to do the storytelling.

Story Starter 1. Jason is playing with his blocks, building a really high tower. Mom calls to him from downstairs, "Jason, please come down here! I want to talk to you about something." Jason doesn't want to leave his blocks right now.

Story Starter 2. Jessica is drawing a picture at the table, when her little brother comes by to see what she is doing. Just as he gets to the table he trips and spills his milk all over her picture. She had worked on it for a long time, and she is very angry!

Story Starter 3. Jason and Jessica are riding in the back seat of the car. Jason bumps his sister accidentally. "Don't!" Jessie yells, and pokes him back. Jason hits his sister, just as Mom turns around and says, "Stop it, you two!"

Prayer Time

Conduct your prayer time as in weeks past.

Bible Time and Closing Prayer Huddle (15 Minutes)

Regathering

As in weeks past, have one facilitator lead the kids in songs or a favorite game or activity.

"Adam and Eve Have a New Baby!"

Present the Bible story (script is on page 61). *Note:* You may want to use visual aids to help tell the story of Cain and Abel.

Memory Verse

Review the verse from last week (Romans 8:38, *ICB*, paraphrased), reminding kids that the Bible tells us that absolutely nothing that happens to us can ever keep God from loving us! Include a few simple motions and say it together a few times:

> **I am sure that nothing can ever stop God from loving me!**

Closing Prayer Huddle

Close the meeting as in weeks past. Use this prayer:

> **Dear God, thank You for giving me my family! Amen!**

Snack and Quiet Games/Stories (15 Minutes)

Have ready a storybook, short video, or coloring page to use after the snack and before parents arrive. The kids may enjoy coloring a picture of Adam and Eve.

Circle Time

Characters

- Skip and his friend

Needed

- Offstage voice of Skip's older brother

The Cereal Bowl

Skip enters with his head down. He paces back and forth, sighing and uttering, "Woe is me!"

Friend	Hi, Skip! Are you ready to play—what's wrong with you? You look awful!
Skip	My mom yelled at me. I wish she wouldn't do that! I feel bad and she feels bad and everyone gets a headache when she does that!
Friend	My mom yells sometimes, too. What happened?
Skip	Nothing! *(Pauses)* Except I guess she wasn't too happy about what I did to my brother.
Friend	What did you do?
Skip	I just threw a little something at him, that's all!
Friend	What did you throw?
Skip	My cereal bowl.
Friend	You threw an empty bowl at your brother?
Skip	Well, maybe it wasn't so empty.
Friend	You mean there was cereal in the bowl when you threw it?
Skip	*(Brightly)* Yeah! You shoulda been there! It was great! Hit him right on the head! There were frosted flakes and little drops of milk running down his nose! He was pretty mad, but I don't care! He deserved it for calling me a little runt! He does that all the time, even when I ask him to stop! Of course, now my brother wants to kill me, and my mom is mad and everyone hates me. What a mess!
Friend	Sounds like you're in trouble!
Skip	Yeah, I like it better when we all laugh and get along. It's all my fault!

| **Friend** | Things like that happen in families all the time! You could say you're sorry to your brother and your mom—that would probably help a lot! |

From offstage, brother yells, "Where are you, you little runt? I want to give you back your cereal bowl!"

| **Skip** | Uh, that's a good idea. Let's think of some more ideas—later, OK? Let's get outta here! |

They run offstage.

Bible Story

From

- Genesis 4:1–8

Characters

- Adam and Eve

Needed

- A few baby items, such as a blanket, rattle, bottle, diapers, etc.
- *Optional:* A video, teaching pictures, or flannelgraph figures to tell the story of Cain and Abel

Adam and Eve Have a New Baby!

Adam and Eve enter and greet the kids. They are carrying the baby items.

Adam	Today you were talking about times we have good feelings and times we have bad feelings in our families. So, we wanted to tell you about when we had our first little boy—Cain. Having a new baby brings all kinds of feelings. How many of you have had a new baby at your house? *(Let kids respond)*
Eve	A new baby can bring lots of different feelings! When you had a new baby at your house, you probably felt happy. But you might have felt sad or angry, too. We learned that when we had our second boy—Abel. We were really happy! But Cain, well, he was feeling something different. Maybe some of you have felt it, too.
Adam	Cain was jealous! When we are jealous, we usually want to act in ways that are hurtful to other people in our families. What things do we do when we feel jealous? *(Get angry, yell at others, go to our room and pout, say things we don't mean, try to hurt the person we are jealous of, etc.)*
Eve	Our poor son, Cain, did all of those things. One day he kicked his brother, another day he yelled at me and said, "I hate you, Mom!" *(Use the visual aids to tell about Cain and Abel at this time)*
Adam	All those actions made our family—and Cain—feel very unhappy! So you see, if you feel sad or unhappy in your family sometimes, just remember that all families have times like that.
Eve	Remember, too, when you feel angry, or jealous or upset, you can handle your feelings better than Cain did. What can you do? *(Talk about your feelings, choose helpful rather than hurtful actions)*
Adam	One other thing you can do—ask God to help you! You can tell Him what you are feeling and ask Him to help you act in helpful ways. Hey! Look at the time! We better go. See you next week!

They exit.

Goals

- Describe how words can hurt or help us
- Use feelings faces connected with various words or tones of voice
- Use the story of Adam and Eve to illustrate how easy it is to hurt others with our words

Needed

- Places around the room for kids to play safely
- Group rules poster
- Happy/sad face masks
- *Optional:* Feelings faces poster
- Story puppets, dolls, or costumes and props for skit
- A puppet family (purchased, or made from wooden spoons or paper bags)
- Copies of "Words Can Hurt, Words Can Help" activity, cut out
- Two paper plates and two dowel sticks (sticks optional) per child
- Prayer notebook or prayer boxes
- Items for regathering, if any
- Costumes, props, or pictures for Bible story
- Memory verse poster
- Snacks or drinks
- Items for quiet games
- Storybook
- Other: _____

Words Can Hurt—Or Help—My Family

Preschool Session 5 Plan

Fill in the name of the person responsible for each activity and post this sheet in the room.

Time: _____

Arrival and Play Centers (20 Minutes)

Greeter _____

Center #1: Free Play _____

Center #2: Telephone Game _____

Time: _____

Circle Time (15 Minutes)

Group Rules and "How Are You Today?" _____

"Sticks and Stones" _____

Time: _____

Small Groups (25 Minutes)

Talk About It _____

"Words Can Hurt, Words Can Help" Face Masks

Prayer Time _____

Time: _____

Bible Time and Closing Prayer Huddle (15 Minutes)

Regathering _____

"Eve Learns to Say Words That Help" _____

Memory Verse _____

Closing Prayer Huddle _____

Time: _____

Snack and Quiet Games/Stories (15 Minutes)

Snack _____

Quiet Games/Stories _____

Words Can Hurt— Or Help—My Family

Preschool Session 5

Opening Play Centers (20 Minutes)

Center #1: Free Play

As before, offer a free-play center where children can play safely.

Center #2: Telephone Game

Have kids sit in groups of three. Begin by whispering a phrase into the ear of one of the kids. Be sure no one else can hear. Have that person then lean over and whisper the same phrase into the ear of the next person. The phrase can only be whispered once to the next child; if the child did not hear it correctly, she must pass on whatever she thinks the phrase is. Pass the phrase to the third child, who then repeats it aloud. See how much it changed as it went through the three sets of ears! Repeat the process as long as time remains. Possible phrases:

> **Humpty Dumpty sat on a wall.**
>
> **Hickory dickory dock.**
>
> **Joey (use a name of one of the kids in the group) is a very special person!**
>
> Confident Kids **is a place to have fun!**

Circle Time (15 Minutes)

Group Rules

Welcome everyone to the group and use your poster to review the group rules.

"How Are You Today?"

As in the last session, use the happy/sad face masks (or the feelings faces poster) to invite kids to tell you how they are feeling today.

"Sticks and Stones"

Introduce the story (script is on page 67):

> In this Confident Kids unit, we are learning about our families. Everyone's family is different. Sometimes living in our families is fun and we feel happy, and sometimes it isn't so much fun and we feel sad or angry. The words we say, and even how we say them, can make us feel happy or sad or angry in our families. Let's watch a story about some kids who learned how words can help—or hurt!

Small Groups (25 Minutes)

Talk About It

Use the following questions to discuss the story:

> Have you ever heard the phrase, "Sticks and stones may break my bones, but words will never hurt me"? *(Let kids respond)* What do you think it means? *(Explain)*

> In the skit, which friend used words that helped Jason? *(Jill)* Which friend used words that hurt him? *(Debbie)*

> When we live in families, we will have times when other family members talk to us—or we talk to them—in ways that hurt. Family members don't usually mean to be hurtful; it just happens. We forget to be careful about what we say and how we say it!

> Can you think of examples of words that hurt? *(Name-calling, shouting "No!" or "I hate you!")*

> But we can work hard to choose words that help, instead of hurt! It's not easy, but you can do it!

> Help me think of words that help. *("I love you." "You're my friend." "Thank you." "I'm sorry.")*

"Words Can Hurt, Words Can Help" Face Masks

Have prepared a set of puppets that represent a full family. Use purchased puppets, or make your own using a set of various-sized wooden spoons or lunch-sized paper bags. Also, prepare two paper plates for each child by lettering *Words Can Hurt* around the rim on the bottom side of one plate, and *Words Can Help* in the same location on the second plate. Cut out the circles from the "Words Can Hurt, Words Can Help" activity sheets (pages 69 and 70), one set per child.

Distribute the face circles, paper plates, and dowel sticks (optional) to each child. Help the kids glue the happy face on the plate that says *Words Can Help* and the sad face on the one that says *Words Can Hurt*, and then tape the plates to the sticks. (Kids can simply hold up the face masks without the sticks, if you are not using them.) Let kids color the plates, if desired.

As they work, point out that our words can hurt instead of help.

> Sometimes we can hurt people with our words when we call them names or say, "I hate you!" We can also hurt people when we use a tone of voice that is angry or hurtful. *(Say "I love you" with clenched teeth and an angry voice, and ask the kids if the words felt loving)* A good rule to follow is this: Say helpful words, and say them in a kind way.

Use the puppet family to present one of the scenarios below. When you finish, ask the kids to choose a face mask that depicts how the words in the scenario made them feel, and hold that mask up in front of their own.

Have the kids help you find words that can help instead of hurt to use in a second version of the scenario. Use the puppets again, presenting this new ending. Then have the kids choose a mask that represents how these words made them feel and hold that mask in front of their faces.

If time allows, repeat using the alternate scenario.

Scenario 1

Mother	*(Upset)* Susie, turn off the TV set now and pick up your toys, like I asked you to do an hour ago!
Susie	*(Yells)* You *always* make me turn off the TV! How come you never tell Jimmy he has to pick up his toys?

Scenario 2

Little Sister	Can I go with you to the park? I want to play on the playground.
Big Brother	Don't be stupid! Why would I want to take a little runt like you with me? I've got better things to do than watch you, dummy!

Prayer Time

Conduct your prayer time as in weeks past.

Bible Time and Closing Prayer Huddle (15 Minutes)

Regathering

As in weeks past, have one facilitator lead the kids in songs or a favorite game or activity.

"Eve Learns to Say Words That Help"

Present the Bible story (script is on page 68).

Memory Verse

In advance, make up a poster of this week's memory verse (Ephesians 4:29, *ICB*, paraphrased), using pictures. Or if you prefer, make up a few motions to teach the verse.

> **Do not say hurtful things. Say words that help others.**

Closing Prayer Huddle

Close the meeting as in weeks past. Use this prayer:

> **Dear God, thank You for giving me my family! Amen!**

Snack and Quiet Games/Stories (15 Minutes)

Have ready a storybook, short video, or coloring page to use after the snack and before parents arrive.

Circle Time

Characters

- Jason, Jill, and Debbie

Sticks and Stones

Jason enters, crying loudly and holding his arm.

Jason	Owwww!
Debbie	*(Enters)* Hey, Jason! What's going on? You dying or something?
Jason	I fell off my scooter and hurt my arm! It hurts and tingles all over!
Debbie	Is that all? Why are you making such a fuss? I don't see blood anywhere. You just hit your crazy bone, that's all!
Jason	*(Still crying)* Well, it hurts a lot, Debbie! Maybe it's broken!
Debbie	*(Laughs)* Broken? You're just a big crybaby, that's all! *(Taunting as she walks away)* Crybaby, crybaby, crybaby—
Jason	Oh, yeah? *(Calls out after her)* "Sticks and stones may break my bones, but words will never hurt me!" *(Sniffles and looks sad as he starts walking in the other direction)*
Jill	*(Enters)* Hey, Jason, what's wrong? I could hear you all the way over in my yard! Should I call 911 or something?
Jason	I fell off my scooter and hurt my arm, Jill! It hurts and tingles all over!
Jill	I tripped once and hurt my arm the same way! It does hurt a lot! Look, I'll help you, OK? I'll get your scooter and walk you back to your house so your mom can take a look at your arm. If she's not home, we can go to my house. Let's go.
Jason	*(Looks relieved)* Thanks, Debbie! I need a friend to help me right now!
They exit.	

Bible Story

From

- Ephesians 4:29

Characters

- Adam and Eve

Eve Learns to Say Words That Help

Adam and Eve enter and greet the kids. They are talking to each other, but they are obviously puzzled.

Adam "Sticks and stones may break my bones"? "Words will never hurt me"? What does that mean? That's a dumb phrase! I mean, it's certainly not true! In fact, words hurt more than sticks and stones!

Eve Hey, Adam, you were hurt by a stick once, remember?

Adam *(Looks puzzled)* A stick? You mean that time I fell over a tree that had fallen in the garden? I'd hardly call that a stick!

Eve *(Laughs)* I know, but I was trying to be kind! I can't believe you just admitted to all these kids that you didn't see a huge tree and you ran right into it! *(To kids)* You should have been there! It was so funny! He was chasing a kangaroo—

Adam *(Looks embarrassed and hurt)* Eve, why are you telling this?

Eve *(Looks at Adam and laughs)* Oh, come on! I'm just having a little fun, that's all!

Adam You're making me look stupid in front of all the kids.

Eve *(Looks shocked)* I am not! Well, at least I didn't mean to. *(Pauses)* I'm sorry, Adam! You know, it really is easy to hurt others with words, isn't it?

Adam It sure is. That's why there is a verse in the Bible about it. Ephesians 4:29 says, "Do not say hurtful things. Say words that help others."

Eve That's a great verse, and I'm going to do what it says—starting right now!

Adam Now those are words that help. I feel so much better! Well, we're out of time! See you all next week! Good-bye!

They exit.

Words Can Help, Words Can Hurt

Goals

- Describe ways to show love for family members
- Define affirmation and illustrate its importance to showing love
- Adam and Eve use Romans 8:39 as an affirmation that God loves us

Needed

- Places around the room for kids to play safely
- Group rules poster
- Happy/sad face masks
- *Optional:* Feelings faces poster
- Story puppets, dolls, or costumes and props for skit
- Copies of "Affirmation Cards" (one per child, plus several extras)
- Prayer notebook or prayer boxes
- Items for regathering, if any
- Costumes, props, or pictures for Bible story
- Memory Verse
- Snacks or drinks
- Items for quiet games
- Storybook
- Other:_____

"I Care About You!"

Preschool Session 6 Plan

Fill in the name of the person responsible for each activity and post this sheet in the room.

Time: _____

Greeter

Center #1: Free Play

Center #2: "Kids' Choice" Game

Arrival and Play Centers (20 Minutes)

_____

_____

_____

Time: _____

Group Rules and "How Are You Today?"

"The Affirmation"

Circle Time (15 Minutes)

_____

_____

Time: _____

Talk About It

Affirmation Cards

Prayer Time

Small Groups (25 Minutes)

_____

_____

_____

Time: _____

Regathering

"Adam and Eve Learn to Affirm"

Memory Verse

Closing Prayer Huddle

Bible Time and Closing Prayer Huddle (15 Minutes)

_____

_____

_____

_____

Time: _____

Snack

Quiet Games/Stories

Snack and Quiet Games/Stories (15 Minutes)

_____

_____

"I Care About You!"

Preschool Session 6

Opening Play Centers (20 Minutes)

Center #1: Free Play

As before, offer a free-play center where children can play safely.

Center #2: Kids Choice

As the kids arrive, ask them to choose a favorite game to play. You might want to be prepared with an idea in case they need help settling on a game everyone can play. Consider using a previous gathering activity the kids enjoyed.

Circle Time (15 Minutes)

Group Rules

Welcome everyone to the group and use your poster to review the group rules.

"How Are You Today?"

As in weeks past, use the happy/sad face masks (or the feelings faces poster) to invite kids to tell you how they are feeling today.

"The Affirmation"

Introduce the story (script is on page 75):

> In this Confident Kids unit, we are learning about our families. Everyone's family is different. Sometimes living in our families is lots of fun and we feel happy, and sometimes it isn't so much fun and we feel sad or angry. Let's watch a story about a little girl who learned that saying kind

words helped make her family a nicer place to be!

Small Groups (25 Minutes)

Talk About It

Use the following questions to discuss the story:

> **Why did Jessica yell at her brother?** *(He spilled water on her painting)*
>
> **How do you think Jason felt when his sister yelled at him?** *(Hurt, sad)*
>
> **How do you feel when someone yells at you?** *(Let kids respond)* **Do you feel loved?** *(Let kids respond)*
>
> **What nice thing did Jessica do for her brother to show him she really loved him?** *(Said he was a good painter, gave him a hug, played with him)*

The best part of living in a family is being loved by the others in your family. But sometimes family members can act in ways that don't make us feel loved at all.

Ask kids to stand in a circle for this next activity. As you read each of the statements below, ask the kids whether they would feel loved or unloved in that situation. Have them act out their response by doing the following: If they would feel loved, stand tall and hug themselves while smiling; if they would feel unloved, slump and look sad.

> **Your mom yells, "You spilled your milk again! Can't we ever get through a meal without you spilling your milk?"**
>
> **Your big sister lets you play games with her and her friends.**
>
> **Your dad takes you to work with him for the day.**

> **Your mom and dad are having a big fight.**

Let kids suggest other things that make them feel loved or unloved.

Affirmation Cards

Give everyone a copy of the "Affirmation Cards" activity (page 78).

> One way we can help others in our families know we love them is by giving them affirmations. Affirmations are simply words that tell others how special they are to us.

Let the kids color the cards and then cut them apart to take home and give to family members. Have extra cards available in case they want to make more or make a mistake on one.

As they work, it might be a good idea for you to make a card for each child in your small group. Give it to them as they leave today.

Prayer Time

Conduct your prayer time as in weeks past.

Bible Time and Closing Prayer Huddle (15 Minutes)

Regathering

Have one facilitator lead the kids in songs or a favorite game or activity.

"Adam and Eve Learn to Affirm"

Present the Bible story (script is on page 76).

Memory Verse

Review the verse from two weeks ago (Romans 8:38, *ICB*, paraphrased), reminding kids that God tells us in the Bible how much He loves us! If you made up motions, review them and say the verse together a few times:

I am sure that nothing can ever stop God from loving me!

Closing Prayer Huddle

Close the meeting as in weeks past. Use this prayer:

Dear God, thank You for giving me my family! Amen!

Snack and Quiet Games/Stories (15 Minutes)

Have ready a storybook, short video, or coloring page to use after the snack and before parents arrive.

Circle Time

Characters

- Jessica and Jason

Needed

- A table with two chairs
- Two pictures and items for painting with watercolors

The Affirmation

Jessica and Jason are sitting at a table painting with watercolors. There is a cup full of water near Jessica's picture.

Jessica	This is so much fun! I haven't painted with watercolors in a long time! I think this is my best picture ever!
Jason	Really? Let me see? *(Clumsily moves toward Jessica's picture and spills the water all over it)* Oops! Uh-oh!
Jessica	*(Yells in an angry voice)* Jason! What's wrong with you! Look what you did! It's ruined! My best picture ever and it's ruined! You clumsy goon!
Jason	*(Looks hurt)* I—I didn't mean to. *(Starts to cry; walks off to the side and sits down with his head buried in his hands)*
Jessica	You did too! You always do dumb—*(Looks at her brother crying and softens)*—stuff like that. *(Pauses, thinking. Looks at Jason's picture, looks back at him. Sighs. Walks over and sits down next to him)* Jason?
Jason	*(Without looking up)* What?
Jessica	Did I ever tell you that you are a really good painter?
Jason	*(Looks up, surprised)* I am?
Jessica	Yeah. Look! *(They get up and go look at Jason's picture that is still on the table)* This is really good. It's much better than I ever did when I was in kindergarten. You're a great painter!
Jason	*(Smiling, gives her a big hug)* Thanks, Jessie!
Jessica	*(Still hugging, says to the kids)* I think I like saying nice things better than yelling. *(To Jason)* Hey, want to go outside and play?

They pick up their things and exit.

Confident Kids © 1997 Linda Kondracki Sibley. Permission granted to photocopy. The Standard Publishing Co.

Bible Story

From

- Romans 8:38

Characters

- Adam and Eve

Adam and Eve Learn to Affirm

Adam and Eve enter and greet the kids. Eve is perky and talkative and rambles on about what a great meeting this was, etc. Adam is feeling low and doesn't say anything. He stays off to the side.

Eve	*(After rambling on for a bit)* Adam, don't you—*(Looks at Adam for a moment and gets serious)* You look so sad! Is something wrong?
Adam	*(Sighs)* No, I'm fine.
Eve	You don't look fine. What are you feeling today?
Adam	Well, since you asked, I am feeling kind of awful. I feel really dumb and stupid.
Eve	*(Surprised)* Why?
Adam	I just saw a platypus.
Eve	So?
Adam	Don't you think that's a really stupid name for an animal? I mean really—platypus! And how about rhinoceros and hippopotamus? Dumb, right?
Eve	I never thought about it. Besides, you named all the animals!
Adam	Exactly! And I did a really bad job of it, too!
Eve	Well, I think you did a great job! Naming all those animals was a big task! I know I never could have done as well.
Adam	*(Brightens)* Really? You know, you've never said that to me. I feel much better just to hear you say that!
Eve	Well, I should have said it sooner! Hey, I just gave you an affirmation, like we learned about in Confident Kids today!

Adam	I guess it really works! I feel much better. Before we go, let's give the kids an affirmation. I know a Bible verse that is God's affirmation to us. You know what I mean?
Eve	You bet. Romans 8:38. Let's review it together: I am sure that nothing can ever stop God from loving me!
Adam	Well, it's time for us to say good-bye! See you next week!
They exit.	

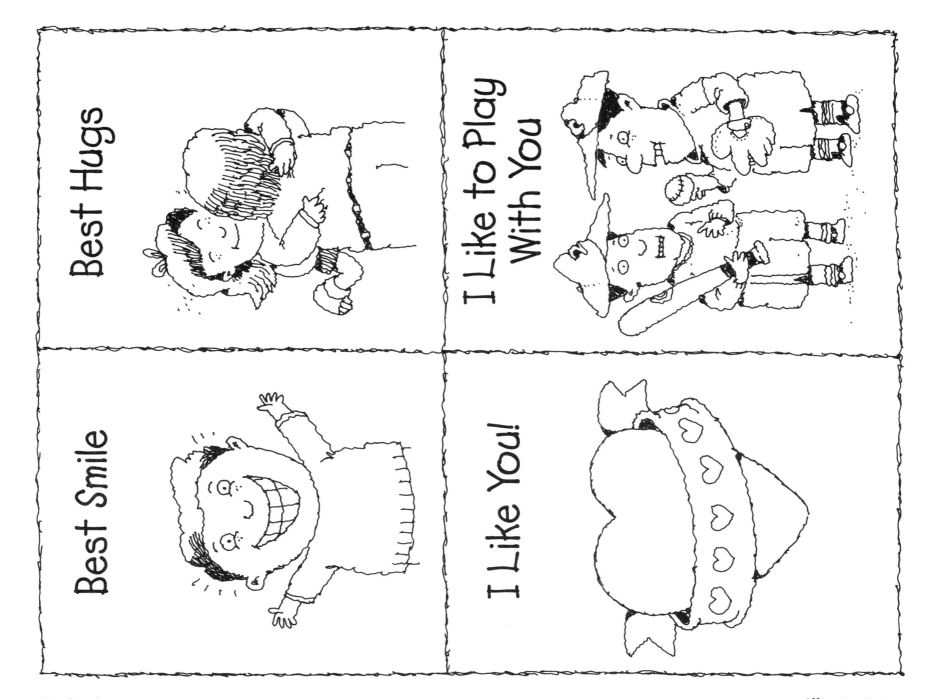

Best Hugs

I Like to Play With You

Best Smile

I Like You!

Affirmation Cards

Goals

- Assure kids of God's love for them, using Matthew 19:13–15
- Explain how kids can belong to two families: their own and God's
- Act out the story of Jesus and the children (Matthew 19:13–15)

Needed

- Places around the room for kids to play safely
- Invitations for Family Night
- Group rules poster
- Happy/sad face masks
- *Optional:* Feelings faces poster
- Story puppets, dolls, or costumes and props for skit
- Copies of "Coming to Jesus" coloring sheet
- Prayer notebook or prayer boxes
- Items for regathering, if any
- Costumes, props, or pictures for Bible story
- Memory verse
- Snacks or drinks
- Items for quiet games
- Storybook
- Copies of "Affirmation Balloons" and unit certificates from Appendix A (pages 371 and 373)
- Other: _____

I Can Belong to God's Family, Too

Preschool Session 7 Plan

Fill in the name of the person responsible for each activity and post this sheet in the room.

Time: _____

    Greeter

    Center #1: Free Play

    Center #2: Invitations for Family Night

Arrival and Play Centers (20 Minutes)

_____

_____

_____

Time: _____

    Group Rules and "How Are You Today?"

    "Coming to Jesus"

Circle Time (15 Minutes)

_____

_____

Time: _____

    Talk About It

    "Coming to Jesus" Coloring Sheets

    Prayer Time

Small Groups (25 Minutes)

_____

_____

_____

Time: _____

    Regathering

    "Adam and Eve Tell a Story"

    Memory Verse

    Closing Prayer Huddle

Bible Time and Closing Prayer Huddle (15 Minutes)

_____

_____

_____

_____

Time: _____

    Snack

    Quiet Games/Stories

Snack and Quiet Games/Stories (15 Minutes)

_____

_____

I Can Belong to God's Family, Too

Preschool Session 7

Center #1: Free Play

As before, offer a free-play center where children can play safely.

Center #2: Invitations for Family Night

As kids arrive, have them work on the invitations for Family Night (page 87). Explain that next week is the final session of this unit. There will be a party and they can invite their family to attend the party with them. Talk about the party enthusiastically so as to get the kids excited about sharing their group experience with their parents. Read the invitations to the kids, and then let each child paste one to the center of a larger piece of paper and fill in the border with various designs.

Circle Time (15 Minutes)

Group Rules

Welcome everyone to the group, and greet them by name. Review the rules again, inviting kids to help you remember them.

"How Are You Today?"

As in weeks past, invite the kids to tell you how they are feeling today. Let everyone have a turn. (Facilitators should participate, too!)

"Coming to Jesus"

Introduce the story (script is on page 83):

> **In this** Confident Kids **unit, we are learning all about families. Everyone has a family,**

but did you know you can have two families? We have our families that we live with, but God wants us to be a part of His family, too. Today's story is about a little boy who lived at the same time Jesus did, and one day he learned how much God loved him.

Small Groups (25 Minutes)

Talk About It

Use the following questions to discuss the story:

> **Why did Samuel want to see Jesus?** *(He was told Jesus loves children)*

> **Why did the disciple tell him to go away?** *(Jesus was already surrounded by a crowd)*

> **What did Jesus tell Samuel about God's love for him?** *(That it is never-ending)*

> Wouldn't it be wonderful if we could all go to Jesus and hug Him and talk to Him right now? Maybe we can't hug Jesus the way Samuel did, but we can all go to Jesus by believing in Him and praying. And what Jesus told Samuel is true for each one of you. God loves you and wants you to be a part of His special family. So, you can belong to two families! You have your own family that you live with, and when you believe in Jesus, you have God's family, too.

"Coming to Jesus" Coloring Sheets

Distribute copies of the "Coming to Jesus" coloring sheet (page 88) and let kids work on solving the maze and making the path to Jesus. As they work, talk about what it means to be a part of God's family.

> **In God's family, we have a Father (God) who loves us very much. And we have lots of brothers and sisters—they are all the people who also believe in God and go to church with us. These people are our family, too. How special it is to have two families!**

Prayer Time

In your prayer time today, emphasize that when we talk to God in prayer, we are talking to our heavenly Father who loves us very much and wants to take care of us. That's why we can tell Him everything we are feeling and bring all of our cares and worries to Him. Follow up on past prayer requests. When you pray, ask God to help each child (by name) feel His special love for them, and know they are a part of God's family.

Bible Time and Closing Prayer Huddle (15 Minutes)

Regathering

Have one facilitator lead the kids in songs or a favorite game or activity.

"Adam and Eve Tell a Story"

Present the Bible story (script is on pages 85 and 86).

Memory Verse

Review the memory verse (Romans 8:38, *ICB*, paraphrased) again:

I am sure that nothing can ever stop God from loving me!

Closing Prayer Huddle

Close the meeting as in weeks past. Use this prayer:

Dear God, thank You for giving me my family! Amen!

Snack and Quiet Games/Stories (15 Minutes)

Have ready a storybook, short video, or coloring page to use after the snack and before parents arrive.

Note

Facilitators will need to take home copies of the "Affirmation Balloons" and the unit certificates from Appendix A (pages 371 and 373). Have them complete one for each child in their small group, so the balloons and certificates can be presented during next week's Family Night program.

Circle Time

From

- Mark 10:13-16

Characters

- Samuel, his mom, Jesus, and a disciple

Needed

- Biblical costumes for all characters

Coming to Jesus

Jesus and a disciple are off to the side, talking. Samuel, excited, enters from the opposite side, dragging his mom along.

Samuel	Come on, Mommy! Today is the day that Jesus is on the hill talking to people. I want to see Him. My friend Jacob saw Him one time and said He is a nice man who loves little kids. I want to talk to Him, too!
Mom	OK, OK! Slow down a little, Samuel. There are going to be lots of people there and it might take us a long time to get to see Him.
Disciple	*(Approaches from offstage)* Wait a minute, you two. Where do you think you are going?
Samuel	Isn't Jesus over there on the hill? I want to go and see Him.
Disciple	Look, I'm sure you would like to see Him. But can't you see all those people over there? There are too many grown-ups there already. Jesus doesn't have time for little kids, at least not today. Why don't you just go back home, OK? *(He exits)*
Samuel	*(On the verge of tears)* Doesn't have time for little kids? I thought He loved little kids. Why doesn't He have time for me, Mommy?
Mom	I don't know, Samuel. I guess He is just too busy for us. Let's go home.
Jesus	*(Enters from offstage)* Samuel! Come here, I want to see you.
Samuel	*(Brightens)* Look, Mommy! It's Him! It's Jesus! *(Runs to Jesus and they hug)* You do have time for little kids, right Jesus?
Jesus	Have time for you? I want you to know that little kids are the most important of all to me, and to God, our heavenly Father. Don't ever forget that no matter what happens to you, God is your Father who loves you, and nothing will ever, ever change that! Will you remember?

Samuel	OK, I will. Thank you for talking to me!
Jesus	You can talk to me and God our Father anytime you want. All you have to do is pray. I have to go back to the others now. Good-bye, Samuel.
Samuel	'Bye, Jesus! I love you! *(Turns to his mom)* OK, now I'm ready to go home!

They exit.

Bible Story

Characters

- Adam, Eve, a disciple, and Jesus

Adam and Eve Tell a Story

Adam and Eve enter and greet the kids.

Eve	Well, I think today's group time was the best of all! Being a part of God's family is more important than anything else!
Adam	Hey, I thought so, too! It's especially important for kids to know that God wants them to be a part of His family. That's because kids are very important to God! Do you remember the story about how Jesus welcomed all the children?
Eve	Yes, I do! Let's tell it right now!
Adam	Better yet, let's get all the kids involved and pretend that the story is actually happening right now!
Eve	OK, let's get ready!

At this point, have Adam and Eve prepare for the story of Jesus and the children by telling the kids the highlights of the story. Explain that you will all be pretending that you were there the day this event happened, and acting out the story together.

Designate one facilitator to be Jesus, and another to be the disciple who tries to keep the kids away. Instruct the kids that in the play, they will be the children and they are to show that they want to see Jesus.

Adam	OK, let's tell this very special story!
Eve	One day Jesus was in town, teaching the people about how much God loves them, and healing everyone who was sick. *(Jesus is on one side of the room, pretending to be talking to people. The disciple is standing near Him)* There were also a lot of children who wanted to see Jesus. They came and asked the grown-up in charge if they could please see Jesus, too! *(Help all the kids move toward the disciple. Have one child say, "Sir, can we please see Jesus?")*
Disciple	No! Go away! Jesus doesn't have time for kids!

Adam	But Jesus saw what was happening and said:
Jesus	What are you doing? Let all the children come to me! God loves children very much and they are an important part of His family! Come here, kids! *(Have the kids run to Jesus and hug Him. Then have them all sit down again)*
Eve	I love that story! It tells just how much God really loves you—every single one of you! I hope you will always remember what the Bible says. Do you remember our memory verse: I am sure that nothing can ever stop God from loving me! Repeat it again. *(Have kids say it together several times)*
Adam	Well, it's time for us to go again! And you know what? Next week is the last week of Confident Kids, and the last time we will visit you, so please don't miss it.
Eve	And we're looking forward to meeting your parents. See you then!

They exit.

An Invitation

To _____

From _____

Please Come!
To Family Night at Confident Kids

A Ministry of Confident Kids

Date _____

Time _____

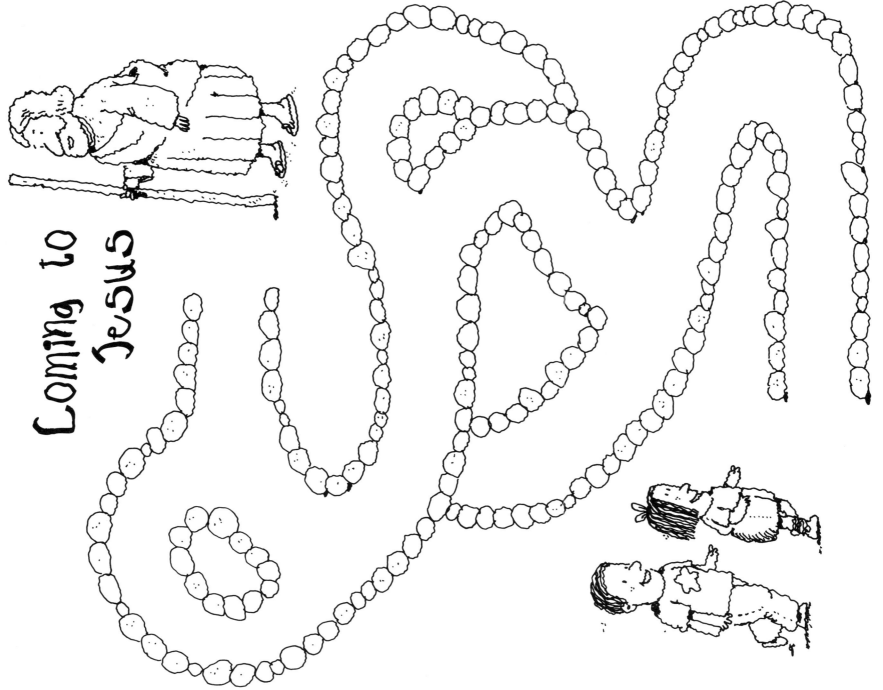

Coming to Jesus

Coming to Jesus Coloring Sheet

Elementary Sessions

Tips for Working With Elementary
Kids in a Support-Group Setting   90

1 There Are No Perfect Families!   93

2 What's a Family For, Anyway!   103

3 Changes Can Upset My Family   111

4 Actions Can Help—Or Hurt—
   My Family   123

5 Words Can Help—Or Hurt—
   My Family   133

6 "I Care About You!"   143

7 I Can Belong to God's Family, Too!   153

Tips for Working With Elementary Kids in a Support-Group Setting

What to Expect From Elementary Kids in *Confident Kids* Groups

The following session plans are for kids in grades one through four. Because there are many differences between first and fourth graders, you will have to adapt this material to fit the grade level you are teaching. Here are a few key points to help you plan for your group:

- **Elementary kids value belonging to the group.**

  First graders are developing their ability to relate to each other in social settings. By fourth grade, the kids' need to be accepted by the group is well established. Having a best friend is important in these years, and there is peer pressure to conform to the group.

- **Elementary kids express their thoughts and feelings in short sentences and in response to direct questions.**

  Kids in your group will talk about their life circumstances, but don't expect them to ramble on and on about what is happening in their lives! Rather, listen for bits and pieces of their stories, especially as they answer direct questions. You'll also learn about them when you ask for prayer requests.

- **Elementary kids like to wiggle, act silly, and express themselves physically in play.**

  Expect lots of physical activity. These behaviors are more prevalent in high-stress kids. Boys, especially, will want to wrestle and hit each other, and girls may fight over who gets to sit next to you! Watch that this behavior does not get out of control and keep you from accomplishing group goals.

- **Elementary kids are increasingly aware of, and distracted by, the opposite sex.**

  First-grade boys and girls can participate in the same small group without many problems. From second grade on, however, coed small groups greatly decrease the kids' ability to focus on the subject at hand. Same-sex groups are most effective at this age.

- **Elementary kids still idealize their parents.**

  Kids at this age deeply want a relationship with their parents, no matter how their parents treat them. They cannot yet separate their parents' behavior from the childhood image of, "My dad (mom) is the best dad in the whole world!" When this discrepancy surfaces, help the child focus on her feelings and *do not attack the parent.* Say, for example, "It really hurts when dads break their promises, doesn't it? I can understand why you feel so sad."

- **Elementary kids learn and absorb a great deal, but offer little feedback.**

  New facilitators may fear they are not "getting through," or making a difference. Never forget that the positive feedback you are fortunate enough to receive is only the "tip of the iceberg." You will never know (except maybe in Heaven) the true extent to which you are influencing the kids' lives.

Minimize Discipline Problems

Because this age group is so physically active, controlling the meeting may be one of the greatest challenges you will have. You will be more successful if you heed the following suggestions:

- **Plan how you will use your physical space.**

  The kids' behavior is affected by their classroom. Before you begin your first session:
  - *Limit the size of your area.* Too much space invites kids to run races rather than pay attention to you.
  - *Remove or mark as "off limits" items that distract.* This includes stacks of extra chairs, boxes of toys, pianos, etc.
  - *Use something physical to define boundaries.* Masking tape on the floor or an area rug can define where the kids are to sit for skits and Bible stories. A table or ring of chairs can establish the area for small groups.

- **Use activity sheets during small group discussions to keep the kids focused.**

  Elementary kids are not yet ready to sit in a circle and listen to one another share. Having something in front of them to work on will help them focus on the activity and lessen the temptation to look around the room or poke a neighbor.

- **Clearly state and consistently enforce rules.**

  All the facilitators in the room must work together to consistently remind the kids of the rules and enforce them. The kids must know that the adults in the room are in control of the meeting. If you give control to the kids, they will not respond to anything you say or try to do—guaranteed!

- **Recruit high schoolers, especially boys, to help in your room.**

  The presence of teens in the classroom has many advantages, but in terms of behavior issues, teens are invaluable. They can play games with the kids, wrestle with the boys at appropriate times, keep the physical energy focused, and help the kids settle down when it's time to listen.

- **Balance active and quiet activities according to the needs of your group.**

If the kids get out of control because the opening activities are too active, start doing table activities! Or, if your kids can't focus on the Bible story after sitting for thirty-five minutes in small group time, use a few stretching exercises or a game of "Simon Says" as a regathering activity. In other words, learn to pay attention to the physical needs of your kids and do what works!

Skits and Bible Stories Are Key Learning Times

The elementary curriculum includes both an opening skit and an ending Bible story. These stories can be told in a variety of ways. Remember that kids today are highly visual and are used to seeing a lot of action in television shows, movies, and video games. Therefore, *be prepared to spend lots of time on the scripts each week to make them come alive.* Better yet, recruit a drama team to care for this part of the session!

- **Use puppets to tell the story.**

  Puppets take some practice and equipment, but the younger kids respond well to puppets.

- **Prerecord the skits on videotape.**

  Videotaped skits allow you the freedom to be creative with the skits and give the kids the familiar experience of watching a "movie" on video. Again, recruiting a team to produce the tapes would be ideal. High schoolers may really enjoy this "high-tech storytelling."

- **Do the skits yourselves.**

  The scripts are simple enough for your team to perform each week. Anything you can do to bring life to them—like adding extra props or characters—will make them more effective. Also, overdramatizing will help draw the kids into the action.

- **Involve the kids.**

  Some of the first and second graders, and most of the third and fourth graders are capable of taking roles in the skits. Assign these roles ahead of time, so the kids can look forward to participating and practicing. Also, all the kids can be recruited to act as a crowd or an army.

- **Use visual aids or videos to tell the Bible stories.**

  Pictures, flannelgraph figures, objects, and animated videos are excellent ways to help the kids focus on the story, especially the younger kids. If you use videos, be sure to have a facilitator summarize the story and apply it to your session theme. If you have an artist available to you, develop your own visual aids.

Have Basic Materials on Hand for All Sessions

Each session plan in the curriculum lists supplies unique to that session. However, before you begin any unit, be sure to set up your room with the following basic supplies. Adding the optional materials will further enhance the group's experience.

- **Basic Supplies**

  Confident Kids postcards and stamps
  Markers, pencils
  Colored drawing paper
  Tape, glue sticks, stapler
  Scissors
  Paper towels and other supplies for clean up
  Paper cups and napkins for snack time
  Extra snacks (in case someone forgets to return the snack tin)

- **Optional Supplies**

  Prop box for skits and role plays
  Glitter, lace doilies, scraps of fabric and ribbon
  Old magazines with lots of pictures
  Cassette tapes of songs for elementary kids
  A variety of stickers
  Elementary games and craft books to supplement the curriculum, if needed
  Books, puzzles, and craft items for first and second graders to fill extra time

Goals

- Get acquainted with each other and establish a warm, caring environment for the group
- Introduce the unit theme that all families are important and special and there are no perfect families
- Help children identify one unique trait about their own family
- Introduce Adam and Eve as the unit Bible story characters

Needed

- Name tags
- Group rules poster
- Props for opening skit
- Copies of "Family Mobile," plus yarn, dowel sticks, or hangers
- Notebooks or two boxes for prayer requests
- Items for regathering, if any
- Props for Bible story
- Memory verse poster (2 Corinthians 6:18)
- Snacks and snack tin

There Are No Perfect Families!

Elementary Session 1 Outline

Opening (30 Minutes)

Name Tags and "In My Family" Circle Game

Introduction of New Kids

Group Rules

"What's Wrong With My Family?"

Small Groups (35 Minutes)

Discussion of Session Theme

"Family Mobiles"

Prayer Time

Bible Time (20 Minutes)

Regathering

"Introducing the First Family"

Memory Verse

Closing Prayer Huddle

Snack (5 Minutes)

The snack can be served during the Bible Time regathering.

There Are No Perfect Families!

Elementary Session 1

Opening (30 Minutes)

Name Tags and "In My Family" Circle Game

As kids arrive, direct them to an area with paper and stickers of things kids would like, such as animals, food, sports, colors, smells, etc. Have them make a nametag by printing their name on a 3"x 5" card and adding stickers that depict things they particularly like. Talk with kids about their selections as they make choices. When all have arrived, begin the following game.

Have the kids sit in a circle. Include only as many chairs in the circle as there are kids. (When new kids arrive, they can join the circle by adding a chair to it.) To play, the facilitator reads the following list of statements that have to do with families. Tell the kids that they are to listen carefully to each statement. If it is true about their family, they must follow the directions given by the facilitator (they will be asked to move a certain number of chairs to the left or right). If it is not true, they will remain seated in their chairs. They must follow the directions precisely, even if it means sitting in a chair where someone else is already seated. (In some cases, kids may end up with three or four sitting on each other's laps!)

1. If you have a mother *and* father living in your house, move two chairs to the right.
2. If you have a younger brother, move three chairs to the right.
3. If you have two grandfathers who are still alive, move one chair to the left.
4. If you have two sisters, move two chairs to the left.
5. If you have only one parent living in your house, move four chairs to the left.
6. If you have a stepparent, move two chairs to the right.
7. If you have a dog at your house, move one chair to the right.
8. If you wish you had a dog at your house, move two chairs to the right.

Nobody's family is perfect!

9. If you have a grandmother who lives in a state other than California (or whatever state you live in), move three chairs to the left.

10. If you ate Christmas dinner with some of your cousins, move one chair to the left.

Now ask all kids to sit in their own chairs. Go through the questions again, asking kids to raise their hands if the statement is true of them. Make this a get-acquainted time, taking note of the different family situations revealed as kids raise their hands. *Note:* If you have primarily first graders, or a combination of older and younger kids, you may want to change the game so the little ones will enjoy it more. For instance, you can have the kids stand in front of each other instead of sit on each other's laps.

Introduction of New Kids

If you have done a Confident Kids unit before, you will likely have both returning kids and new kids in the group. Welcome the new ones by calling each one to the front of the room. Ask the new children to tell the others their name, grade, and one unique thing about themselves. When they are finished, lead the group in yelling, "Welcome, *[child's name]!*" and give each one a round of applause.

Group Rules

If you did not use the introductory session, "Welcome to Confident Kids," last week, you will need to make a group rules poster. (See page 15 in the "Getting Started" section for complete directions on generating a list of rules for your group.) Spend some quality time doing this, as the group rules are crucial to the success of your support-group experience.

If you did use the introductory session, display the poster you made last week and review it. Be sure everyone understands the rules and the consequences for breaking them.

"What's Wrong With My Family?"

You will need to decide how the skits will be handled each week. (See page 91 in the "Tips for Working with Elementary Kids" for ideas.) This session's script is on page 98. Dismiss to small groups after the skit is performed.

Small Groups (35 Minutes)

Discussion of Session Theme

Use the following questions to discuss the session theme, "Nobody's family is perfect!"

> Have you ever felt like Joey in today's skit? *(Let kids respond)*

> What did he do or say that you can identify with? *(Responses could include wanting to watch TV but not being allowed to; having a father who works too much; wishing you lived in someone else's family, or a TV family)*

> What do you think Billy would have said if Joey had told him that he would rather live in Billy's family than his own? *(He might have agreed that his was better; or, he might have said that he wasn't so crazy about living in his family, either!)*

> Is any family perfect? *(Let kids respond)* If so, what do you think that family would be like? *(Kids describe characteristics of what they would consider to be the perfect family)*

> Sometimes it is easy for us to look at another family or a family on TV and think that in comparison, ours is the pits.

We can think, "If only my dad didn't work so much," or "If only my parents hadn't gotten a divorce," or "If only I had my own room." *(Change or add statements to describe family issues affecting your kids)* **In the next few weeks, we are going to talk about what it means to live in our families. Tonight, we need to talk about the fact that even though your family may have things about it that you don't like and wish you could change, your family is your family, and for you it can be a special place. To begin, let's find out about each other's families.**

Family Mobiles

Give each child a copy of the "Family Mobile" (pages 101 and 102), a dowel stick or hanger, and a 3' length of yarn or string. Guide children to thoughtfully complete their mobiles, talking with them about how each family is different. Ask kids to share with everyone what they write or draw in the shape labeled, "My Family Is Special Because. . ." When they have finished, cut out the pieces, punch a hole at the top of each one, and assemble it (house at the top).

Prayer Time

Each week you will spend the last seven or eight minutes of your group time in prayer. The purpose of this time is to help the kids learn that God's presence and power are significant resources as they face the circumstances in their lives. To make this time tangible, set up a prayer notebook for your group to keep track of requests and answers. Younger kids might enjoy using prayer boxes. Set up two boxes, one labeled *Requests* and the other *Answers*. Review the requests each week and talk about what God has done in response to that request. When a clear answer has been given, write it in the notebook, or if you are using the boxes, record the answer and move the slip to the *Answers* box.

To begin your prayer journey, ask the group for one or two prayer requests for your notebook or box. Be sure you add one of your own. Pray for these requests. End by thanking God for each family represented in your group.

Bible Time (20 Minutes)

Regathering

Assign one facilitator each week to lead the kids in a favorite game, song, or activity (see Appendix B, "Resources," for ideas) as they come from their small groups to the Bible story area. This facilitator will have to finish her small group time a few minutes early to be ready to gather the kids as they dismiss from their groups. *Note:* Some groups prefer to serve the snacks at this time, with the rule that the snacks will be served as soon as everyone has arrived and is quiet.

"Introducing the First Family"

As with the opening skit, you will have to decide how the Bible stories will be handled each week. Using teaching pictures, flannelgraph pieces, or short videos to tell the "real" Bible story before or during this week's skit (script is on page 99) is highly recommended, especially for younger children.

Memory Verse

Before class, prepare a poster of this week's memory verse (2 Corinthians 6:18):

> **"I will be your father, and you will be my sons and daughters, says the Lord All-Powerful."**

The poster will be used by Adam and Eve to introduce the verse.

Closing Prayer Huddle

Each week the meetings will close in the same way. Gather all the kids into a tight circle and instruct them to stack their hands on top of each other in the middle of the circle. As they stand in this position, have them recite the following prayer together:

> **Dear God, thank You for my family.**
> **Please make it a special place for all of us**
> **who live in it! Amen!**

Have them raise their hands out of the stack and over their heads as they yell out, "Amen!"

Snack (5 Minutes)

The facilitators should bring the snack the first night. Before the kids leave, choose a child to take the snack tin home for next week. (See page 14 in "Getting Started" for more information about handling the snack.)

Opening Skit

Characters

- Joey and his mother

Needed

- A telephone

Suggested

- A VCR with a tape containing a few minutes of a family sit-com that portrays the "perfect" family. Select a segment that shows a particularly "perfect" scene, such as the family happily talking together, or the father solving a problem with great wisdom, etc. Have the tape ready to play as the skit begins.

"What's Wrong With My Family?"

Joey enters and turns on the TV.

Joey	Oh, boy! *[Name the show you taped or Joey is pretending to watch]*! My favorite!
Mother	*(If you are using a real tape, let it play for a minute or so)* Joey! How many times have I told you, no TV until your room is clean and your homework is done? You got a D on your last geography test. Have you done your geography homework today?
Joey	Not yet, but I'll do it right after this show is over! It's my favorite!
Mother	I said no. Turn off the TV now and go to your room. And when your father comes home, he'll have something to say to you. *(Exits)*
Joey	*(Turns the set off, pouting)* Humph! My father. He never comes home! Last week he missed my big game—said he had to work. He's always got some excuse for why he can't be with me. *(Thinks for a moment)* I'll bet *[Refer to the perfect father on the TV show or name one from a popular TV show]* never misses any of his kids' games. I hate my family! We're always yelling at each other. Oh, well. *(Pauses; walks to phone)* I think I'll call Billy! Maybe his family would let me come and live with them. His family is really neat. Except for his sister. She's always calling him names. But even so, living in his family would be better than living in mine! *(Pretends to dial phone)*

Bible Story

From

- Genesis 1 and 2

Characters

- Adam and Eve

Needed

- Simple costumes
- Memory verse poster (2 Corinthians 6:18)

Suggested

- Teaching pictures, flannel-graph figures, or a short video to tell the events of Genesis 1 and 2

Introducing the First Family

Adam and Eve enter, talking excitedly about how glad they are to be here, and how anxious they are to meet all these kids.

Adam	Well, we are so glad to be here. My wife and I have come a long way. By the way, our names are—well, maybe we'll let you guess who we are. The first hint is that you can read about us in the Bible. Anyone think they know who we are? *(Allow one guess, and if it is wrong, offer more clues until kids guess)*
Eve	We are going to be with you for the next few weeks while you are talking about families. Of course, things were very different when we started our family. *(Briefly tell the events of Genesis 1 and 2)*
Adam	Being the very first family, we had it a little bit harder than most of you. We didn't know anything about what families are supposed to be like because there had never been one before!
Eve	But we did the best we could. Some things about our family were very good. Adam got to name all the animals! We laughed so hard some days! Hippopotamuses and orangutans are the most fun to me!
Adam	Actually, platypus was my favorite.
Eve	*(Stares at Adam)* Since when? You've never said that before!
Adam	Sure I did—you just weren't listening!
Eve	I wasn't listening! You should know—you are the all-time worst listener that— *(Turning to kids)* See what I mean! Even people in the Bible didn't have perfect families!
Adam	But there is one thing we do agree about. In those first days of figuring out what a family was supposed to do and be like, God always took good care of us. We made some bad mistakes, and sometimes God had to discipline us for it, but He never left us alone. He was, and still is, a Father to us.

Eve	We're here to tell you that no matter what your family is like here on earth—and we all know that no families are perfect—God is your Father, too. And He takes care of you. So, in the next few weeks, as we learn about things that happen in our families, let's remember 2 Corinthians 6:18. *(Shows poster)* Let's read it together.
Adam	Knowing that God was our Father and taking care of us all the time helped us get through some pretty hard times. We'll tell you more about that next time, but now it's time for us to go. Good-bye for now!
They exit.	

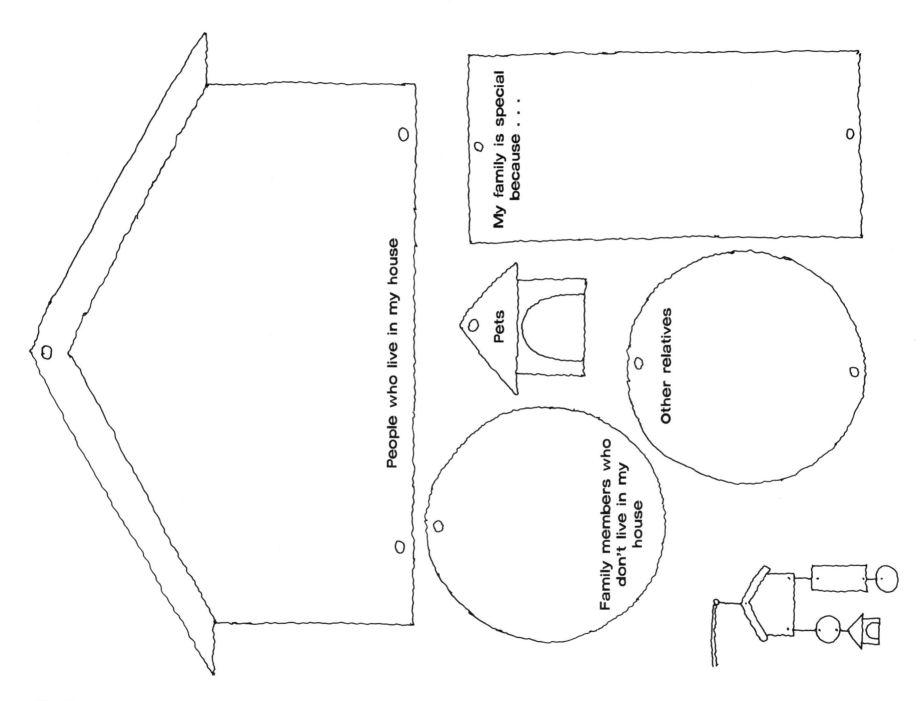

People who live in my house

My family is special because . . .

Pets

Other relatives

Family members who don't live in my house

Goals

- Identify the functions of families and what they do for us
- Emphasize that our family will not always provide everything we need (there are no perfect families)
- Have kids list the strengths and weaknesses of their own families
- Use the story of Adam and Eve to affirm that God created families to be places of belonging and caring

Needed

- Strip of butcher paper, shelf paper, or several sheets of poster board
- Lots of magazines and other sources of pictures of things families do for us
- Group rules poster
- Props for opening skit
- A puzzle depicting your family, which you have made on a blank, precut puzzle purchased from a craft or teacher supply store
- *Optional:* Blank puzzles for all the kids
- A spinner with six sections, or a pair of dice for each small group
- Items for regathering activity, if any
- Props for Bible story
- Memory verse (2 Corinthians 6:18) written on an erasable board

What's a Family For, Anyway?

Elementary Session 2 Outline

Opening (30 Minutes)

    "What's a Family For?" Montage

    Group Rules

    "The Runaway"

Small Groups (35 Minutes)

    Discussion of Session Theme

    "Finish This Sentence" Game

    Prayer Time

Bible Time (20 Minutes)

    Regathering

    "Adam Isn't Lonely Anymore"

    Memory Verse

    Closing Prayer Huddle

Snack (5 Minutes)

    The snack can be served during the Bible Time regathering.

What's a Family For, Anyway?

Elementary Session 2

Opening (30 Minutes)

"What's a Family For?" Montage

You will need a 3' strip of butcher or shelf paper or several sheets of poster board and a wide variety of magazines or other sources of pictures depicting things our families do for us. As kids arrive, direct them to the pictures and ask them to begin cutting out pictures to add to the montage of things our families do for us. Direct them toward appropriate pictures. Possibilities include pictures that depict:

- Physical needs *(Food, clothes, shelter, care when sick)*
- Emotional needs *(Love, talking and listening to each other, affirmation)*
- Guidance *(Instruction on how to do things, setting rules)*
- Companionship *(Having fun together)*

As the kids find pictures, they can tape or glue them to the montage in a random and overlapping fashion. Try to find enough pictures to fill the whole paper so there are no white areas visible. To complete the montage, take a very wide marker and write words over the top of the pictures. You can start with a title in the middle, such as, "We need our families!" Then add smaller words, such as "Love," "Food," and "Protection."

Note: If you have first and second graders, you may want to cut out the pictures in advance and have the kids sort them into piles before placing them on the montage. You can write the words over the top as kids suggest them. Older kids can cut out their own pictures and write the words themselves.

Group Rules

Use your group rules poster from last session to review the rules and the consequences you have established for breaking them.

"The Runaway"

Use the script on page 107 to introduce the session theme. Dismiss to small groups after the skit.

Small Groups (35 Minutes)

Discussion of Session Theme

Use the following questions to discuss the session theme, "Who needs a family?"

> **Have you ever felt like running away from your family?** *(Lots of kids feel like that sometimes, and many of them actually do run away)*
>
> **What do you think life would be like if you left your family and tried to live on your own?** *(Let kids respond)*
>
> **What did Suzy discover about her own family when she ran away?** *(That even though her family had some problems, they loved her and wanted her to be part of the family)*
>
> **Pretend you are Suzy, and you are alone in the park. What do you miss about your family?** *(Let kids respond)* **What do you think they miss about you?** *(Let kids respond)*
>
> **Even though none of us lives in a perfect family, we need to understand how important our families are to us. Families give us love, protection, guidance, and teach us how to live in the world. We can think of our families like a puzzle.** *(In advance, depict your family on a blank, precut puzzle purchased from a craft or teacher supply store. Show it, unassem-*

bled, to the kids now) **Each puzzle has a design on it.**

Hold up a piece and ask the kids if that piece alone tells you what design is on the puzzle. Take two pieces that do not fit together and ask a volunteer to try to make them fit. Then work with the kids to put the pieces together to see the completed design.

> **When our families are working together well, they are like these puzzles. Everyone in the family is important to the whole family.**
>
> **But sometimes things happen and a piece is missing.** *(Take a piece out)* **When that happens, the family is not the same, but it is still a family, and all the rest of the pieces still fit and can work together to make the family an important place for everyone. Remember, your family is not just a bunch of people living in the same house! It is made up of people who are all important to each other, and your family is not complete without you in it!**

"Finish This Sentence" Game

Place a spinner that has at least six divisions on it (or a pair of dice) in the middle of the table. To play the game, kids take turns spinning the spinner or throwing one of the dice. They must then answer the question below that corresponds to the number they come up with. Keep playing until all the kids have had a chance to answer at least two different questions:

1. I wish my family was more _____.
2. I'm glad my family _____.
3. I wish my family would _____.
4. My family thinks I am _____.
5. The one thing about my family I wish I could change is _____.
6. The one thing about my family I would never want to change is _____.

Who needs a family?

Optional: If time allows, you could give all the kids blank, precut puzzles to make a puzzle of their families. Or, if you prefer, use the puzzles instead of the sentence game.

Prayer Time

Use your prayer journal to follow up on last week's prayer requests and ask for new ones. Give special emphasis to needs kids mention regarding their family situations.

Bible Time (20 Minutes)

Regathering

As you did last week, have one facilitator lead the kids in songs or a favorite game or activity as they regather from small group time.

"Adam Isn't Lonely Anymore!"

If you used visual aids last session to tell the creation story, have them available again today to review the creation of Eve as a companion for Adam. The script is on pages 109 and 110.

Memory Verse

Write this week's memory verse, 2 Corinthians 6:18, on a chalkboard or whiteboard and have the kids read it together. Then erase two words and have them read it again, filling in the missing words. Continue erasing words until they are gone and kids can say the verse from memory.

Closing Prayer Huddle

Close your meeting with the prayer huddle, as you did last week. Use this prayer:

> **Dear God, thank You for my family.
> Please make it a special place for all of us
> who live in it! Amen!**

Snack (5 Minutes)

Distribute the snack the child brought. Before the kids leave, choose another child to take the snack tin home for next week.

Characters

- Suzy, a policeman, and Suzy's big sister

Needed

- A school backpack for Suzy
- Two chairs placed side by side to make a park bench
- A policeman's hat or badge

The Runaway

Suzy enters carrying the backpack and walking dejectedly. She wanders over and sits down on the bench. She sighs heavily.

Policeman	*(Enters, sees Suzy on the bench, and walks up to sit beside her)* Hey, there! Isn't it a little late for you to be out in the park by yourself? What are you doing here?
Suzy	Well—I—uh, I guess I'm running away.
Policeman	I see. Won't you be missing your supper?
Suzy	I have a peanut butter sandwich in my bag.
Policeman	Oh. And what are you going to do when that's gone?
Suzy	Umm—I don't know.
Policeman	And where are you going to sleep tonight? Won't you be cold sleeping on this bench? Wouldn't your own bed be better than this?
Suzy	No! Anything is better than living at my house. They don't want me there.
Policeman	Why do you say that?
Suzy	My dad hated me so much he moved away. And now my mom has to work and when she comes home she yells a lot and says she's too tired to talk to me. I'm just in the way.
Policeman	I see. So, you think your dad left because he hates you. And now you think your mom would be better off without you there. Got any brothers and sisters?
Suzy	Yeah, one of each. They're older than me and they pick on me. I guess I bother them, too.

Confident Kids © 1997 Linda Kondracki Sibley. Permission granted to photocopy. The Standard Publishing Co.

Policeman	Well, it hurts when things aren't the way we want them to be. But what do you think living in the park is going to be like? You really think sleeping in the cold and not having any food or toys or people around who care about you will be better than living at your house?
Big Sister	*(Enters the park and yells to Suzy)* Oh, Suzy! There you are! What are you doing here? Mom and Davey and I were so worried about you! You can't run away—we need you! Who would I pick on if you weren't there? And who would sleep in your bed? Look, Suzy, things aren't so great right now, but we're a family, and we need each other. We need you! Come on, squirt, let's go home!

They exit with their arms around each other.

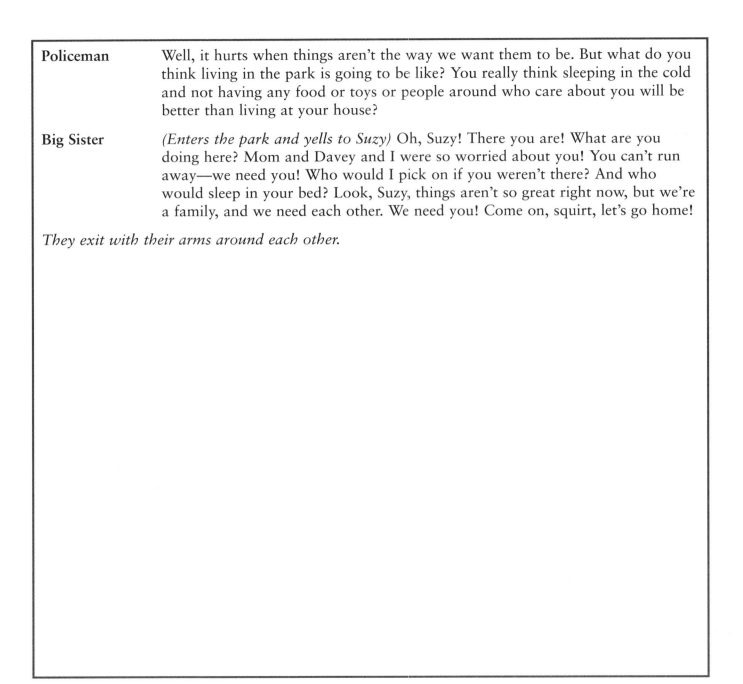

Bible Story

From

- Genesis 2:18-25

Characters

- Adam and Eve

Needed

- Costumes for Adam and Eve

Suggested

- If you used visuals last week, use them again to tell the story of Eve's creation

Adam Isn't Lonely Anymore!

Adam and Eve enter and greet the children.

Adam	You know, I was really interested in listening to Suzy talk about why she ran away from home and how she was feeling. She never said it, but I know what she was feeling! She was lonely. She didn't think anyone in her family cared about her or needed her anymore. That's not a comfortable feeling for any of us! I can say that because if anyone knows what it means to be lonely, it's me! You see, when God created me, there weren't any other people around at all. I felt very lonely.

Use visual aids or the following paragraph to review the story of how God provided animals to be companions for Adam, but they weren't adequate, so He created Eve.

Adam	Of course, it was a beautiful world I lived in. The garden was beautiful and at first I had fun getting to know about all those different animals. But it didn't take long before I began to feel lonely. Animals are fun, but they can't talk to you or take care of you. I wanted someone like me to be my friend and helper. So I told God that I wanted someone else to be in the garden with me, and He said He agreed! In fact, I remember His exact words: "It's not good for you to be alone, Adam. I will make a companion for you." *(Puts his arm around Eve)* And that's when Eve was created!
Eve	Ta-da! And here I am! Together, we made a family and we took care of each other and had fun together. Especially getting to know the animals and plants and trees. It was all so new!
Adam	The best part was I wasn't lonely anymore!
Eve	I guess God knew that putting people together into families was the best way for people to live—and it still is today! Even if, like Suzy, you think your parents got a divorce because of you or that your mom doesn't have time to listen to you all the time, you are still important to your family and your family

	is important to you. Whatever is happening, if you try to face it alone, you will feel lonely.
Adam	But, when you remember that your family is the place God has given you to belong and to be taken care of, you won't be lonely. You will have each other.
Eve	Before we go, we also want to remind you that God, your heavenly Father, is always present with you. He cares for you even more than your family does!
Adam	Hey! Look at the time! We'd better get going—quickly!
Eve	Why such a hurry?
Adam	We've got to get home to feed Arnold the aardvark. You know how he gets when we don't feed him on time!
Eve	Oh, my, let's go! When he's hungry, Arnold will eat anything! Last week he ate our bedspread and a bar of soap! He was breathing bubbles for two days! We'll be back next week. Good-bye for now!

They exit, saying "Let's hurry!" "What did we leave out that he could eat?" etc.

Goals

- Make a list of changes that can disrupt family stability
- Have the children identify changes that have occurred within their own families and discuss how each family reacted to the change
- Identify healthy ways to cope with change
- Assure children that they still have a family even when significant change occurs
- Use the story of Adam and Eve to discuss God's presence in the midst of difficult change

Needed

- Group rules poster
- Props for opening skit
- Copies of "Putting Humpty Dumpty Together Again" puzzle
- Prayer journals
- Items for regathering, if any
- Items for Bible story
- Memory verse poster (Romans 8:38, 39)

Changes Can Upset My Family

Elementary Session 3 Outline

Opening (30 Minutes)

    "Fruit Basket Upset"

    Group Rules

    "The Divorce"

Small Groups (35 Minutes)

    Discussion of Session Theme

    "Putting Humpty Dumpty Together Again" Puzzle

    Prayer Time

Bible Time (20 Minutes)

    Regathering

    "A Big Change for Adam and Eve"

    Memory Verse

    Closing Prayer Huddle

Snack (5 Minutes)

    The snack can be served during the Bible Time regathering.

Changes Can Upset My Family

Elementary Session 3

Opening (30 Minutes)

"Fruit Basket Upset"

This favorite old game is fun, yet ties into the lesson on change. To play, have everyone sit in chairs in a circle. Go around the circle and whisper the name of a fruit (apple, orange, pear, or banana) in everyone's ear as a way to divide them into groups. Designate one person as "it," and remove his chair from the circle. "It" stands in the middle of the circle and calls out the name of one of the fruits (apple, orange, pear, or banana). Everyone who is in that group must now get up from their chair and find a new one, including "it." The person who does not get a chair is the new "it" and calls out the next fruit. The person who is "it" can call out more than one fruit at a time, or she may call out "Fruit Basket Upset," and everyone in the circle must get up and find a new seat. Play the game as long as time allows.

Group Rules

Use your group rules poster to review the rules and the consequences for breaking them.

"The Divorce"

Present the skit (script is on pages 115 and 116). Dismiss to small groups after the skit is presented.

Small Groups (35 Minutes)

Discussion of Session Theme

Use the following questions to discuss the session theme, "Change upsets my family!"

What happened in Jenny's family? *(Parents divorced)* **How did that change things for her?** *(She had to help with household chores more, she saw her dad on weekends, etc.)* **For her parents?** *(Mom had to go back to work, Dad had to get a new place to live and adjust to only seeing his kids on weekends, etc.)*

How was Jenny feeling? *(Angry, sad, guilty, embarrassed)* **Did she tell anyone about her feelings?** *(Except for telling her best friend, she kept her feelings locked up inside)*

Most of us would rather that things in our lives never changed. Even adults don't like to go through change. But it is a fact of life that things change. When things change in our families, we go through a time of adjustment that is usually hard to deal with. Lots of things can change in our families and disrupt our lives. Let's think of some.

Help kids brainstorm a list. Challenge them to make the list as long as possible. Write their answers down so they can see the list grow. Possibilities include divorce, birth of a baby, death of family member, long-distance move, serious illness, parent goes to work, stepfamily established, grandparent moves in, or family member abuses alcohol or drugs.

When change happens, people react in different ways. What are some of the feelings and ways people can react when change occurs? *(Get angry, cry and be sad, feel it was my fault, take it out on someone else, not talk to anyone, feel afraid, pretend it didn't happen, run away, etc.)*

Change is always going to happen in our families. We can't stop that. But we can

learn ways to respond to changes that will help us rather than hurt us. Let's think some more about how we can do that.

"Putting Humpty Dumpty Together Again" Puzzle

In advance, copy the "Putting Humpty Dumpty Together Again" activity sheets (pages 119–121) back to back. Be careful to line the sides up so the squares will cut apart correctly. Distribute these copies and ask:

How many of you know the nursery rhyme about Humpty Dumpty? *(Say the rhyme together)* **When change happens in our lives, we can feel like Humpty Dumpty—all broken up and thinking things will never be put back together again! But change does not have to break us apart. We can get through it when we learn to handle it in healthy ways.**

To use the puzzle, follow these directions. *Note:* Older kids can work on their own; younger ones will need help. You might want to do just one puzzle per small group for younger kids.

1. Cut the squares apart.
2. As a group, read the words on each square and decide which ones describe healthy ways of dealing with change. If the square describes an unhealthy way of dealing with change, set it aside.
3. When you have all the squares that describe healthy ways of dealing with change in front of you, turn them over and use them to form a picture. If you have chosen correctly, you will be able to make a picture. If you have chosen incorrectly, you will not be able to form a complete picture and will need to rethink your choices about what are healthy and unhealthy ways to deal with change.

Nine pieces (with positive statements) are used to make a complete picture. Seven pieces (with unhealthy statements) make an incomplete picture. (See page 119.)

Change upsets my family!

The squares that should be eliminated are:
- Yell at your friends
- Watch TV every moment you are awake
- Stop playing with your friends
- Hit your brother
- Make yourself sick, or pretend to get sick
- Hold all your feelings inside
- Blame yourself

Prayer Time

Refer to your prayer journal as you conduct your prayer time. Give particular attention to any requests concerning changes happening in the kids' families.

Bible Time (20 Minutes)

Regathering

Have a facilitator lead a favorite song, game, or activity.

"A Big Change for Adam and Eve"

Present the Bible story (script is on pages 117 and 118).

Memory Verse

Prepare a poster of Romans 8:38, 39 (*ICB*), to review with the kids:

Yes, I am sure that nothing can separate us from the love God has for us. Not death, not life, not angels, not ruling spirits, nothing now, nothing in the future, no powers, nothing above us, nothing below us, or anything else in the whole world will ever be able to separate us from the love of God that is in Christ Jesus our Lord.

Closing Prayer Huddle

Close with the huddle, as in past meetings. Use this prayer:

Dear God, thank You for my family. Please make it a special place for all of us who live in it! Amen!

Snack (5 Minutes)

Distribute the snack the child brought. Before the kids leave, choose another child to take the snack tin home for next week.

Characters

- Mr. Foster (a principal), Jenny, and Mrs. James (Mr. Foster's secretary)

Needed

- A small table and two chairs

The Divorce

Mr. Foster, Jenny's principal, is sitting behind a table. Jenny is sitting in a chair next to it.

Mr. Foster	Well, Jenny. This is the third time this week you have been sent to the principal's office. So I called your mom this morning to find out what's going on. She told me about the divorce. That helps me understand! Why didn't you tell me before?
Jenny	*(Looks down and kicks her feet)* I dunno. I guess I don't want anyone to know.
Mr. Foster	That's a pretty big secret to be keeping all to yourself. Have you told anyone?
Jenny	Only my best friend, and I made her swear not to tell anyone else or I'd pull her tongue out!
Mr. Foster	You sound pretty angry.
Jenny	Wouldn't you be if you didn't have a family anymore?
Mrs. James	*(Enters from offstage; looks flustered)* Excuse me Mr. Foster, but—
Mr. Foster	Not now, Mrs. James. I'm having an important conversation with Jenny.
Mrs. James	Yes, but—
Mr. Foster	Whatever it is, I'll take care of it later! *(Mrs. James shakes her head and leaves)*
Mr. Foster	Now Jenny, where were we? Oh, yes. You just lied to me.
Jenny	*(Looks surprised)* What?
Mr. Foster	You said you don't have a family anymore. That's not true.
Jenny	Well I don't call it a family! A real family doesn't have a dad that lives in another house and only comes to visit you once a week. And a real family doesn't have a mother that has to take care of everybody and makes the kids do

Confident Kids © 1997 Linda Kondracki Sibley. Permission granted to photocopy. The Standard Publishing Co.

	things like laundry and cook supper. I'm the oldest, you know, so it's my job to be sure everything's OK.
Mr. Foster	Did your mother or father tell you that?
Jenny	No—but who else is going to take care of my mother now that my dad's gone? Besides, its all my fault.
Mrs. James	*(Enters again, looking more upset)* Mr. Foster, I'm sorry! But you have to come!
Mr. Foster	*(Annoyed)* I'm not finished yet! I'll be out in a few minutes. Nothing can be that important!
Mrs. James	OK, but if I were you, I'd hurry! *(Exits)*
Mr. Foster	Look, Jenny. I'm going to have to go. But we'll talk again. In the meantime, I want you to think about some things for me, OK? *(Jenny nods agreement)* First of all, all kids think it's their fault when parents get a divorce. But it's not. You didn't do anything wrong. It is going to mean some big changes for your family. It's not easy to go through changes. Everyone in your family, including your mom and dad, will have to adjust to a new way of life. No one likes change, Jenny, but your family is still a family, and you can all find ways to get through this. We'll talk again—
Mrs. James	*(Bursts into the room, panic stricken)* Mr. Foster, you have to come now! Jared knocked over the frog tank in the science lab! All 500 frogs are loose in the school! The girls are screaming and the boys are stuffing frogs in their pockets! And unless you want frog soup for lunch, you'd better do something before they get to the cafeteria!

Mr. Foster looks horrified, Jenny starts to laugh and clap her hands, and all three of them leave in a hurry.

Bible Story

From

- Genesis 3:1-7

Characters

- Adam and Eve

Needed

- A large stuffed or rubber snake (the bigger the better)
- A visual aid to tell the story of the fall
- Memory verse poster (Romans 8:38, 39)

A Big Change for Adam and Eve

Adam and Eve enter and greet the children. Adam is carrying a stuffed or rubber snake. Eve is walking a few steps behind Adam, obviously upset that he has brought the snake. She grumbles things like, "For goodness sake, Adam, get rid of that thing. You know I can't stand snakes—yuck! No one here likes them either."

Adam   *(To kids)* Never mind Eve—she gets this way around snakes. When I found out you talked about changes in families today, I wanted to bring this guy *(Holds up snake)* along. After all, it was a snake that brought about the first big change in our lives!

Eve   Do we have to talk about this? It's so embarrassing. *(To kids)* I make one little mistake, and he *(Points to Adam)* never lets me forget it!

Adam   It wasn't a little mistake, Eve. And don't forget, I was there too! I'm just as much to blame as you are.

Eve   Oh, sure, but just ask anyone on the street, "Who was responsible for the first sin?" What do they say? Eve, that's who! Not Adam and Eve, not that miserable, lying deceitful snake, but Eve! Me! I always get blamed! It's downright embarrassing! I—

Adam   *(Puts hand over her mouth)* Enough! You've been blaming yourself for thousands of years now. When are you going to give it a rest? *(Looks at kids)* Well, by now I guess you all know what we're talking about. *(Use a visual aid to tell the story of the fall, ending with Adam and Eve leaving the garden)*

Eve   I'm so depressed! *(Sits down with her head in her hands)*

Adam   You know, it really wasn't Eve's fault, but she has blamed herself ever since. I'll bet some of you can relate to what she is feeling today. I know some of you are blaming yourselves for the changes in your families. And when you blame yourself, it's easy to get stuck saying, "If only."

Eve	*(Looks up and says loudly)* If only I hadn't listened to that dumb snake! *(Puts head down. Just before Adam can start talking again, raises head again and speaks)* If only I hadn't been hungry!
Adam	That's the "If only's." Have you ever said, "If only I had been better, my dad wouldn't have left?" Or, "If only my little sister hadn't been born, my parents would have more time for me?" Well, take it from me, the "If only's" are not a healthy way to get through change.
Eve	*(Rises and joins Adam)* He's right, you know. After we disobeyed God, we had to leave our beautiful garden, and I thought life would never be good again! I mean, everything changed!
Adam	That's right. Well, everything but one thing. Even though He had to discipline us, God never stopped loving us. He was still there in every part of our lives, and many days, that was the only thing that helped us adjust to our new life outside the garden.
Eve	After awhile, we began to get used to our new life. It wasn't long before we looked at each other one day and realized we weren't hurting anymore! God was taking care of us, and we were happy in our new life.
Adam	And so, we wanted to tell you tonight that no matter what happens in your family, you still have a family, and you can make it through—and God will help!
Eve	Here's a special verse for you to remember. *(Displays verse poster and lead the kids in saying it several times)* Good-bye!
They exit.	

Complete puzzle with healthy statements

Incomplete puzzle (2 pieces missing)
with unhealthy statements

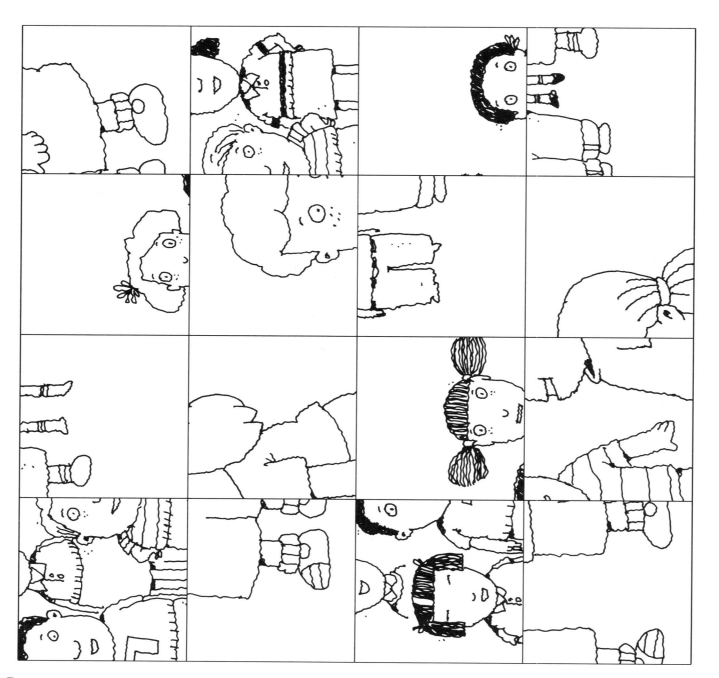

TOP

Position or photocopy these pages so that the TOP of the text (page 121) aligns with the TOP of the puzzle art (page 120). Use a glue stick to glue puzzle art to statements.

Humpty Dumpty Puzzle Pieces—Front

Tell your parents or other adults what you are feeling.

Hit your brother.

Feel angry for awhile.

Stop playing with your friends.

Come to Confident Kids.

Blame yourself.

Cry and feel sad for awhile.

Hold all your feelings inside.

Ask other family members what they are feeling.

Make yourself sick, or pretend to get sick.

Ask for what you need.

Watch TV every moment you are awake.

Yell at your friends.

Tell God what you are feeling; ask Him to help.

Ask for a hug.

Talk to your friends about what happened.

Position or photocopy pages 120 and 121 so that the TOP of the puzzle art (page 120) aligns with the TOP of the text (page 121).

Goals

- Identify various pleasant and unpleasant feelings we have in our families and the actions that produce them
- Role-play actions that help us bring more pleasant feelings into our family life
- Use the story of Cain and Abel to illustrate how unpleasant and hurtful actions can affect families

Needed

- Group rules poster
- Items for opening skit
- "Feelings/Actions Cards" (one set per small group), each copied on a different color paper and cut apart
- "Feeling Good/Feeling Bad" chart (one per small group)
- A variety of hand puppets for each small group
- Prayer journals
- Items for regathering, if any
- Items for Bible story
- Memory verse poster (Romans 8:38, 39)

Actions Can Help— Or Hurt—My Family

Elementary Session 4 Outline

Opening (30 Minutes)

"Feelings" Charades

Group Rules

"The Cereal Bowl"

"Feelings/Actions Cards" Search

Small Groups (35 Minutes)

Discussion of Session Theme

"Feeling Good/Feeling Bad" Chart

"Finish This" Stories

Prayer Time

Bible Time (20 Minutes)

Regathering

"Adam and Eve Have a Baby"

Memory Verse

Closing Prayer Huddle

Snack (5 Minutes)

The snack can be served during the Bible Time regathering.

Actions Can Help— Or Hurt—My Family

Elementary Session 4

Opening (30 Minutes)

"Feelings" Charades

Since this lesson is about the different feelings we experience in our families, play "Feelings" charades as the kids arrive. Ask kids to volunteer, and whisper a feelings word to them for them to act out. You may want to use the same words that are listed on the "Feelings/Actions" cards, which you will be using later.

Group Rules

Use your group rules poster to review the rules. Emphasize any that the group is having difficulty following.

"The Cereal Bowl"

Use the script on pages 127 and 128 to introduce today's theme. Dismiss to small groups after the skit has been presented and the cards have been gathered. (See below.)

"Feelings/Actions Cards" Search

Before the kids arrive, copy one set of the "Feelings" cards and one set of "Actions" cards (pages 131 and 132) for each small group. Color code them so the kids from each group can collect a complete set of one color. Hide them around the room in obvious places so it won't take the kids long to find them.

Just before dismissing the kids to their small groups, tell them about the cards and ask them to find the twenty-four cards coded with their small group's color. Have them keep looking until all the cards have been found and brought to their small group areas. (If you prefer, do not hide the two "Write Your Own" or the two blank cards.)

Small Groups (35 Minutes)

Discussion of Session Theme

Before class, take a piece of poster board or butcher paper and prepare a "Feeling Good/Feeling Bad" chart.

Feels Good		Feels Bad	
Feeling	Action	Feeling	Action

Use the following questions to discuss the session theme, "My actions make a difference in my family."

Why was Skip feeling so bad? *(His family had a fight at breakfast and everyone had left the house that morning upset)*

What had he done to contribute to the angry feelings in his family? *(He threw a bowl of cereal at his brother)*

What did he decide he could do to help himself and everyone else feel better? *(Apologize)*

Refer to the "Feeling Good/Feeling Bad" chart and the "Feelings/Actions" cards the kids collected earlier. Say:

Wouldn't it be nice if everything that happened in our families made us feel really good and happy? Unfortunately, life isn't like that. Living together always involves times when we get on each others' nerves, and times when we say and do things without thinking that upset other family members. But we can make choices about what we will do—or not do—that will help us have more good feelings in our families and fewer upset feelings! Let's see how this works.

Put the chart on a table or on the floor. Spread out the cards. Decide where each feeling word fits on the chart. Put it in the appropriate column. Then look at the actions cards and match them to the feelings they produce. When everyone is satisfied that all the cards have been placed correctly, glue them in place. Ask the kids to think of more feelings and actions to write or draw and add to the chart. Try to get them to talk about specific things that happen in their own families. Continue as long as the kids have things to add. Tape the chart to the wall.

Talk about the chart by pointing out that feelings in their families are a result of the actions they (and other family members) choose. When family members consistently choose actions that produce upset feelings, the family will not be a comfortable or safe place. However, when all family members work hard at choosing actions that produce good feelings, the family will be much closer and safer for everyone!

Conclude by asking kids to identify one behavior they can work on changing so their family will be a better place. Help them think of something they do that upsets the family, or they get in trouble for, on a consistent basis (e.g., doing homework or chores without being told repeatedly, keeping their rooms clean, teasing younger siblings, losing their tempers, lying, causing scenes at the dinner table, refusing to get along with stepsiblings). *Note:* Although we do not want to communicate to the kids that they alone are responsible for all the feelings in their family, this discussion will help them focus on their behavior (that they can change). They will recognize how behavior affects the total family atmosphere.

"Finish This" Stories

Introduce the activity by saying:

Let's practice choosing actions that can bring good feelings to our families, and rejecting actions that will upset the family.

Read one of the following stories to the kids. Work together as a group to make up an ending to the story that will show the family members (including parents)

My actions make a difference in my family

choosing actions that will upset the family. Then make up a second ending to the story, showing the family members choosing actions that will bring pleasant feelings to the family.

Story 1. A mother (or father) comes home from work and the kids, Susie and Joey, rush into the room wanting to tell her (him) all about the play, *Star Crasher*, they tried out for at school. Joey tried out for the part of Luke Skyrunner, and Susie tried out for the part of Princess Linda. Mother (father), however, has had a bad day and doesn't want to talk right now.

Story 2. Two brothers are riding home from school in the car. The younger brother says, "Look, Mom, at the paper I made in school today." The older brother reaches over and grabs the paper, saying, "Let me see it, twerp. What baby stuff did you do in school today?"

Conclude by saying:

> **Rejecting actions that bring unpleasant feelings is very hard! But you can work hard at making wiser choices!**

If time allows, move on to the other story. *Note:* If you have older kids, you could divide them into two teams and ask one team to write the first story ending, and the other the second. Let the teams share their story endings with each other.

Prayer Time

Focus your prayer time on God's great power to help us change our actions.

> **Learning to do more of the actions that bring good feelings to our family and fewer of the actions that bring bad feelings is hard to do! But God promises to help us do it when we ask Him!**

Ask each child to pray a one-sentence prayer, asking God to help them change the behavior they identified early in the session. For example:

> **Dear God, please help me to clean my room the first time my mom asks so she won't have to yell at me. Amen.**

Remind kids to use the "right to pass" rule if they don't want to pray.

Bible Time (20 Minutes)

Regathering

Have one facilitator lead the kids in a song, game, or activity.

"Adam and Eve Have a Baby"

Present the Bible story (script is on pages 129 and 130).

Memory Verse

Use your memory verse poster to review Romans 8:38, 39 with the kids.

Closing Prayer Huddle

Close your meeting as in weeks past.

Snack (5 Minutes)

Distribute the snack the child brought. Before the kids leave, choose another child to take the snack tin home for next week.

Opening Skit

Characters

- Skip (a puppet) and a facilitator

Needed

- A puppet and a simple puppet stage, which can be made from a table turned on its side, or a sheet (or blanket) held up by two facilitators

The Cereal Bowl

Skip enters and walks back and forth with his head drooping, looking sad, and sighing. "Woe is me!" is uttered occasionally.

Facilitator	*(Enters)* Hey, Skip! How are you? Ah—not so good, I guess! What's wrong?
Skip	Nothing.
Facilitator	I don't believe that. You're not your usual perky self today!
Skip	Well, OK. I'm upset 'cause my mom yelled at me before I left for school this morning. I wish she wouldn't do that. I feel bad and she feels bad and everyone gets a headache when she does that!
Facilitator	Did you do something to get her to yell at you?
Skip	No!
Facilitator	*(Disbelieving)* Skip?
Skip	Well—I guess she wasn't too happy about what I did to my brother.
Facilitator	What was that?
Skip	It was his fault, really! He called me a runt, so I threw something at him.
Facilitator	Yeah, keep going—what did you throw?
Skip	Just some cereal.
Facilitator	Umm. Just picked some up in your hand, did you?
Skip	They were in my cereal bowl.
Facilitator	And what happened to the bowl?
Skip	It stayed with the cereal.

Facilitator	I see. Was this before or after you put the milk on?
Skip	After. *(Pauses)* It was great! Got him right in the head! He had little flakes of cereal and drips of milk all over his head! You should 'a seen him! He started to cry— *(Pauses, looks sad)* and that's when my mom yelled at me.
Facilitator	Sounds like you had quite an unpleasant morning! How did you work it out?
Skip	*(Looks sad)* We didn't. When I left for school, everyone was mad at everyone else. I guess it was all my fault. I feel awful inside and don't want to go home. I like it better when we all laugh and talk and get along. But we always seem to mess it up and get mad.
Facilitator	Well, that's normal. Sometimes it's hard to get along when we live together all the time. But you can do something about it!
Skip	I can?
Facilitator	Sure! Maybe you messed up this morning, but I'll bet you can think of something you can do this afternoon that will bring pleasant feelings to your home again.
Skip	Like what?
Facilitator	Think about it! What can you do to make things feel good in your family again?
Skip	*(Thoughtfully)* Well, I could 'pologize to my mom! *(Brightens)* Yeah, she'd like that, and probably give me a hug! Hey! I just thought of something else! Thanks! I'll see you around! *(Exits)*
Facilitator	*(Calls after him)* Hey, wait a minute, Skip! How about apologizing to your brother? *(Shakes his head)* Oh well, maybe he'll think of that, too! *(Exits)*

Bible Story

From

- Genesis 4:1-8

Characters

- Adam and Eve

Needed

- A few baby items, such as a blanket, rattle, bottle, a disposable diaper, etc.
- *Optional:* A video, teaching pictures, or flannelgraph figures to tell the story of Cain and Abel

Adam and Eve Have a Baby

Adam and Eve enter and greet the kids. They are carrying the baby items.

Adam	Last week we were talking about changes in our families, and today we're talking about feeling good and feeling bad in families. We sort of put the two things together, and we both thought of the same thing—
Adam and Eve	*(Together)* Cain and Abel!
Eve	You know, we were so proud when we had our first baby! Of course, I didn't have all these wonderful things to take care of him, like you do today! *(Holds up a disposable diaper)* Do you know how much I would have loved something like this when Cain was a baby? Making diapers out of fig leaves and deer hides is pretty difficult, believe me!
Adam	After Cain was born, we were feeling really good in our family for a long time.
Eve	And when I found out I was going to have another baby, we were really excited! *(Pauses)* Unfortunately, Cain wasn't very happy about it.
Adam	After Abel was born, we began to see some changes in Cain. It was clear that he was feeling a very unpleasant feeling: jealousy. From that time on, he chose actions that came from his jealousy, and it made for some very unpleasant times in our family.
Eve	Whenever we tried to talk to Cain about his feelings of jealousy, he would get really mad and run away from us!
Adam	That's a really unhealthy way for anyone to handle their feelings. It hurts everyone—Cain, Abel, Eve, and me! We felt so sad because of his actions!
Eve	But Cain was hurting the most, and the sad part was he wouldn't tell us about his feelings. He just kept all that anger and jealousy inside, until—well, you know what happened! *(Use a visual aid to help you briefly tell the story of Cain killing Abel)*

Adam	That's why we are here with you in Confident Kids. We want you to learn that holding your feelings inside is dangerous, and there are much better ways to handle your feelings! You can make choices, and we hope you will choose to talk about your feelings!
Eve	I've got a secret!
Adam	*(Looks at her, puzzled)* What?
Eve	I said, "I've got a secret!"
Adam	Here we are talking about Confident Kids and feelings and remembering how our son killed his brother, and out of nowhere you say, *(Mimicks)* "I've got a secret"? What are you talking about?
Eve	I just wanted to tell the kids that they can have a secret weapon to help them learn how to be honest with their feelings and help bring more pleasant feelings to their families.
Adam	A secret weapon?
Eve	Yes! It's prayer. *(To kids)* God has lots of power to help you. We tried to teach Cain to ask God to help him when he was feeling angry and jealous, but he never learned to trust God to help. Don't be like Cain! Ask God to help you, and I know He will!
Adam	Hey, we have to go! Have a great week, everyone, and we'll see you next week!
They exit.	

Confident Kids © 1997 Linda Kondracki Sibley. Permission granted to photocopy. The Standard Publishing Co.

Love	Belonging	Anger	Jealousy
Cared for	Left out	Having fun	Hurt
Listened to	Disappointed	Write your own	Write your own

Goals

- Illustrate how our words can help or hurt others in our family
- Present four principles for using words that help—not hurt—others in our family
- Practice using the principles through role playing with puppets
- Have Adam and Eve use the memory verse (Ephesians 4:29) to reinforce the need to use words that help—not hurt

Needed

- Four wooden spoons of various sizes or four paper lunch bags (one set per small group), plus scraps of cloth, pieces of ribbon, yarn, and steel wool (optional)
- Group rules poster
- Items for opening skit
- Copies of "Talking Together in My Family"
- A set of hand puppets per small group (if you did not make them during the gathering activity)
- Prayer journals
- Items for regathering, if any
- Props for Bible story
- Memory verse poster (Ephesians 4:29)

Words Can Help— Or Hurt—My Family

Elementary Session 5 Outline

Opening (30 Minutes)
> "Telephone Game" or "Puppet Construction"
>
> Group Rules
>
> "Sticks and Stones"

Small Groups (35 Minutes)
> Discussion of Session Theme
>
> Puppet Role Plays
>
> Prayer Time

Bible Time (20 Minutes)
> Regathering
>
> "Eve Learns to Use Words That Help"
>
> Memory Verse
>
> Closing Prayer Huddle

Snack (5 Minutes)
> The snack can be served during the Bible Time regathering.

Words Can Help— Or Hurt—My Family

Elementary Session 5

Opening (30 Minutes)

"Telephone Game" or "Puppet Construction"

The "Telephone Game" illustrates how poor communication can cause misunderstandings and hard feelings. To play, have everyone sit in a circle. Begin by whispering a phrase into the ear of one of the kids. Be sure no one else can hear. That person must then lean over and whisper the same phrase into the ear of the next person. Continue passing the phrase around until it reaches the last person. The only rule of this game is that the phrase can be whispered only once to each person. If the child did not hear it correctly, he must pass on whatever he thinks the phrase is. When the phrase reaches the last person, she should repeat it aloud. In all likelihood, everyone will enjoy a good laugh as they see how much it has changed as it has gone around the circle! Repeat the process as long as time remains. Here are some possible phrases:

- The red, red robin comes bob-bob-bobbing along.
- Follow the yellow brick road.
- Peter Piper picked a peck of pickled peppers.
- *[One of the kids in the group]* is a very special person!
- Confident Kids is a place to have fun!

You may prefer to have the kids make puppets to use during the small group time. Each small group will need one set of puppets to represent a family. You can use various-size wooden spoons, paper lunch bags, or other items of your choice. Have items available to decorate the puppets, such as scraps of cloth or ribbon, yarn, and bits of steel wool.

Group Rules

Use your poster to review the rules.

"Sticks and Stones"

Use the script on page 138 to introduce today's theme of the power of words.

Small Groups (35 Minutes)

Discussion of Session Theme

Use the following questions to discuss the session theme, "My words can help—or hurt—others in my family."

Have you ever heard the phrase, "Sticks and stones may break my bones, but words will never hurt me"? Do you think it's true that words can never hurt us? *(Let kids respond)*

How did words hurt Jason? *(Debbie's namecalling and put-downs made him hurt more and feel alone)*

In the skit, how did words help Jason? *(Jill's words of kindness and offer to help put him at ease and made him feel like he wasn't alone)*

Can you think of a time someone used words that hurt you? *(You can start the sharing by telling an incident from your own life)*

How about a time words helped you? *(Again, begin with an illustration from your own life)*

Last week we talked about how the actions we choose can help make our family a good place, or a hurtful place to be. *(Refer to the actions kids identified that they wanted to change and ask if any*

of them remembered to make better choices) It's hard to remember to act in ways that help, not hurt, isn't it? Today we're talking about how the words we choose can either help or hurt others in our families. Sometimes we can hurt each other with words more than we can in any other way! Words can hurt very much!

But like Jason discovered in the skit, words can also help, too! When others talk to us in kind, helpful, loving ways, we can handle whatever happens to us. Unfortunately, people who live together in families are not always careful about the way they talk to each other. Many families have lots of yelling and hurtful words that make living there difficult. But we can work to make our families a better place by learning to choose our words carefully. Here are some principles about using words that can help.

Distribute copies of "Talking Together in My Family" (page 141). Let kids fill in the blanks and color the sheets as you present the following information. *Note: If you have first and second graders, you will have to simplify the following principles, perhaps focusing on just one or two that are particularly problematic for your kids.*

Say words that help, not hurt. You have great power to make others feel good or bad by what you say. Your words do make a difference!

Say them in a kind way, with no namecalling or put-downs. Watch your tone of voice. A sarcastic, angry tone of voice is as hurtful as the words themselves. Remember how it feels to be called names or cut down with words. *(Spend*

My words can help— or hurt— others in my family

time helping the kids understand how destructive it is to use words in this way)

Say what is true. Calling someone stupid, saying "I hate you" or "I'm never going to talk to you again" is not truthful. "I'm really angry" or "I don't like what you are doing" are examples of true statements.

Speak for yourself. Use "I" statements such as "I'm really angry" or "I don't like what you are doing." This will help you own your own feelings. "You make me so mad" or "You're driving me crazy" are blaming and shaming statements that shut down communication and wound the other person.

Puppet Role Plays

You will need a set of puppets that represent a full family, either those made during the gathering activity, or ones you have brought with you. To do this activity, follow these instructions:

1. Read one of the scenarios listed below.
2. Ask for volunteers to use the puppets to act them out.
3. Ask kids to identify which communication principles are being violated.
4. Ask kids to rewrite the sentences so that they are consistent with the principle (one possible way is suggested for you).
5. Ask for volunteers to use the puppets to role-play the situation using the principle properly.
6. Do as many scenarios as time allows.

Scenario 1

Mother	Susie, turn off the TV set now and do your homework.
Susie	*(Yells)* You *always* make me turn off the TV! How come you never tell

Jimmy he has to go do his homework? *(Pouts)*

Principles Violated:

Tone of voice, saying what is true.

Rewrite:

Susie	If you will let me finish this program, I will turn off the set and go do my homework then.

Scenario 2

Mother	Susie, you will never get good grades if you keep watching all that junk on TV. Now go to your room and get busy!
Susie	I hate you! *(Storms out)*

Principles Violated:

Mother's words were not helpful! Susie does not hate her mom.

Rewrite:

Mother	I understand you want to finish this program. But until your grades improve, you may not watch TV until your homework is done.
Susie	I don't want to do my homework. *(But turns TV off and goes to room)*

Scenario 3

Younger Sibling	*(To older sibling)* Tony, will you play a game with me?
Tony	Are you nuts? Why would I want to play with a little cheat like you?

Younger Sibling	Please? I won't cheat! I really want to play!
Tony	Look, brat, can't you see I've got homework to do? Oh, I forgot! You don't get any homework in that baby class you're in! Now get out of here!

Principles Violated:

Tony's words are not helpful or kind.

Rewrite:

Tony	I don't feel like playing now, and I have homework to do. Please leave me alone now so I can do it.

Scenario 4

Younger Sibling	*(Angrily)* You never play with me anymore! You could do this dumb homework later! *(Exits)*
Tony	*(Angrily)* Hey! You messed up my paper! You'll die for this, you brat! *(Chases after younger sibling)*

Principles Violated:

It's not true that the older brother never played with him; his words and actions were not kind or helpful.

Rewrite:

Younger Sibling	Maybe you could do your homework after we play! (If *that doesn't work,* simply say *"OK"* and *leave him alone*)

Prayer Time

Conduct your prayer time as in weeks past.

Bible Time (20 Minutes)

Regathering

Have one facilitator lead the group in a song, game, or activity.

"Eve Learns to Use Words That Help"

Present the Bible story (script is on pages 139 and 140).

Memory Verse

Introduce this week's memory verse (Ephesians 4:29, ICB). Emphasize the importance God places on how we talk to and with each other. Have kids read it together a few times. If you have time, use a memory verse game. (See Appendix B, "Resources," for ideas.)

> When you talk, do not say harmful things. But say what people need—words that will help others become stronger. Then what you say will help those who listen to you.

Closing Prayer Huddle

Close your meeting as in weeks past.

Snack (5 Minutes)

Distribute the snack the child brought. Before the kids leave, choose another child to take the snack tin home for next week.

Characters

- Jill, Jason, and Debbie

Sticks and Stones

Debbie and Jason enter from different sides of the room. Jason is walking slowly and looks sad.

Debbie	Hi, Jason! Hey, what's wrong?
Jason	I can't believe it, Debbie. My parents are going to get a di—a div—I can't even say it!
Debbie	A divorce? Hey, no big deal! Lots of parents get divorced! Besides, your parents were jerks anyway. All they ever did was fight and get on your case!
Jason	What are you talking about? My family is falling apart! Don't you care?
Debbie	Why should I care? It's your family. You always were a big crybaby anyway. *(Taunting, as she walks away)* Crybaby, crybaby, crybaby!
Jason	Oh, yeah! *(Calls out after her)* "Sticks and stones may break my bones, but words will never hurt me!" *(Cries a little and sits down with head in hands)*
Jill	*(Enters and sits next to Jason)* Hey, Jason, what's wrong? You look so sad!
Jason	I can't believe it, Jill. My parents are going to get a di—a div—I can't say it!
Jill	A divorce? Gosh, Jason, I'm really sorry. You must feel really hurt about it. Is there anything I can do?
Jason	I don't think so. Maybe just walk the long way home with me. I don't really feel like going home just yet and I don't really want to be alone.
Jill	Sure! *(They stand)* Do you want to stop at my house on the way?

Jill puts her arm through his. They talk softly as they exit.

Bible Story

From

- Ephesians 4:29

Characters

- Adam and Eve

Needed

- Memory verse poster (Ephesians 4:29)

Eve Learns to Use Words That Help

Adam and Eve enter and greet the kids. They are talking to each other, looking puzzled, scratching their heads, etc. They say, "Sticks and stones will break my bones?" "Words will never hurt me?" "What does that mean?" "I don't know. It's certainly not true, is it?" etc.

Eve	Well, the kids have been talking about this tonight. Maybe we should ask them what it means! *(Asks kids to explain the phrase)*
Adam	That's a dumb phrase! I mean, it's certainly not true! Words hurt more than sticks and stones!
Eve	True! Hey, Adam, you were hurt by a stick once, remember?
Adam	*(Looks puzzled)* A stick? You mean that time I fell over a tree that had fallen in the garden? I'd hardly call that a stick!
Eve	*(Laughs)* I know, but I was trying to be kind! I can't believe you just admitted to all these kids that you didn't see a huge tree and you ran right into it! *(To kids)* You should have been there! It was so funny! He was chasing a kangaroo—
Adam	It was an elephant.
Eve	*(Looks at Adam and laughs)* Oh, come on! An elephant? You never chased an elephant in the garden! You have the worst memory of anyone I know! Anyway, the point is—I forget the point. What was I saying?
Adam	You were making me look stupid in front of all the kids.
Eve	What? *(Looks shocked)* I was not! Well, at least I didn't mean to.
Adam	Whether you meant to or not, you did. Your words hurt me, Eve.
Eve	I'm sorry, Adam! *(Pauses)* You know, it really is easy to hurt others with words.

Adam	That's why God's word says so much about being careful about what we say! In fact, it's so important, we have a new memory verse that talks about it. *(Displays poster of Ephesians 4:29. Read it aloud with the kids)* "When you talk, do not say harmful things. But say what people need—words that will help others become stronger. Then what you say will help those who listen to you."
Eve	That's a great verse, and I'm going to do what it says—starting right now! I'm really sorry, Adam!
Adam	Now those are words that help! I feel so much better! Well, we're out of time! See you all next week! Good-bye!

They exit.

Talking Together in My Family

1. Say words that _____, not _____.

2. Say them in a _____ way; no _____ or _____.

3. Say what is _____.

4. Speak for _____.

Goals

- Present the importance of caring for each other in families
- List the behaviors that make us feel cared for and not cared for
- Define affirmation and discuss how affirming one another is a powerful way of caring for each other
- Make affirmation badges for other family members as a way to practice giving affirmations
- Use Adam and Eve to talk about how God affirms us

Needed

- Two indoor play balls
- Group rules poster
- Props for opening skit
- "Affirmation Badges" (one copy per child, plus a few extras) and 2"x 3" plastic pin back nametag holders (four per child)
- Prayer journals
- Items for regathering, if any
- Props for Bible story
- Memory verse posters (Romans 8:38, 39; Ephesians 4:29)

"I Care About You!"

Elementary Session 6 Outline

Opening (30 Minutes)

    "Patterns" Game

    Group Rules

    The Conference

Small Groups (35 Minutes)

    Discussion of Session Theme

    Affirmation Badges

    Prayer Time

Bible Time (20 Minutes)

    Regathering

    "Adam and Eve Learn to Affirm"

    Memory Verse

    Closing Prayer Huddle

Snack (5 Minutes)

    The snack can be served during the Bible Time regathering.

"I Care About You!"

Elementary Session 6

"Patterns"

"Patterns" is a cooperation game that reinforces the need for everyone to work together. You will need two balls, such as Nerf soccer balls, or red indoor play balls. Have all the kids stand in a circle. Begin by establishing the pattern. To do this, tell the kids that you will throw the ball to one of them, who will in turn throw it to someone else in the circle. They must remember who threw them the ball, and whom they are throwing it to, because when everyone has had the ball once, they will have to throw it around the circle again in exactly the same order. This is called the pattern. Practice the pattern several times until the kids can throw it around easily, without having to stop and think who they are receiving it from or throwing it to.

For Third and Fourth Graders

When the pattern has been learned, add a second ball to the circle. After the first ball has been thrown to the third or fourth person, start the second ball at the beginning of the pattern. Encourage the kids to concentrate and help each other keep both balls moving smoothly through the pattern.

Group Rules

Use your group rules poster to review the rules, if needed.

"The Conference"

Introduce the skit.

> Our theme today is about how we can care for others in our families. In the skit, you will see the same scene presented twice. Your job is to listen and see which

Everyone needs to feel cared for in my family!

one shows family members caring for each other.

Present the skit (script begins on page 147). Dismiss to small groups after the skit is presented.

Small Groups (35 Minutes)

Discussion of Session Theme

Use the following questions to discuss the session theme, "Everyone needs to feel cared for in my family!"

Which scene showed family members who were not caring for each other? *(The first one)* What did they do that was uncaring? *(Dad wouldn't listen to his son's explanation; the sister taunted and called her brother names; Dad's words were hurtful and he never even got to the main problem)*

Which scene showed family members who were caring for each other? *(The second one)* What did they do that was caring? *(Dad used words that were caring and he identified the real problem; sister didn't call brother names and she chose a restaurant that he would like; Richard was apologetic for his behavior and for making his dad miss some work)*

Which family do you think you would rather live in? *(Let kids respond)*

Which family reminds you more of your own? *(Let kids respond)*

One important part of living in families is that all the members act in ways that show that they love and care for each other. But that can only happen when everyone works together to show that they care for each other.

What do parents do to show they love their kids? *(Provide food, shelter, clothing; listen; spend time with them; etc.)*

What do brothers and sisters do to show that they care about each other? *(Play together, don't use put-downs or namecalling, treat each other as they would want to be treated, etc.)*

Who in your family shows you they love and care about you? *(Let kids respond)* What do they do to show you? *(Let kids respond)*

Is there anyone in your family who doesn't treat you in ways that feel loving and caring? *(Let kids respond)* What does that person do that makes you feel that way? *(Let kids respond)*

It's nice when others in our family show us they love and care for us. However, we have to do our part, too, by showing others we love and care about them. There are many ways we can do that, and one of the best is to use words. When we tell people nice things we think about them, we are giving them a positive message about how special they are to us. We call these messages affirmations.

For instance, if I say to *[Choose one of the kids in your group]* that I think she has a wonderful smile, I am caring for her by giving her an affirmation. Or, if I tell *[Choose another one of the kids in your group]* that I think he is the best artist in the group, I am giving him an affirmation. Let's think of an affirmation for everyone

in our group. (*Ask kids to think of positive messages to give one another. Be sure they understand that these messages must be true, at least in their opinion. Have one in mind for each of your kids, in case they have trouble doing this*)

Now let's think about how we can give affirmations to others in our families.

Affirmation Badges

Give everyone in your group a sheet of "Affirmation Badges" (page 152) and one plastic badge holder for each member of their family. (Have a few extras available as well.) Have them read through the designs on the sheet and choose one that describes each member of their family. If they can't find one on the sheet that is appropriate, they can create their own design. The point is to make a gift for each family member that affirms them by the message it contains. Ask them to give the badges to family members in the morning to wear all day (or at least during breakfast or dinner when the family is together) and to share with each family member why they chose that particular message for them.

It is also important that we know how to affirm ourselves. Ask kids to choose a badge for themselves, and then talk to them about why they chose the design they did. Also, it would mean a lot to the kids if you made a badge for each of them and gave it to them before they leave today. You can do this in advance and bring it with you, or work on them as the kids work on theirs.

Prayer Time

Conduct your prayer time as in weeks past. In your concluding prayer, thank God for how much He loves and cares for each one of us!

Bible Time (20 Minutes)

Regathering

Have one facilitator lead in a song, game, or activity.

"Adam and Eve Learn to Affirm"

Present the Bible story (script is on pages 150 and 151).

Memory Verse

Review Ephesians 4:29, using it to reinforce the importance of giving affirmations to others in our family.

Closing Prayer Huddle

Close your meeting as in weeks past.

Snack (5 Minutes)

Distribute the snack the child brought. Before the kids leave, choose another child to take the snack tin home for next week.

Characters

- Richard, his teacher, his father, and Richard's sister Vicki

Needed

- Two areas: one with a desk and chairs for a parent/teacher conference; the other with four chairs to represent the front and back seats of a car

The Conference

Scene 1

Richard and his dad are meeting with the teacher. Richard looks withdrawn and disinterested; his father looks irritated and angry. Vicki is waiting in the "car."

Teacher	Thank you for taking time off work to come, Mr. Bennett. I think we can make this meeting short.
Dad	Just get to the point. What sort of trouble is Richard in now?
Teacher	Well, it seems Richard has not turned in any homework for the past two months. When I ask him where it is, he always has some excuse about why he doesn't have it.
Dad	*(Angry)* Two months? Believe me, this will end now! I won't have any lazy kids in my family! You send me copies of all the stuff he hasn't done and he'll do it! Let's go, Richard! *(Teacher exits; Richard and Dad get into the "car")*
Vicki	So what did you do now, creep?
Richard	Shut up, Vicki! It's none of your business!
Dad	Well it is my business! I can't believe a son of mine would be so lazy as to skip his homework for two months—and lie to the teacher about it, besides!
Vicki	Ha! You got caught! Now you're in big trouble, jerk!
Richard	*(Yells)* Who asked you, Vicki? *(Tries to explain)* Look, Dad—
Dad	I don't want to hear it, Richard! Just don't expect to go out of the house for the next two weeks!

Scene 2

Richard and his dad are meeting with the teacher. Richard looks sad and embarrassed; his father looks concerned. Vicki is waiting in the "car."

Teacher	Thank you for taking time off work to come, Mr. Bennett. I think we can make this meeting short.
Dad	No problem. Is Richard in some sort of trouble?
Teacher	Well, it seems Richard has not turned in any homework for the past two months. When I ask him where it is, he always has some excuse about why he doesn't have it.
Dad	*(Looks shocked)* Really? That doesn't sound like my son.
Teacher	That's why I called you here. This is a definite change in his behavior. Did something happen two months ago?
Dad	I don't think so—wait a minute! *(Turns to Richard)* Your birthday was two months ago. Is this about that Nintendo your grandmother gave you?
Richard	Dad, it's not that—
Dad	*(To teacher)* I think I can straighten this out. If you send me copies of all the work he's missed, I'll see that he does it. Let's go, Richard. *(They go to the "car")*
Vicki	*(Looks concerned)* What happened? Are you OK, Richard?
Richard	I don't know yet.
Dad	He's fine. He's just having a little trouble with his Nintendo. Richard, what was the rule you agreed to when I let you keep that thing?
Vicki	Uh-oh! You got caught! Told you this would happen!
Richard	That I'd do my homework before I played with it.

Dad	And have you been doing that?
Richard	Yes! Well, mostly—not. But I'm better at *Star Crashers* than anyone in my class!
Dad	I guess it's time to take it away.
Richard	Dad, I'm sorry! It's all my fault that you had to take time off work to talk to my teacher and I lied to you about the Nintendo and everything! I'm so stupid!
Dad	Hey, you just made some bad choices, that's all! You're not stupid and I don't ever want to hear you say that again! You're my kid, and I'm proud of you. I'm just going to help you with this Nintendo thing until you can get back on track in school. Now, where should we go for dinner?
Vicki	I know! Let's go to Geronomo's! That's Richard's favorite and I think he needs a treat!
Dad	We're on our way!

They exit.

Bible Story

From

- Romans 8:38, 39

Characters

- Adam and Eve

Needed

- Memory verse poster
  (Romans 8:38, 39)

Adam and Eve Learn to Affirm

Adam and Eve enter. Eve is feeling perky and talkative. She greets the kids by name, comments on what a great meeting it was, etc. Adam is feeling low. He slinks in with his hands in his pockets, head hanging, doesn't greet kids, etc.

Eve	*(Looks at Adam with a smile on her face, then looks in his eyes for a long moment and gets serious)* You look so sad! Is something wrong?
Adam	*(Sighs)* No, of course not. What makes you think anything is wrong?
Eve	Well, your face, for one thing! *(Looks concerned)* Adam, what is wrong?
Adam	I feel fine. *(With head hanging and a long face)* I'm happy, really.
Eve	Adam, you are not saying what is true.
Adam	OK, OK! I'm feeling—uh—well, I guess I'm feeling dumb and, well, worthless about sums it up.
Eve	Why?
Adam	Well, I just saw a platypus.
Eve	*(Looks at Adam, waiting for him to go on)* So?
Adam	Well, don't you think that's a pretty stupid name for an animal?
Eve	I never thought about it. Besides, you named all the animals.
Adam	That's what I mean. I got to thinking about what a rotten job I did of it. I mean, platypus. What a dumb name. And how about rhinoceros? Or hippopotamus?
Eve	*(Giggling)* I always thought cow was pretty stupid. *(Looks at Adam who is obviously hurt by that statement)* Oh, I forgot—that's your favorite name. Well, anyway, Adam. Naming all those animals was a huge job, and I think you did great! I couldn't have done it.

Adam	*(Brightens)* Really? You know, you have never said that to me before!
Eve	*(Surprised)* Well, I should have! I thought it lots of times. In fact, I think you do lots of wonderful things. And I love you! But I know you already know that!
Adam	But it's still good to hear you say it. You gave me an affirmation—I just learned that word today—and it really helped me feel better. Thanks!
Eve	Giving and getting affirmations is fun. Say, let's give an affirmation to all the kids before we go!
Adam	OK! And I know the best affirmation we can give. *(Displays poster of Romans 8:38, 39)* This is God's affirmation to you! I want everyone here to go home tonight knowing that you are loved by God. He loves you because He created you, and He didn't make anyone else in the whole world like you.
Eve	That means no one else anywhere in the whole world could ever replace you! That's how special God created you! So remember: *(Have kids read the poster aloud with you)*
Adam	Well, we have to go! We'll see you next week!

They exit.

Affirmation Badges

I'm Huggable—
Hug ME!

I'm Growing
Up Good

I'm a Great

I'm Lovable

I'm Fun to Be
Around

I'm an
Encourager

Goals

- Make a clear presentation of God's invitation to join His family
- Create an opportunity for children to respond to God's invitation
- Identify ways the church family functions as an extended family in caring for our needs
- Use the parable of the lost son to assure kids of how much God loves them and wants to include them in His family

Needed

- Family night invitations
- Group rules poster
- Props for opening skit
- Copies of "Adoption Invitations" (If possible copy page 165 onto the back of page 164. If not, staple 2 pages together and fold to make an invitation.)
- Copies of "The Parable of the Lost Son"
- Prayer journals
- Items for regathering, if any
- Props for Bible story
- Memory verse poster (2 Corinthians 6:18)
- Copies of "Affirmation Balloons" and unit certificates from Appendix A (pages 371 and 373)

I Can Belong to God's Family, Too!

Elementary Session 7 Outline

Opening (30 Minutes)

    Family Night Invitations

    Group Rules

    "The New Family"

Small Groups (25 Minutes)*

    Discussion of Session Theme

    Adoption Invitations

    Prayer Time

Bible Time (30 Minutes)*

    Regathering

    "Adam and Eve Present 'The Parable of the Lost Son'"

    Memory Verse

    Closing Prayer Huddle

Snack (5 Minutes)

    The snack can be served during the Bible Time regathering.

*Note time difference.

I Can Belong to God's Family, Too!

Elementary Session 7

Family Night Invitations

Next week is the final session of this unit, which is a Family Night. Tell the kids that next week you will host a party, and they can invite their parents to come with them. Talk about the party enthusiastically to build a sense of excitement for sharing the group with their parents. Have the kids make invitations (page 163) or use purchased party invitations.

Group Rules

Review the group rules again this week, if necessary.

"The New Family"

Present the opening skit (script is on pages 157 and 158).

Small Groups (35 Minutes*)

Discussion of Session Theme

Use the following questions to discuss the session theme, "God wants me to belong to His family!"

> **Why do you think Larry didn't want to be adopted by the Davis family?** *(He was scared of the unknown)*
>
> **How would life be different for Larry and Carrie in a family than in a children's home?** *(Refer to the things Carrie talked about: a real family to love them, Christmas presents, their own rooms, etc.)*

*Note time difference

God wants me to belong to His family!

Even though the Davises were eager to adopt Larry, what did he have to do before that could happen? *(Agree to it, make a commitment by signing the release paper)*

Have you ever wished a family other than your own would adopt you? *(Let kids respond)* Why? *(Let kids respond)*

Because our families are imperfect, they cannot meet our needs all of the time. There will be times in your family when others mess up, let you down, or hurt you. During those times, it is easy to look around and wish we could find a different family. Sometimes we may wish we could be adopted by other families we know, or we make up a perfect family in our minds and pretend we belong to it. Unfortunately, neither of these options help us get through the times when our families are not meeting our needs. But there is another family we can belong to that will help us in ways our own family cannot. There is a family with a loving Father who wants to adopt us and take care of us. This family has lots of people in it who care for one another in special ways. That Father is God, and His family is the church. We can belong to God's family at the same time we belong to our own family. In fact, we very much need both families!

Adoption Invitations

Distribute folded copies of the "Adoption Invitation" (pages 164 and 165). Then say:

In a way, we are all like Carrie and Larry in the skit. Each of us is invited to become a member of God's family. But being a

member of God's family is not automatic. We are not born into God's family the way we are born into our own families. We are invited to become a member of God's family, just like Carrie and Larry were invited to join the Davis family. And, just like Carrie and Larry, we have to decide if we will accept God's invitation. No one can do that for us. We have to decide on our own.

Use the "Adoption Invitations" to talk about how we become members of God's family. Discuss the invitation at the top of the inside, helping kids fill in the blanks. Note that the answers come from John 3:16:

- Because he *loves* you.
- By *believing* in Jesus.
- *For ever!* (Eternity)

Next, look at each picture and talk about these benefits to becoming a member of God's family. Kids can color and decorate their certificates as you talk. Finally, read through the prayer on the back, which encourages them to accept God's invitation to join His family.

Optional: If you have pamphlets describing how kids can give their lives to Jesus, distribute them at this time. The children's ministry department of your church will most likely have such a resource. If not, check with your local Christian bookstore for material consistent with your beliefs.

Prayer Time

Since this is the last small group of the unit, be sure to spend a few minutes reviewing the answers to prayer that have happened during the last few weeks. Encourage kids to keep praying for the requests that are still current. As you close in prayer, focus on accepting God's invitation to become a member of His family. Give kids an opportunity to read the prayer on their "Adoption Invitations." Help them understand the concept of commiting their lives to Jesus. To avoid peer pressure, give them time to pray silently and invite them to tell you what they prayed when the group is dismissed.

Bible Time (20 Minutes*)

Regathering

Have one facilitator lead in a song, game, or activity.

Adam and Eve Present "The Parable of the Lost Son"

During this time, Adam and Eve will help the kids dramatize the parable, which you may want to have the kids present during the closing program next week. You will need copies of "The Parable of the Lost Son" (pages 161 and 162) and any props you may want to bring to add interest to the play. The script and directions are on pages 159 and 160.

Memory Verse

Use 2 Corinthians 6:18 (*ICB*) as your final affirmation of the relationship we can have with God.

> "I will be your father, and you will be my sons and daughters, says the Lord All-Powerful."

Closing Prayer Huddle

Close your meeting as in weeks past.

Snack (5 Minutes)

Distribute the snack. Thank all of the children who brought snacks during this unit.

Characters

- Carrie and Larry, Mr. and Mrs. Davis

The New Family

Carrie and Larry are getting ready to be adopted out of a children's home. They enter, arguing.

Carrie *(Very upset)* What do you mean, you don't want to do it?

Larry Read my lips— *(Slowly and deliberately)* I don't want to do it!

Carrie You are such a noodle brain! This is what we've wanted for years! This is our big chance to have a real family!

Larry Then you go!

Carrie I intend to! *(Pauses; softens)* But I don't want to go without you, Larry. We've been together in this children's home for three years. Besides being my brother, you're my best friend.

Larry Well, what's so bad about this place anyway? Let's just stay here.

Carrie *(Upset again)* What? You were the one who kept talking about getting adopted! You said being with a real family is better than being alone! You said we'd get more stuff at Christmastime! You said you wanted your own room! You said you wanted a real mom to hug you after school! You said—

Larry All right! I get the idea! So I changed my mind.

Carrie *(Ready to burst)* Why? The Davises really want us and they'd give us plenty of stuff at Christmas! We'd even have our own rooms! What kind of wiggly worm has gotten into your brain?

Larry Maybe they don't want us! Maybe they'd give us back someday! Maybe they'd give us stuff at Christmas we don't want! Maybe they'd put snakes in our bed!

Carrie Oh, gross! Only you could think of something so dumb!

Larry And they'd probably have all kinds of rules and chores and stuff we'd have to do!

Carrie	Of course they do! That's part of being in a family. We'll all have to work together and that means sometimes doing stuff we don't like, but we have to because that's just the way it is. Look, Larry, you can stay here and be afraid if you want, but I'm going to have a new family. A real family with real parents and—

Mr. and Mrs. Davis enter.

Mr. Davis	There you are! We are so excited about having you two come to live with us! Your rooms are all ready and waiting.
Mrs. Davis	You know, we looked at fifteen different children's homes, and thought about asking twenty different children to become a part of our family. But when we saw both of you, we knew you were just the kids we were looking for. We loved you from the first.
Mr. Davis	There's only one thing left to do. You have to sign the papers saying you want to join our family. Are you ready to do that?
Carrie	*(Excited)* Yes! *(Looks at Larry)* Well, at least I am. How about you, Larry?

They exit.

Bible Story

From

- Luke 15:11-24

Characters

- Adam and Eve

Needed

- Copies of "The Parable of the Lost Son" (pages 161 and 162)

Adam and Eve Present "The Parable of the Lost Son"

Adam and Eve enter and greet the kids.

Eve	It's hard to believe, but our time with you is almost over. Next week is the last week of this unit, and the last week we will be here. I feel sad because I will miss coming here each week!
Adam	Me too! Besides, Eve has learned some important lessons right along with you!
Eve	*(Looks surprised)* Me? What about you? You've learned some things you needed, too!
Adam	Are you kidding? I've learned more than everyone!
Eve	I think the most important lesson of all was today's. Belonging to God's family is more important than anything! I am always amazed that God loves us so much, that He longs and yearns for each one of us to be His son or daughter!
Adam	Right! And nothing tells us that better than the story Jesus told about the lost son. That's why we want to get all of you involved in a little play that will help us tell the story. If we do a good job on our play, we may even present it to your parents next week.
Eve	Let's get ready for that by reading the story together and thinking about the parts of it.

For the remainder of the time, Adam and Eve work together to accomplish the following:

Distribute copies of "The Parable of the Lost Son." Read the parable and discuss the following:

In what ways is the father in the story like God? *(He loves us as we are; He waits anxiously for us to come to Him; He cares for our needs)*

What can we learn from the son? *(We don't have to be afraid to go to God with our feelings, even when we feel guilty or unlovable; living with God is better than living without Him)*

Now organize the kids to act out the parable. The simplest way to do this is through pantomime. One child acts as narrator while the rest act out what is being read. Assign a part to everyone in the group. This will include the father, two sons, servants, pigs, and townspeople. Talk through the play, helping kids think of what they can do to depict the action. For example, in the first verses, the father can put his arms around his son's shoulders to show his affection; the son can pretend he is drinking and laughing hysterically with townspeople to show "wild living," etc. Ask the kids:

What can you do to help those watching understand this part of the story?

When all the actions have been established, practice going through the play until all are comfortable with their parts.

When complete, Adam and Eve say good-bye and exit.

The Parable of the Lost Son

From Luke 15:11-24 (ICB)

A man had two sons. The younger son said to his father, "Give me my share of the property." So the father divided the property between his two sons.

Then the younger son gathered up all that was his and left. He traveled far away to another country. There he wasted his money in foolish living. He spent everything that he had.

Soon after that, the land became very dry, and there was no rain. There was not enough food to eat anywhere in the country. The son was hungry and needed money. So he got a job with one of the citizens there. The man sent the son into the fields to feed pigs. The son was so hungry that he was willing to eat the food the pigs were eating. But no one gave him anything.

The son realized that he had been very foolish. He thought, "All of my father's servants have plenty of food. But I am here, almost dying with hunger. I will leave and return to my father. I'll say to him: Father, I have sinned against God and have done wrong to you. I am not good enough to be called your son. But let me be like one of your servants." So the son left and went to his father.

While the son was still a long way off, his father saw him coming. He felt sorry for his son. So the father ran to him, and hugged and kissed him. The son said, "Father, I have sinned against God and have done wrong to you. I am not good enough to be called your son."

But the father said to his servants, "Hurry! Bring the best clothes and put them on him. Also, put a ring on his finger and sandals on his feet. And get our fat calf and kill it. Then we can have a feast and celebrate! My son was dead, but now he is alive again! He was lost, but now he is found!" So they began to celebrate.

Confident Kids © 1997 Linda Kondracki Sibley. Permission granted to photocopy. The Standard Publishing Co.

An Invitation

To _____

From _____

Please Come!
To Family Night at Confident Kids

A Ministry of Confident Kids

Date _____

Time _____

Will You Accept God's Invitation?

Dear God,

Thank You for wanting me to join Your family! I want to accept Your invitation. I believe in You, and that Your Son, Jesus, died on the cross for me. I invite You to live inside me and teach me how to live as Your child for the rest of my life. And someday, I know we will live together in Heaven because I belong to Your family!

Love,

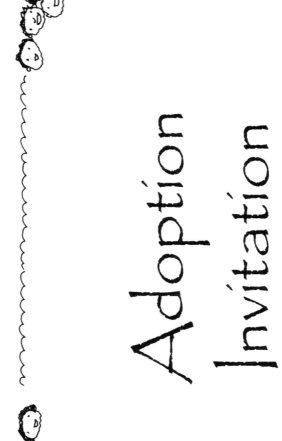

Adoption Invitation

God Invites You to Join His Family

Why?

Because He _____ you.

How? By _____ in Jesus.

For How Long? _____

John 3:16

For God loved the world so much that He gave His only Son. God gave His Son so that whoever believes in Him may not be lost, but have eternal life.

Living in God's Family Means...

God is always with us.

God's Word teaches us how to live.

The church family is my family, too!

Preteen Sessions

Tips for Working
With Preteens in a
Support-Group Setting   168

There Are No Perfect
Families!   171

What's a Family For, Anyway? 179

Changes Can Upset My Family 187

Actions Can Help—
Or Hurt—My Family   199

Words Can Help—
Or Hurt—My Family   213

"I Care About You!"   225

I Can Belong to God's
Family, Too!   237

Tips for Working With Preteens in a Support-Group Setting

What to Expect From Preteens in Confident Kids Groups

Preteens are at a much different developmental level than younger elementary kids, and function in and respond to the support-group experience uniquely. Here are a few key points to help you plan for your group:

- **Preteens are developing skills of abstract and cause-and-effect thinking and therefore will have less difficulty with the process-oriented concepts in the Confident Kids material.**

  Dealing with issues such as feelings, grief, and evaluating the results of choices are well within the range of preteens' emerging thinking capabilities. Take advantage of this, but don't be alarmed if the kids don't understand everything perfectly.

- **Preteens are letting go of "magical thinking."**

  About the age of ten, kids' perspectives broaden beyond the restrictions of their own home environments. Until this time, their home and parents—regardless of how good or bad things actually were—were magically interpreted by the child to be the "best in the world." But now, they begin to see that there are other families and other parents who are different—maybe even better—than their own. If there are problems in the family, this can be a particularly agonizing time for kids as they let go of their idealized view of the parent and begin to see reality. You will see kids in your group struggling with these issues. Be patient if they bounce back and forth between realism and magical thinking!

- **Preteens are entering puberty.**

  Be prepared for the accompanying effects of puberty: emotional upheaval; "love/hate" attraction to, but awkwardness around, the opposite sex; and many complaints about things being "babyish." Although the curriculum does not address the issues connected to puberty directly, you are likely to get into discussions in your small groups about the many changes that are taking place. Sixth graders may be particularly curious.

- **Preteens have defense mechanisms that are deeply internalized and mostly subconscious.**

  By this age, the behaviors kids have developed to defend themselves from emotional pain will significantly affect the way they relate to the world at large. In addition, many of them will enter your groups feeling "too cool" to open up about the painful points of their lives. You may have to work hard to establish trust with your kids, and wait patiently for them to feel safe enough to lower their defenses with you. Once the kids do, however, you will be rewarded with the opportunity for extended conversations on healthy ways to deal with the emotional stress points in their lives.

Skits and Bible Stories Are Key Learning Times

Fifth and sixth graders *love* the skits! Invest a lot of energy in these parts of the session. Here are a few tips to help you do so:

- **Be prepared.**

  Be sure to read each skit at least a week in advance so you can prepare adequately. You can also recruit a drama team to manage this part of the program to free you to focus on building relationships with the kids.

- **Give the kids adequate time to prepare for skits in which they will participate.**

  When the scripts call for the kids to participate, they need time to get ready! Prepare them by having them practice during the gathering activity, or better yet, choose skit participants a week in advance and send scripts home with them to study. Also, if you recruit a drama team, be sure the kids are involved as much as possible! It is one of the most important ways the kids bond with the group!

- **Use adults to be the main Bible story characters.**

  We recommend that the same adults play the main Bible characters each week. This ensures consistency, and allows the adults to properly emphasize the biblical concepts written into the stories. Do not assign kids to these roles.

- **Add as many props and visuals as possible.**

  Remember that today's kids are highly visual! The more you put into the skits, the more effective a communication tool they will be!

Competition, Projects, and Outings Motivate Preteens

Competition, projects, and outings help you keep your preteens involved with the group. Here are some tips for using these three motivators with your kids.

Competition

Kids at this age *love* to compete. But competition can be motivating *or* destructive to the participants, depending on how it is handled. Be sure:

1. To play down the competition by not making a big deal over who wins and who loses. Simply move on to the next activity.
2. Everyone wins sometimes.

3. To avoid giving big prizes to winners. If you want to use prizes, be sure they are small and that over the course of the unit, all of the kids receive prizes at one time or another.
4. To recognize when some of your kids can't handle the competition, and stop using it!

Projects

Preteens can be motivated to work together on projects, especially when the projects accomplish a specific goal. Kids this age enjoy working together on community service projects, or preparing a program or teaching materials for the younger kids. You can also have them start working on a skit or other presentation for the Family Night program early in the unit.

Outings

Plan an end-of-the-unit outing for the kids. Early in the unit, set a group goal that if the kids work hard each week, they will have a party, overnight retreat, or other outing to enjoy. Maximize this motivator by having the kids spend a few minutes each week making plans for their special outing. They can vote on what they would like to do, and then plan a few details each week.

Adapt the Session Plans to Fit Your Kids

There is more material in each of the preteen session plans than you can probably do in one session! As you get to know the kids in your group, you will begin to see what works with them and what elicits the best response. Find your own comfort level with the material and prioritize the things you most want to accomplish each week. Also, there is nothing magical about this material. Make whatever changes are necessary for you to most effectively connect to your kids, in your setting.

Have Basic Materials on Hand for All Sessions

Each session plan in the preteen curriculum lists supplies unique to that session. However, before you begin any unit, be sure to set up your room with the following basic supplies. Adding the optional materials will further enhance the group's experience.

- **Basic Supplies**

  Confident Kids postcards and stamps
  Markers, pencils
  Colored drawing paper
  Tape, glue sticks, stapler

  Scissors
  Paper towels and other supplies for clean up
  Paper cups and napkins for snack time
  Extra snacks (in case someone forgets to return the snack tin)

- **Optional Supplies**

  Prop box for skits and role plays
  Small prizes
  Cassette tapes of songs for preteens
  Preteen games and craft books to supplement the curriculum, if needed

Goals

- Get acquainted with each other and establish a warm, caring environment for the group
- Introduce the unit themes: there are no perfect families; it takes work to live in families
- Have kids introduce their family by doing a paper cup family sculpture
- Affirm God's plan for families through an interview with Adam and Eve

Needed

- Half sheets of various colors of construction paper
- Group rules poster
- Props for opening skit
- Paper or Styrofoam cups (five per child)
- Prayer journal for the group's prayer requests
- Items for regathering, if any
- Props for Bible skit
- 2 Corinthians 6:18 written on poster board and cut into puzzle shapes (at least one piece per child)
- Snacks and snack tin

There Are No Perfect Families!

Preteen Session 1 Outline

Opening (25 Minutes)

Animal Name Tags and "In My Family" Circle Game

Introduction of New Kids

Group Rules

"That's It! I'm Moving to Joe's House"

Small Groups (40 Minutes)

Discussion of Session Theme

Paper Cup Family Sculptures

Prayer Time

Bible Focus (20 Minutes)

Regathering

"Lifestyles of the Biblically Famous"—I

Memory Verse

Closing Prayer Huddle

Snack (5 Minutes)

The snack can be served during the Bible Focus regathering.

There Are No Perfect Families!

Preteen Session 1

Opening (25 Minutes)

Animal Name Tags and
"In My Family" Circle Game

As kids arrive, direct them to a table where they will find a variety of half sheets of colored paper. Instruct them to choose an animal and a color that they feel is representative of themselves, then have them tear the paper into the shape of that animal. As they work, ask them about their choice of color and animal. When all have arrived, play the "In My Family" circle game:

Ask the kids to sit in a circle. Include only as many chairs in the circle as there are kids. (When new kids arrive, they can join the circle by adding a chair to it.) To play, read to the kids the following statements that have to do with families. Tell the kids that they are to listen carefully to each statement. If the statement pertains to their family, they must follow the directions given by the facilitator (they will be asked to move a certain number of chairs to the left or right). If it does not pertain to them, they should remain seated in their chairs. They must follow the directions precisely, even if it means sitting in a chair where someone else is already seated. (In some cases, three or four kids may be sitting on each other's laps!)

1. If you have a mother and father living in your house, move two chairs to the right.
2. If you have a younger brother, move three chairs to the right.
3. If you have two grandfathers who are still alive, move one chair to the left.
4. If you have two sisters, move two chairs to the left.
5. If you have only one parent living in your house, move four chairs to the left.
6. If you have a stepparent, move two chairs to the right.
7. If you have a dog at your house, move one chair to the right.

8. If you wish you had a dog at your house, move two chairs to the right.
9. If you have a grandmother who lives in a state other than California (or whatever state you live in), move three chairs to the left.
10. If you ate Christmas dinner with some of your cousins, move one chair left.

Now ask the kids to sit in their own chairs. Go through the questions again, as a get-acquainted time, taking note of the different family situations revealed as kids raise their hands.

Introduction of New Kids

If you have done a *Confident Kids* unit before, you will likely have both returning kids and new kids in the group. Welcome the new ones by calling each one to the front of the room. Ask the new children to tell the others their name, grade, and one unique thing about themselves. When they are finished, lead the group in yelling, "Welcome, *[child's name]!*" and give each one a round of applause.

Group Rules

If you did not use the introductory session last week, you will need to make a group rules poster. (See page 13 in the "Getting Started" section for complete directions on generating a list of rules for your group.) Spend some quality time doing this, as the group rules are crucial to the success of your support-group experience.

If you did use the introductory session, display the poster you made last week and review it. Be sure everyone understands the rules and the consequences for breaking them.

"That's It! I'm Moving to Joe's House!"

Use the script on page 176 to set the theme for the session. *Note:* Decide in advance how you want to

handle the skit for this and future sessions. You may want to have the facilitators do it or choose two kids to perform it, giving them a few minutes during the opening game to practice. See "Tips for Working With Preteens in a Support-Group Setting" (page 168) for more ideas. Dismiss to small groups after the skit is performed.

Small Groups (40 Minutes)

Discussion of Session Theme

Use the following questions to discuss the session theme, "There are no perfect families!"

Have you ever felt like Jake in today's skit? *(Let kids respond)* **What specific things happen in your family that make you feel that way?** *(Let kids respond)*

Why do you think Joe was so surprised to hear Jake say he thought living in his family would be really great? *(He probably had times of wishing he could live in someone else's family, too!)* **What do you think he probably said next?** *(Let kids respond)*

If, right now, we could design a perfect family, what would it be like? *(Let kids respond)* **Are there any families that are like the one we just described?** *(Let kids respond)* **Why not?** *(Let kids respond)*

Sometimes it is easy for us to look at another family or a family on TV and think that in comparison, ours is the pits. We can think, "If only my dad didn't work so much," or "If only my parents hadn't gotten a divorce," or "If only I had my own room." *(Change or add*

There are no perfect families!

statements to describe family issues affecting your kids) **In the next few weeks, we are going to talk about what it means to live in our families. Tonight, we need to talk about the fact that even though your family may have things about it that you don't like and wish you could change, your family is your family, and for you it can be a special place. To begin, let's find out about each other's families.**

Paper Cup Family Sculptures

Have available a supply of paper or Styrofoam cups. Have the kids take one cup for each member of their families. Give them a few minutes to draw faces or write names on the cups to identify each family member. Then instruct the kids to think of a way to place all the cups to represent their families. For instance, if their father does not live with them, they can place that cup a distance away from the others. Or, if they feel a special relationship exists between two family members they can place those cups close to each other and the others a little distance off. Encourage the kids to be creative with this and spend some time building a clear picture of what their family is like. When all are done, have them use the sculptures to introduce their families to each other. Introduce this activity by sharing a sculpture of your own family of origin. This will give an opportunity for the kids to get to know you, too.

Note: Be aware that some of your kids may dramatically reveal strong negative feelings about family members. Take special note of this information, but resist the urge to "fix" the problem by telling kids what they should—or shouldn't—feel or do in the situation. For example, don't say, "You shouldn't feel that way about your dad. I'm sure he's doing the best he can." Rather, use a validating response, such as, "It must be very hard to see so little of your dad."

Prayer Time

Each week you will spend the last seven or eight minutes of your group time in prayer. The purpose of this time is to help the kids learn that God's presence and power are significant resources as they face the circumstances in their lives. To make this time tangible, set up a prayer notebook for your group to keep track of requests and answers. Review the requests each week and talk about what God has done in response to that request. Write the answers in the notebook.

Bible Focus (20 Minutes)

Regathering

Assign one facilitator each week to lead the kids in a favorite game, song, or activity (see Appendix B, "Resources," for ideas) as they come from their small groups to the Bible story area. This facilitator will have to finish her small-group time a few minutes early to be ready to gather the kids as they dismiss from their groups. *Note:* Some groups prefer to serve the snacks at this time, with the rule that the snacks will be served as soon as everyone has arrived and is quiet.

"Lifestyles of the Biblically Famous!"—I

This skit (script is on pages 177 and 178) is an interview with the Bible's very first family, Adam and Eve.

Memory Verse

In advance, print the memory verse (2 Corinthians 6:18) on a piece of poster board and then cut it into enough puzzle pieces so everyone gets at least one piece. Following the skit, distribute the puzzle pieces to the kids and have them work together to assemble and tape it together. Then have everyone read it aloud. Remind kids that no matter what life is like in their families—or what their earthly dad is like—God takes care of them. He is their heavenly Father, and can always be counted on to be with them. Here is the verse *(ICB)*:

> **"I will be your father, and you will be my sons and daughters, says the Lord All-Powerful."**

Closing Prayer Huddle

Each week the meetings will close in the same way. Gather all the kids into a tight circle and instruct them to stack their hands on top of each other in the middle of the circle. As they stand in this position, have a volunteer or a facilitator lead in short closing prayer. Have them raise their hands out of the stack and over their heads as they yell out, "Amen!"

Snack (5 Minutes)

The facilitators should bring the snack the first night. Before the kids leave, choose a child to take the snack tin home for next week. (See page 14 in "Getting Started" for more information about handling the snack.)

Characters

- Jake, Jake's mom, and Joe

Needed

- TV
- Dishpan and dishes
- *Optional:* Sound effects to simulate a TV show

"That's It! I'm Moving to Joe's House!"

Jake enters and turns on the TV. Sound effects start to play loudly.

Jake	All right! "Micro Power Blasters From Pluto!" My favorite show! I'm been waiting for this all day!
Mom	*(Offstage)* Jake! That's not the TV I hear, is it? You'd better not be watching anything by the time I get to the living room!
Jake	Mom! Lay off, would ya? This is my favorite show!
Mom	*(Enters)* Don't you use that tone of voice with me, young man! You know the new rules. No TV until the dishes and all your homework are done. The spaghetti is drying on the plates in there! Let's go—now!
Jake	*(Turns off the TV and stomps off to the "kitchen" and mimics doing dishes)* I hate being in this family! No one in the whole world has as rotten a family as I do! I think I'll run away to Pluto and be a Micro Power Blaster!
Joe	*(Enters through the "kitchen door")* Knock-knock! Can I come in? I've got something to show you. Hey, are you ticked at something?
Jake	Just my dumb family! I hate living here! *(Brightens)* Hey, Joe, can I come and hang out at your house for about a year? You have the greatest family! Your dad lives with you and he always makes me laugh and your mom makes the best tacos in the whole world! I think it would be the greatest to live in your family!
Joe	*(Looks shocked)* You think living in my family would be the greatest? You got a screw loose, or what?
Jake	*(Looks surprised)* What do you mean by that?

Focus on Session Theme

TAKE ONE

Bible Focus

From

- Genesis 1 and 2

Characters

- Adam, Eve, and Robin Church (program host)

Needed

- A TV talk show set. You can put as much or as little energy into this as you wish.

  Minimal: A microphone, chairs, and a placard that says: "Welcome to 'Lifestyles of the Biblically Famous!' with your host—Robin Church!"

  Optional: Recorded theme music for the show, a cardboard TV frame to serve as a stage, and costumes for Adam and Eve

"Lifestyles of the Biblically Famous!"—I

As the theme music plays, Robin enters holding up the placard. He speaks energetically into the microphone.

Robin   Welcome to "Lifestyles of the Biblically Famous" with your host—me—Robin Church! Tonight we travel back to the beginning of time on earth; to those days when life was peaceful and quiet and animals inhabited the land and the population count was up to exactly—two! Yes, you've read about them in the book of Genesis and now you will meet them right here in our studio tonight! Please welcome the very first biblically famous people—Adam and Eve! *(Applause)*

Adam and Eve enter, looking confident but a bit overwhelmed.

Adam   Thank you so much. Wow! What a reception. This is great. Thanks for having us!

Robin   Welcome to this century. I suppose you know why we've invited you here to our show.

Adam   Well, I believe we're going to be with you for the next few weeks while you're talking about families. Of course, Eve and I, we were the very first family, and so we had it a little bit harder than most of you. We didn't know anything about what families are supposed to be like because there had never been any before!

Eve   But we did the best we could. Some things about our family were very good—like when Adam taught me the names of all the animals! We laughed so hard some days! Hippopotamus and orangutan were the funniest!

Adam   Actually, platypus was my favorite.

Eve	*(Stares at Adam)* Since when? I've never heard you say that before!
Adam	Oh, I've said it! You just weren't listening!
Eve	I wasn't listening! You should know! You are the all-time worst listener—
Robin	*(Looks nervous)* Whoa, wait a minute here. If I didn't know better, I'd think you were going to have a fight, right here on national TV!
Eve	*(Laughs)* See what we mean? Even Bible people didn't have perfect families! In fact there have been problems in families ever since they were created!
Adam	That's one thing that hasn't changed in all these centuries! But there's something else that hasn't changed, either. In those first days of figuring out what a family was supposed to do and be like, God always took good care of us. We made some big mistakes, and sometimes God had to discipline us for them, but He never left us alone. He was, and still is, a father to us.
Robin	So what you're saying is that God was an important part of helping you live in your family. Do you think God can do anything for us in our families today?
Eve	We're here to tell you that no matter what your family is like here on earth— and we all know that no family is perfect—God is always with you. He is your Father, too, and He'll take care of you just like He took care of us.
Adam	Knowing that God was our Father and taking care of us all the time helped us get through some pretty hard times. Robin, do you think we can come back and talk about some of those times?
Robin	Is next week soon enough? *(Laughs)* Until then, this is Robin Church saying good-bye and see you next time on "Lifestyles of the Biblically Famous!"
They exit.	

Goals

- Identify the functions of families and what they do for us
- Emphasize that our family will not always provide everything we need (there are no perfect families)
- Play a game to discover things kids value about their own families, and things they wish they could change
- Use Adam and Eve to show how God created families as places of caring

Needed

- Letter cards for "Unit Slogan" game
- One copy of "Family Introductions," cut into sections
- "Finish This" sentences, cut apart and attached to small pieces of candy or trinkets (one set per small group)
- Prayer journal
- Items for regathering, if any
- Props for Bible skit
- Memory verse (2 Corinthians 6:18) written out on sheets of 9"x 12" colored paper, one or two words per sheet

What's a Family For, Anyway?
Preteen Session 2 Outline

Opening (25 Minutes)
> "Unit Slogan" Game
>
> Group Rules
>
> "Will the Real Family Please Stand Up?"

Small Groups (40 Minutes)
> Discussion of Session Theme
>
> "Finish This Sentence" Game
>
> Prayer Time

Bible Focus (20 Minutes)
> Regathering
>
> "Lifestyles of the Biblically Famous"—II
>
> Memory Verse
>
> Closing Prayer Huddle

Snack (5 Minutes)
> The snack can be served during the Bible Focus regathering.

What's a Family For, Anyway?

Preteen Session 2

"Unit Slogan" Game

In advance, prepare a set of cards (each card approximately 6"x 6") that will spell out the phrase, "There are no perfect families." Place only one letter on each card. Pin these to a bulletin board, or tape them to the wall in order, but so the letters cannot be seen. To play, let kids take turns guessing a letter. If the letter is in the phrase, turn the card over so it can be read. Have kids continue guessing letters until someone wants to guess what the phrase is. To guess, they must raise their hands and not just blurt it out. If the person guessing is correct, turn all the cards over and lead the group in loud applause. If all the kids have arrived at that point, go on with the lesson. If it is still early, let the one who guessed correctly think of a word or short phrase to write on the board and lead the kids in another round. *(Note:* You could add some fun by dividing the kids into teams and keeping score.)

Group Rules

Review the group rules from last week and remind the kids of the importance of the rules to your group experience.

"Will the Real Family Please Stand Up?"

In advance, copy the "Family Introductions" worksheet (page 185) and cut it apart. Divide the kids randomly (by numbering off, for instance) into four groups, and give each group one of the family introductions. Give the groups a few minutes to read their sheet and prepare a way to introduce their family to the rest of the group. For instance, one family member may choose to do all the talking or each family member may choose to speak for themselves. They just need to be sure they get all the information on their sheets communicated in some way.

The facilitators can roam among groups, giving suggestions, if needed, and helping them accomplish the task as quickly as possible.

When all the groups are ready, gather everyone together and ask each family to introduce themselves. At the conclusion of this time, have all the "families" sit together (if they are not already doing so). Then, say that you are looking for a "real family" among them. Give each group a few minutes to consider if they are a real family or not, and why. Then focus everyone's attention and say, "Will the Real Family please stand up?" At this point, each group that decided they were a real family should stand up. Hopefully, all the groups will stand, even though you have given them the impression that only one family is a real family! If any group did not stand, ask them to tell the others why they did not consider themselves to be a family. Then dismiss to small groups.

Small Groups (40 Minutes)

Discussion of Session Theme

Use the following questions to discuss the session theme, "Who needs a family?"

Did you think all the families were "real" families? *(Let kids respond)* **Why or why not?** *(Let kids respond)*

What do you think makes a family a family? *(Let kids respond)*

What specific things do families provide for the family members? *(Let kids respond)*

Use a piece of paper to brainstorm a list of the things family members do for each other. Your goal is to generate a list such as this:

Physical Needs	Emotional Needs
Food	Love
Shelter	Listen to each other
Clothes	Stick up for each other
Care when sick	Have fun together

When your list is complete, discuss the following two questions:

What makes it hard for families to do these things? *(Let kids respond)*

On a scale of one to ten, with one being "the pits" and ten being "the best," rate your family. *(Have each child respond)*

Even though none of us lives in a perfect family, we need to understand how important our families are to us. Families give us love, protection, guidance, and teach us how to live in the world. We can think of our families as a puzzle. Everyone in the family is important to the whole family, just as every puzzle piece is important to make up the whole puzzle. But sometimes things happen and a piece is missing. When that happens, the family is not the same, but it is still a family, and all the rest of the pieces still fit and can work together to make the family an important place for everyone. Remember, your family is not just a bunch of people living in the same house! It is made up of people who are all important to each other. Your family is not complete without you!

"Finish This Sentence" Game

In advance, make one copy of the "Finish This Sentence" worksheet (page 186) and cut the questions apart. Attach each question to a small piece of candy or a trinket and place all of them in a basket or paper bag. To introduce the activity, say:

Who needs a family?

Confident Kids © 1997 Linda Kondracki Sibley. Permission granted to photocopy. The Standard Publishing Co.

It is important for each of us to think about the things we consider to be really good about our families, and those things that are not perfect that we would change if we could. Let's play a game to help us talk about those things.

Have one person at a time pull a question out of the basket or bag and read the question aloud. Have the child keep the candy or trinket, but everyone in the group must answer the question before the next question is asked.

Prayer Time

Use your prayer journal from last week to review prayer requests and add new ones. Give special emphasis to concerns kids mention regarding their family situations.

Bible Focus (20 Minutes)

Regathering

Have one facilitator lead in a favorite song, game, or activity.

"Lifestyles of the Biblically Famous"—II

Present the Bible skit (script is on pages 183 and 184).

Memory Verse

In advance, print the memory verse (2 Corinthians 6:18, *ICB*) on sheets of 9"x 12" colored paper, one word per sheet. Mix them up and distribute them to the kids. Have them stand up and arrange themselves in the proper order so the verse can be read. Then hide all the sheets and have the kids say the verse from memory.

Closing Prayer Huddle

Close the meeting in the same way as last session.

Snack (5 Minutes)

Distribute the snack the child brought. Before the kids leave, choose another child to take the snack tin home for next week.

Bible Focus

From

- Genesis 2:18-25

Characters

- Adam, Eve, and Robin Church (program host)

Needed

- The same TV talk show set as last week (see last week for directions)

"Lifestyles of the Biblically Famous!"—II

As the theme music plays, Robin enters holding up the placard. He speaks energetically into the microphone.

Robin	Welcome to "Lifestyles of the Biblically Famous" with your host—me—Robin Church! Tonight we have with us once again, direct from the book of Genesis, our ancient family members—Adam and Eve! Let's bring them out *(Applause)*

Adam and Eve enter, looking confident and excited.

Eve	Thank you so much. This is great. Thanks for having us back!
Robin	You're welcome. Glad you could join us. Now then, at the end of last week's show I believe you were telling us about some hard times you had as the first family on earth. That's pretty hard to believe, living in the garden of Eden and all. Compared to a lot of what goes on in our world today, most of us would say you had it pretty good!
Adam	At first we did! The garden of Eden was beautiful, there's no doubt about that. But the best part of living in the garden was the evening.
Eve	Oh, yes! The whole garden would get very quiet and peaceful just as the sun was setting, and Adam and I would settle down and watch the colors creep across the sky and wait for God to come.
Robin	*(Surprised)* Ah—God to—come?
Adam	Yes! In the garden, God himself would visit us every evening. We would talk and laugh about different things that happened during the day. You know, just visit!
Robin	So, let me get this straight. God came to talk to you in the garden?

Eve	Well, actually, He came to make sure we had everything we needed.
Robin	But you were living in the garden of Eden! What could you possibly have needed?
Adam	I guess the biggest thing I needed *(Puts his arm around Eve)* was Eve! As you know, I was the first one God created and for a long time I really enjoyed all the beauty and the fun of naming the animals and all that. But after a while, I began to get sad and, well—lonely. Let's face it, it's lonely being the only man on earth! So one evening, when God came to the garden, He said, "Adam, I've been thinking. It's not good for you to live alone. You need a companion, someone like you who can be with you during the day and keep you company. And—"
Eve	*(Interrupts)* And, bingo! There I was! And Adam and I became the first ever husband and wife.
Robin	So God created you, Eve, so Adam would not have to be alone.
Eve	Right. From the very beginning of time, God placed people together to care for each other by being in families. In all these years, that has never changed.
Robin	Now wait a minute. Last week you talked about having hard times in your family. So far, I'd change places with you any day!
Adam	Ah, but remember, we didn't live in the garden for very long! You know the story about how we were removed—
Eve	Removed! We were kicked out of the garden! One big celestial boot and all our days of ease and comfort in the garden were gone for good! All because of one little mistake!
Robin	Now we're getting to it! Oh, but look at the time! I guess we'll have to save that part for next week. You will join us again, won't you? Of course you will! *(To audience)* Until then, this is Robin Church saying good-bye and see you next time on "Lifestyles of the Biblically Famous!"
They exit.	

Our Family ...

There are four people who live in our house:

A father, whose name is _____
A mother, whose name is _____
A son, whose name is _____
A daughter, whose name is _____

Father goes to work each day in an office. Mom works part-time in a department store at the mall. On holidays we often visit our grandparents and other relatives. We have a large extended family.

Our Family ...

There are three people who live in our house:

A mother, whose name is _____
A son, whose name is _____
A stepson, whose name is _____

Mother has been divorced twice. The son was from her first marriage, and the stepson from her second. The stepson lives with us because his father does not want him to live with him. Both boys see their fathers occasionally.

Our Family ...

There are two people who live in our house:

An aunt, whose name is _____
A niece, whose name is _____

Aunt has never been married. The niece came to live with her when she was eight years old because her mother went away somewhere and her father couldn't take care of her. Sometimes on weekends and holidays the father comes to visit them.

Our Family ...

Two sisters, whose names are _____ and _____, live with their dad and stepmom and three stepbrothers, whose names are _____, _____, and _____.
The girls live at their mom's house four days a week, and at their dad's house three days a week. Their mom is also remarried and there are two stepsisters living with them there. The girls have trouble figuring out who their real grandparents and other extended family members are.

I wish my family was more...

I'm glad my family...

I wish my family would...

My family thinks I am...

One thing about my family
I wish I could change is...

One thing about my family
I would never change is...

The best thing our family
ever did together was...

My favorite family member
who does not live with us is...

Confident Kids © 1997 Linda Kondracki Sibley. Permission granted to photocopy. The Standard Publishing Co.

Goals

- Make a list of changes that can disrupt family stability and identify possible reactions to such changes
- Have the kids name changes that have occurred within their own families and discuss how they and other family members responded to those changes
- Role-play healthy and unhealthy ways of coping with family changes
- Use the story of Adam and Eve to discuss God's presence in the midst of difficult changes

Needed

- Paper, crayons, watercolors, brushes, water containers, newspapers
- Group rules poster
- Copies of "The Divorce" skit
- "Handling Changes in My Family" scenarios, cut into strips and placed in a basket or paper bag (one set per small group)
- *Optional:* Props for kids to use in the "Handling Changes" role plays
- Prayer journals
- Items for regathering, if any
- Items for Bible skit
- Memory verse poster (Romans 8:38, 39)

Changes Can Upset My Family
Preteen Session 3 Outline

Opening (25 Minutes)

 "Fruit Basket Upset" or "Watercolor/Crayon Resist"

 Group Rules

 "The Divorce"

Small Groups (40 Minutes)

 Discussion of Session Theme

 "Handling Changes in My Family" Role Plays

 Prayer Time

Bible Focus (20 Minutes)

 Regathering

 "Lifestyles of the Biblically Famous"—III

 Memory Verse

 Closing Prayer Huddle

Snack (5 Minutes)

 The snack can be served during the Bible Focus regathering.

Changes Can Upset My Family

Preteen Session 3

Opening (25 Minutes)

Choose one of the following activities:

"Fruit Basket Upset"

This favorite old game is fun, yet ties into the lesson on change. To play, have everyone sit in chairs in a circle. Go around the circle and whisper the name of a fruit (apple, orange, pear, or banana) in everyone's ear, as a way to divide them into groups. Designate one person as "it," and remove his chair from the circle. "It" stands in the middle of the circle and calls out the name of one of the fruits (apple, orange, pear, or banana). Everyone who is in that group must now get up from their chair and find a new one, including "it." The person who does not get a chair is the new "it" and calls out the next fruit. The person who is "it" can call out more than one fruit at a time, or she may call out "Fruit Basket Upset," and everyone in the circle must get up and find a new seat. Play the game as long as time allows.

"Watercolor Crayon Resist"

As another way to prepare the kids for the theme of family changes, create an art project that "changes" before their eyes. Have kids draw pictures, using heavy strokes of crayons in bright colors. When done, they can wash watercolors over the crayon, changing the picture significantly by adding a background color, or mixing colors by using several colors that run together. Let the kids have fun with the project and be sure to have lots of cleanup supplies on hand.

Note: Also during this time, choose kids to participate in "The Divorce" skit and give them copies of the script (pages 192 and 193). Give the actors a few minutes to practice.

Group Rules

If needed, review the group rules again this week. Ask the kids if they can think of any other rules that would make the group a safer place.

"The Divorce"

During the gathering activity, choose kids to play the kids in this skit. Have the facilitators and kids doing the skit take a few minutes to practice.

Introduce the skit by saying:

> Tonight's theme is about changes that happen in our families. Handling changes in our families can be difficult. Let's watch as one family faces a big change.

Present the skit (script is on pages 192 and 193).

Small Groups (40 Minutes)

Discussion of Session Theme

Use the following questions to discuss the session theme, "Change upsets my family!"

> What's your first reaction to how this family is dealing with this change? (*Let kids respond*)

> How many different reactions to change did you see in the skit? (*Kevin was angry, Adam was quiet and withdrawn, Beth was fearful, and Mom had a disinterested "I don't care" reaction*)

> In addition to divorce, what other big changes can happen to disrupt a family? (*Let kids respond*)

Using the last question as a springboard, brainstorm a list of family changes and write them out on a piece of paper or on a board. Possibilities include moving, a new baby, remarriage/stepfamily, a parent loses a job, death or serious illness of a family member, etc.

Under this list, create another list of different ways family members can react when serious changes happen in their families. Include both positive and negative coping mechanisms. Possibilities include anger, fear, blaming yourself, crying, silence/withdrawal, pretending it didn't happen, running away, finding someone to talk to, expressing feelings in a journal, taking it out on someone else, etc.

When the list is complete, ask kids to look it over and identify changes that have actually happened in their families and how they reacted to each change. Can they identify ways other family members reacted to the change? Then say:

> Most of us would rather that things in our lives never changed. Even adults don't like to go through change. But it is a fact of life that things change. Change is always going to happen in our families; we can't stop that. But we do have a choice about how we will deal with changes when they happen. When things change in our families, we go through a time of adjustment that is usually hard to deal with. We can choose healthy ways that will help us get through the time of adjustment, or unhealthy ways that will probably just make things worse. Let's see if we can tell the difference.

"Handling Changes in My Family" Role Plays

In advance, cut the "Handling Changes in My Family" scenarios (page 197) into strips and place all of them in a basket or paper bag. Have kids draw a scenario and then take a moment to act it out for the group. They can ask other kids to help them or use pantomime and monologue to communicate what is happening in the situation, but they should not just read the scenario to

Change upsets my family!

the group. After each presentation, have the kids guess what coping mechanism is being presented, and discuss if this is a healthy or unhealthy means of dealing with changes, and the reasons they think so. Ask them to consider whether acting in this way will help them get through the change or just make it worse. Do as many scenarios as time allows (you most likely cannot do them all).

Scenario 1

Your mom just told you that your family is going to move to New York. You don't want to go! You react by telling her you hate her and then you push your little brother out of the way as you leave the room. *(Coping response: Anger)*

Scenario 2

Three weeks ago your father was diagnosed with cancer. The whole family has had to adjust to him being sick and Mom spending long hours at the hospital. You feel alone and scared. You decide to help yourself feel better by writing a long letter to your dad telling him how you feel. *(Coping response: Writing about your feelings)*

Scenario 3

You are trying to do your homework, but your parents are having another fight about their divorce. You feel too upset to concentrate. You put on your running shoes and go outside to run around the block a few times. When you come back, you feel calmer and can concentrate again. *(Coping response: Physical exercise)*

Scenario 4

Your mom is getting remarried to a man you really like. But you are not so sure how you are going to like sharing your mom with the new stepbrothers who are coming to live with you, too. You are spending a lot of time in your room, thinking about it. When your mom comes in and asks, "What's wrong?" you say,

"Nothing. I just want to be left alone." *(Coping response: Silence/withdrawal)*

Scenario 5

You just found out your older brother is involved in a neighborhood gang. The whole family is worried, but no one is talking about it. You decide to tell your mom how you feel and ask if the family can sit down and talk together. *(Coping response: Talk about your feelings)*

Prayer Time

Use your prayer journal to review past requests and add new ones. Give particular attention to requests concerning changes happening in the kids' families.

Bible Focus (20 Minutes)

Regathering

Have one facilitator lead in a favorite song, game, or activity.

"Lifestyles of the Biblically Famous!"—III

Present the Bible skit (script begins on page 194).

Memory Verse

Display the memory verse poster (Romans 8:38, 39, *ICB*) and read it aloud together several times:

> **Yes, I am sure that nothing can separate us from the love God has for us. Not death, not life, not angels, not ruling spirits, nothing now, nothing in the future, no powers, nothing above us, nothing below us, or anything else in the**

whole world will ever be able to separate us from the love of God that is in Christ Jesus our Lord.

Closing Prayer Huddle

Close with the huddle as in past meetings. In the prayer, thank God for His unchanging love in the midst of the difficult changes in our lives.

Snack (5 Minutes)

Distribute the snack the child brought. Before the kids leave, choose another child to take the snack tin home for next week.

Focus on Session Theme

Characters

- Mom, Dad, Kevin, Adam, and Beth

Needed

- A living room scene (chairs arranged as a couch, easy chair, etc.)

The Divorce

The family is in the living room. Dad is seated on the couch, Mom is standing off to the side looking disinterested, Kevin is pacing and angry, and Adam and Beth look dazed. Adam is quiet and wants to be alone; Beth is fearful. (It will help if characters have name tags.)

Kevin	*(Angry)* What do you mean, you're moving out? How could you do this to us, Dad? Are you nuts, or what?
Dad	Look, I know this is hard—
Beth	*(Fearfully)* You can't go! Who will take care of us? Where will we live?
Dad	Beth, just because I'm moving out doesn't mean I won't still take care of you. Your mother can get a job and I'll still pay for things.
Mom	*(Under her breath)* Yeah, right!
Kevin	You're ruining this family, Dad! None of us will ever be able to face our friends again!
Dad	Kevin, many of your friends have parents that are divorced. You'll fit right in!
Beth	Who cares about them? This is our family and we'll never make it without you! Daddy, I'm scared! Please don't go! Don't do this! Mom, make him stay.
Mom	Let him go, Beth. It's probably best. At least we won't be fighting all the time anymore.
Adam	I'm going to my room. *(Starts to leave)*
Dad	Oh, no you're not. Adam, we aren't through yet. And you haven't said anything at all. What are you thinking about all this?
Adam	I don't know. I just want to go to my room, OK?
Dad	No. Stay right here until we can work this out.

Kevin	Work it out? The only way we can work it out is for you to tell us you're not going.
Dad	Kevin, there are other ways to work this out. I know this is a shock and a big change for our family, but we can get through it.
Beth	Where will we stay? Who will buy food? Who will—
Mom	Beth, we will still be here for you. This divorce is not about you kids, it's about your dad and me.
Adam	If it's not about us, why do I feel so bad? Can I go now?
Dad	No! We're not through yet!
Kevin	Why not? What else is there to talk about?

From

- Genesis 3:1-7

Characters

- Adam, Eve, and Robin Church (program host)

Needed

- The same TV talk show set as last week (see last week for directions)
- A rubber or stuffed snake (the bigger the better)

"Lifestyles of the Biblically Famous!"—III

As the theme music plays, Robin enters holding up the placard. He speaks energetically into the microphone.

Robin Welcome to "Lifestyles of the Biblically Famous!" with your host—me—Robin Church! Tonight we have with us once again, direct from the book of Genesis, our ancient family members—Adam and Eve! Let's bring them out! *(Applause)*

Adam and Eve enter and greet Robin. Adam is carrying a stuffed or rubber snake. Eve is walking behind Adam a few steps, obviously upset that he has brought the snake. She grumbles things like, "For goodness sake, Adam, get rid of that thing. You know I can't stand snakes. Yuck! No one here likes them either."

Adam Never mind my wife—she gets this way around snakes!

Robin Looks like we're off to quite a start. Would you like to tell us why you brought the snake?

Adam Well, if you remember, we ended last week with a reference to being removed—I believe kicked out was the phrase my wife used—of the garden of Eden, and I promised to tell you about it this week.

Eve Do we have to talk about this? It's so embarrassing. I make one little mistake, and he *(Points to Adam)* never lets me forget it!

Adam It wasn't a little mistake, Eve. And don't forget, I was there too! I'm just as much to blame as you are.

Eve Oh, sure, but just ask anyone on the street, "Who was responsible for the first sin?" What do they say? Eve, that's who! Not Adam and Eve, not that

	miserable, lying deceitful snake, but Eve! Me! I always get blamed! It's downright embarrassing!
Robin	I think I've got the picture. You're referring, of course, to the time you were removed from the garden because Eve listened to the snake and took a piece of fruit from the tree of knowledge of good and evil.
Eve	I'm so depressed! *(Puts her head in her hands)*
Adam	You know, it really wasn't Eve's fault, but she has never gotten over what happened. The fact that Satan lied to her, and that I also ate the fruit doesn't keep her from blaming herself. She's stuck in the "If Only's."
Eve	*(Looks up and says loudly)* If only I hadn't listened to that dumb snake! *(Puts head down, pauses, then raises head again and speaks)* If only I hadn't been hungry!
Robin	I think a lot of kids in our audience can relate to you, Eve. They handle changes in their families with the "If Only's," too. They say, "If only I had been better, my dad wouldn't have left" or, "If only my little sister hadn't been born, my parents would have more time for me."
Adam	Well, take it from me, the "If only's" are not a healthy way to get through change. It's better to face what happened openly and trust God to help you adjust to your new way of life.
Eve	He's right, you know. After we disobeyed God, we had to leave our beautiful garden, and I thought life would never be good again! I mean, everything changed! Well, everything but one thing—God never stopped loving us. Even when He disciplined us, He still loved us! And then, after awhile, we began to get used to our new life. One day we looked at each other and realized we weren't hurting anymore! God was helping us to be happy in our new life.
Adam	And so, we wanted to tell everyone tonight that things may change but that doesn't change the fact that God loves you and is taking care of you! Here's a special promise from the Bible to help you remember that. *(Displays and reads the Romans 8:38, 39 poster)*

Robin	Wow! That's a lot of stuff for us to think about. But I have a feeling you have even more to tell us next week! *(To audience)* Until then, this is Robin Church saying good-bye and see you next time on "Lifestyles of the Biblically Famous!"

They exit.

Goals

- Make a chart that lists various pleasant and unpleasant feelings we have in our families and identifies the actions that contribute to them

- Set one personal goal to change a behavior that is causing unpleasant feelings in the family

- Use the story of Adam and Eve to illustrate how unpleasant and hurtful actions can affect families

Needed

- Group rules poster
- "Life in My Family" scripts (two copies)
- Blank poster board (one per small group)
- "Actions and Feelings in My Family" cards, cut apart (one set per small group)
- "My Growth Goal" worksheet (one per child)
- Prayer journals
- Items for regathering, if any
- Items for Bible skit
- Memory verse poster (Romans 8:38, 39)

Actions Can Help— Or Hurt—My Family

Preteen Session 4 Outline

Opening (25 Minutes)

 "Feelings" Charades

 Group Rules

 "Life in My Family" Mini-Skits

Small Groups (40 Minutes)

 Discussion of Session Theme

 "Actions/Feelings Chart" and Setting "Growth Goals"

 Prayer Time

Bible Focus (20 Minutes)

 Regathering

 "Lifestyles of the Biblically Famous"—IV

 Memory Verse

 Closing Prayer Huddle

Snack (5 Minutes)

 The snack can be served during the Bible Focus regathering.

Actions Can Help— Or Hurt—My Family

Preteen Session 4

Opening (25 Minutes)

"Feelings" Charades

Since this session is about the different feelings we experience in our families, begin with a game of "Feelings" charades. As the kids arrive, direct them to a table where one facilitator is seated, armed with paper and pencil. Ask the kids to work together to generate a list of feelings words by going through the alphabet one letter at a time and calling out as many feelings words beginning with that letter as they can think of. When the list is complete, ask for volunteers to begin the charades game. To play, have the facilitator choose a word from the list and show it secretly to one of the kids, who will act it out. The person who guesses the correct feeling is the next actor. You can also add some fun for this age group by adding a little team competition to the game.

Group Rules

Review the group rules again this week.

"Life in My Family" Mini-Skits

Divide the kids into four small groups and give each group two copies of one of the "Life in My Family" mini-skit scripts (pages 203–207). *Note:* If you have fewer than eight kids in your room, divide them into two groups and use only two of the scripts. If you have more than eight, they can share the scripts and decide how to present the skit, adding characters if they like.

Give the groups a few minutes to prepare their skit and then bring everyone back together again. Ask each group to present their skit. Add some fun to this by having one facilitator act as a movie director, introducing each skit with the words, "Let's have quiet on the set! Film rolling for Skit 1, Scene 1! Ready! Action!" At the end of the skit, yell, "Cut!" Make a big deal about not having good feelings about how that played out and call for a retake. Ask the second group to come up and take their places, and use the same lines as above, substituting "Skit 1, Scene 2" in the intro. When complete, yell "Cut!" again and express satisfaction with the changes. If you are doing the third and fourth skit, repeat all of the above for them.

Small Groups (40 Minutes)

Discussion of Session Theme

Before class, prepare a poster board or butcher paper as follows:

ACTIONS AND FEELINGS IN MY FAMILY

Feels Good		Feels Bad	
Action	Feeling	Action	Feeling

Place the chart and the "Actions and Feelings in My Family" cards (page 211) in the center of your group area. Begin by saying:

> Wouldn't it be nice if everything that happened in our families made us feel really good and happy? Unfortunately, life isn't like that. Living together means that there will be good times and unhappy times. When we understand that, we can work harder at having more good times in our family and fewer difficult times.

Use the following questions to discuss the session theme, "My actions determine my feelings in my family."

In the first skit, scene 1, what was going on? *(Older sibling picked on a younger*

one) **What feelings were going on in this family?** *(Let kids respond)* **Does this family feel like a good place to be for all the members?** *(No)*

In the second scene, what changed? *(The older sibling made a conscious choice to change his behavior. Instead of harassing his brother, he apologized and took interest in how his brother's day had been)* **What happened to the feeling tone of this family?** *(It improved)* **Does this family feel like a good place to be?** *(Yes)*

In the second skit, scene 1, what was going on? *(Daughter forgot to tell her mom about the play practice)* **What feelings were going on in this family?** *(Let kids respond)* **Does this family feel like a good place to be for all the members?** *(No)*

In the second scene, what changed? *(Instead of blaming her mom for her mistake, Jill decided to take responsibility for her actions and find a constructive way to deal with her problem)* **What happened to the feeling tone of this family?** *(It improved)*

The point we are trying to make today is that how family members choose to act determines what life is like in the family. When we use actions that are hurtful to others or blame others, our families will not feel like good places to be. When family members treat each other with courtesy and respect and take responsibility for their own actions, life in our families improves dramatically.

Now spread the six cards out on the table and look at each one. Decide where each would fit on the chart and paste it down in that column. Next to it, write the

My actions determine my feelings in my family

feeling the actions would produce in the family. Now ask the kids to think of specific actions and the corresponding feelings that happen in their own families and add them to the chart. Try to keep going until the poster is full.

Setting "Growth Goals"

Distribute a copy of the "My Growth Goal" worksheet (page 212) to each child. Say:

> **We can each take responsibility to make life in our families better. We can learn to do more of the actions that make the family feel good, and fewer actions that upset the family. It's hard work, but we can do it!**

Ask kids to share one action they do that causes unpleasant feelings in their families. Use the activity sheet to help them set a growth goal to change that behavior. Emphasize the term "growth goal," since this is what personal growth is all about—replacing negative behavior with positive behavior. Motivate the kids by sharing a personal growth goal of your own and filling out and signing your own growth goal worksheet. Have them sign their worksheets and encourage them to put the paper somewhere it can remind them to work on that behavior during the week.

Prayer Time

Conduct your prayer time as you have in weeks past. Focus particularly on asking God to give the kids in your group the wisdom and power to accomplish their growth goals. *Note:* Send a postcard to your kids this week reminding them to keep working on their goals. Do not mention the exact goal as that would be a breach of confidentiality if the parents read the cards first. You may prefer to call each one.

Bible Focus (20 Minutes)

Regathering

Have one facilitator lead in a favorite song, game, or activity.

"Lifestyles of the Biblically Famous!"—IV

Present the Bible skit (script begins on page 208).

Memory Verse

Use the Romans 8:38, 39 memory verse poster to encourage the group to create motions that could be added to the verse. Let them know that if they do a good job on this, the verse could be performed on Family Night.

Closing Prayer Huddle

Close your meeting as in weeks past. In the prayer, ask God for wisdom and courage to follow through with the growth goals to improve life in our families this week.

Snack (5 Minutes)

Distribute the snack the child brought. Before the kids leave, choose another child to take the snack tin home for next week.

Characters

- Jason (age 11) and Tim (age 7)

Needed

- Two chairs to serve as the backseat of a car
- A child's school paper

"Life in My Family" Mini-Skit I

The Ride Home, Scene 1

Jason and Tim are riding home in the car from school. Tim is looking at a paper he is bringing home from school.

Tim	*(Holds up his paper, with pride)* Hey, Mom! Look what we did in our class today! My teacher said—
Jason	*(Interrupts and grabs the paper away)* Let me see that, you little twerp! What kind of baby stuff did you do today? Looks like garbage to me!
Tim	*(Looks surprised and hurt)* Hey! Give that back, Jason! It's mine and it's not baby stuff! I'm learning how to write and my teacher said I did really good and put a sticker on it! Give it to me! *(Tries to grab paper)*
Jason	*(Holds on to paper and pulls it away so it tears. Speaks in a mocking tone)* Oh, my, how careless of me! The baby paper with the sticker just ripped in two! It's stupid anyway! *(Throws it back at Tim)*
Tim	*(Starts to cry)* Jason, you're a jerk and I hate you!
Jason	*(Pokes him in the arm)* Oh, now you're a crybaby, too! Come on, Timmy! Crybaby, cry some more! Told you you're a baby! *(Laughs)*
Tim	*(Turns away and yells)* Just leave me alone! Just wait till we get home—I'm going to break something of yours, Jason!
Jason	Oh, I'm so scared of a crybaby! *(Pokes at him again)*

The Ride Home, Scene 2

Tim *(Holds up his paper, with pride)* Hey, Mom! Look what we did in our class today! My teacher said—

Jason *(Interrupts and grabs the paper away)* Let me see that, you little twerp! What kind of baby stuff did you do today? Looks like garbage to me!

Tim *(Looks surprised and hurt)* Hey! Give that back, Jason! It's mine and it's not baby stuff! I'm learning how to write and my teacher said I did really good and put a sticker on it! Give it to me! *(Tries to grab paper)*

Jason *(Holds on to paper and pulls it away so it tears. Speaks in a mocking tone)* Oh, my, how careless of me! The baby paper with the sticker just ripped in two! It's stupid anyway! *(Throws it back at Tim)*

Tim *(Starts to cry)* Jason, you're a jerk and I hate you!

Jason *(Sighs)* Hey, Tim. I'm sorry, OK? I didn't mean to tear your paper

Tim *(Crying)* Why are you always so mean to me? I didn't do anything to you! How would you like it if I broke something of yours when we get home?

Jason I wouldn't like it and I'd be mad! *(Pauses)* So, Tim, what else did you do in school today? Play any good games at recess?

Charac

ters

- Jill and her mother

Needed

- A table and two chairs

"Life in My Family" Mini-Skit II

The Play Practice, Scene 1

Jill and her mother are sitting at the breakfast table.

Jill	You don't have to pick me up until 4:30 today, Mom, OK? Tonight's our first play practice, and I'm so excited!
Mother	*(Looks surprised)* What are you talking about?
Jill	You know, I told you last week that I'm going to play Juliet in our class production of *Romeo and Juliet,* condensed for sixth grade.
Mother	*(Getting mad)* Oh, I remember you got the part, all right. What I don't remember is anything about a play practice today! Jill, you did it again, didn't you? You just expect me to do whatever you want without telling me in advance. Well, this time it's too late, young lady. I'm taking Sarah to the dentist at 4:15 today—we both have appointments and we won't get back home until 5:30. Sorry, no play practice for you!
Jill	*(Looks horrified)* But I have to be there! I have the lead! How come you can always do stuff for Sarah but never for me! She always gets anything she wants and you always mess up my plans!
Mother	Don't you talk to me like that! I have a good mind to call your teacher and tell her you can't be in that play at all! If you had told me ahead of time about the practice, I might have been able to do something. It's your tough luck that you can't be at the practice today.
Jill	Please, Mom, it's really important to me! Ask Mrs. Shelly to pick me up, or something!

Mother	*(Angrily)* Just forget it, Jill. Maybe next time you'll remember to tell me in advance.
Jill	*(Storms away from the table)* I'll bet if Sarah wanted you to pick her up, you'd find a way to do it!

The Play Practice, Scene 2

Jill	You don't have to pick me up until 4:30 today, Mom, OK? Tonight's our first play practice, and I'm so excited!
Mother	*(Looks surprised)* What are you talking about?
Jill	You know, I told you last week that I'm going to play Juliet in our class production of *Romeo and Juliet,* condensed for sixth grade.
Mother	*(Getting mad)* Oh, I remember you got the part, all right. What I don't remember is anything about a play practice today! Jill, you did it again, didn't you? You just expect me to do whatever you want without telling me in advance. Well, this time it's too late, young lady. I'm taking Sarah to the dentist at 4:15 today—we both have appointments and we won't get back home until 5:30. Sorry, no play practice for you!
Jill	*(Looks horrified)* But I have to be there! I have the lead! How come you can always do stuff for Sarah but never for me! She always gets anything she wants and you always mess up my plans!
Mother	Don't you talk to me like that! I have a good mind to call your teacher and tell her you can't be in that play at all! If you had told me ahead of time about the practice, I might have been able to do something. It's your tough luck that you can't be at the practice today.
Jill	Please, Mom, it's really important to me! *(Pauses)* OK, I know it's my fault. Mrs. Winters gave us a practice schedule last week and I kept forgetting to bring it home. Can we work it out? I could ask Mrs. Shelly to pick me up, or

	something! And I promise I'll bring the schedule home tonight so you can put all the practices on the calendar. Please?
Mother	I should teach you a lesson and say no. But, OK. Go call Mrs. Shelly and if she can bring you home and you have a play practice schedule in your hand when you get here, we'll make it work.
Jill	Thanks, Mom! *(Runs off to make her call)*

Bible Focus

From

- Genesis 4:1–8

Characters

- Adam, Eve, and Robin Church (program host)

Needed

- The same TV talk show set as last week (see last week for directions)
- A few baby things (bottles, rattles, disposable diaper, etc.)
- A teaching picture of Cain and Abel

"Lifestyles of the Biblically Famous!"—IV

As the theme music plays, Robin enters holding up the placard. He speaks energetically into the microphone.

Robin	Welcome to "Lifestyles of the Biblically Famous!" with your host—me—Robin Church! Let's bring out our guests! *(Applause)*

Adam and Eve enter and greet Robin, carrying the baby items.

Robin	Well, well! Do we have "show and tell" tonight?
Eve	When we heard you were going to be talking about feeling good and feeling bad in families today, Adam and I immediately thought of the same thing—
Adam and Eve	*(Together)* Cain and Abel!
Robin	Ah, yes! Your two sons!
Eve	You know, we were so proud when our first son was born! Of course, I didn't have all these wonderful things to take care of him, like you do today! *(Holds up a disposable diaper)* Do you know how much I would have loved something like this when Cain was a baby? Making diapers out of fig leaves and deer hides is pretty disgusting, believe me!
Adam	Having a first baby brought a lot of good changes to our family! We were feeling terrific for a long time.
Eve	And when I found out I was going to have another baby, we were really excited! *(Pauses)* Unfortunately, Cain wasn't as thrilled.
Robin	What do you mean?

Adam	After Abel was born, we began to see some changes in Cain. It was clear that he was feeling a very unpleasant feeling: jealousy. From that time on, he chose actions that came from being jealous, and it made for some very unpleasant times in our family.
Eve	And whenever we tried to talk about his feelings of jealousy, he would just get really mad and run away from us!
Adam	His actions hurt everyone—Cain, Abel, Eve, and me!
Eve	But Cain was hurting the most, and the sad part was that he wouldn't tell us about it. He just kept all his anger and jealousy inside, until—well, you know what happened!
Robin	Ah, I can't say as I do. Please elaborate.
Adam	*(Shows teaching picture)* Maybe this will help. Here's a picture of our boys when they were grown. It is so hard to believe that Cain could hate his brother so much—he actually killed him!
Robin	No!
Adam and Eve	*(Together)* Yes!
Adam	We want to encourage everyone to make good choices about how they act in their families, and to work hard on their growth goals to do what they can to make their family a good place to be!
Robin	Sounds like a great note to end on for tonight.
Eve	Wait! There's one more thing! Don't forget to tell them about their secret weapon—
Adam	*(Interrupts)* That's right! God wants to give you His power to help you in your family. We tried to teach Cain to ask God to help him when he was feeling angry and jealous, but he never learned to trust God to help. Don't be like Cain! Ask God to help you, and I know He will!

Robin   An important point to add! But now we really are out of time! So, until next week, this is Robin Church saying good-bye and see you next time on "Lifestyles of the Biblically Famous!"

They exit.

Confident Kids © 1997 Linda Kondracki Sibley. Permission granted to photocopy. The Standard Publishing Co.

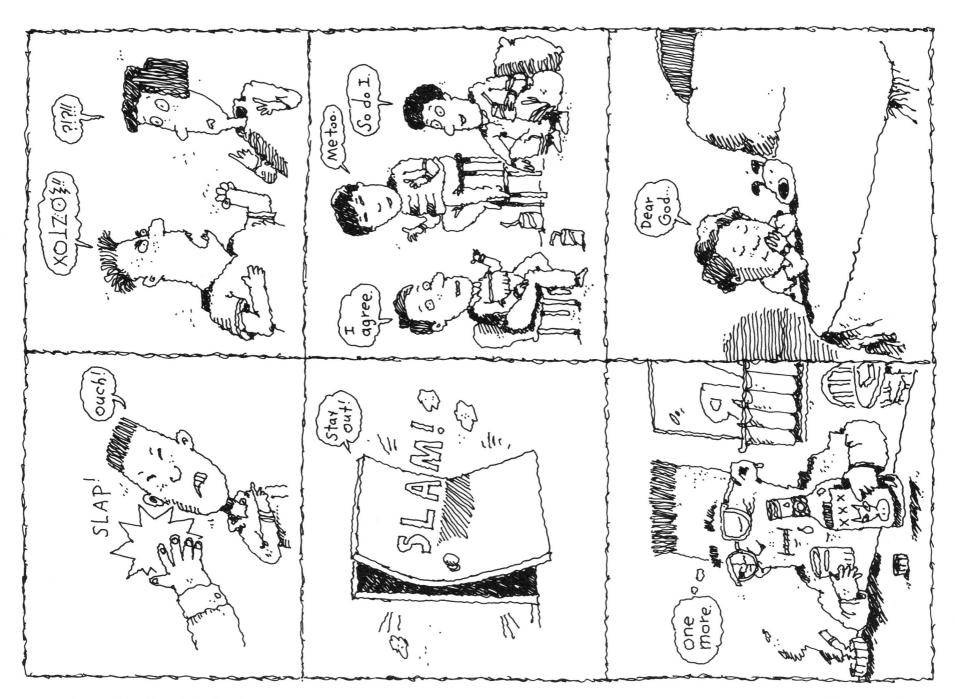

A growth goal is an agreement we make with ourselves and another person to work on changing behaviors we see in ourselves that we don't like and want to change. Changing our behavior is hard, but we can do it! And God will help.

My Family Is a Better Place When I...

_____ Walk away from my sibling(s) instead of yelling and fighting.

_____ Do my homework and chores without complaining.

_____ Use words of encouragement and kindness instead of anger or put-downs.

_____ Clearly ask for what I need instead of whining and complaining.

_____ Other

_____ Other

My Growth Goal...

Behavior I want to change:

One specific thing I will do this week to begin to change:

Asking God to help me, I agree to do the above.

Signed:
Date:

Goals

- Illustrate the importance of learning to speak in ways that help—not hurt—our families
- Generate four principles for talking together in helpful ways
- Have the kids identify subjects they would like to discuss with their parents and role-play ways to open up these subjects with them
- Have Adam and Eve use the memory verse (Ephesians 4:29) to reinforce the need to change negative communication patterns into positive ones

Needed

- A 3' length of butcher paper and sets of waterbased markers
- Group rules poster
- Poster board or overhead transparency (and projector) with family communication rules written on it
- Copy of "Talking Together in My Family," Elementary Session 5, page 141
- "Can We Talk?" worksheets
- Prayer journals
- Items for regathering, if any
- Items for Bible skit
- Memory verse poster (Ephesians 4:29)

Words Can Help—
Or Hurt—My Family
Preteen Session 5 Outline

Opening (25 Minutes)
"Graffiti Wall"

Group Rules

"Talking Together in My Family" Scenarios

Small Groups (40 Minutes)
Discussion of Session Theme

"Can We Talk?"

Prayer Time

Bible Focus (20 Minutes)
Regathering

"Lifestyles of the Biblically Famous"—V

Memory Verse

Closing Prayer Huddle

Snack (5 Minutes)
The snack can be served during the Bible Focus regathering.

Words Can Help— Or Hurt—My Family

Preteen Session 5

Opening (25 Minutes)

"Graffiti Wall"

Before the kids arrive, attach a 3' length of butcher paper or white shelf paper to the wall. Using water-based markers (permanent markers will bleed through to the wall), divide the paper in half and prepare as follows:

Let's Talk!	No Talk!

Using words or pictures, have the kids write words or actions that make it easy for them to talk to others (open up communication) on the left half. On the right half, have them write words or actions that stop them from talking (shut down communication). As they arrive, direct the kids to the graffiti wall, and explain what they are to do. If the kids have trouble thinking of things to write or draw, suggest a few focus questions, such as:

> **What things make it easy to talk to your mom or dad or friends? What things make it hard? Impossible?**
>
> **What things do people do or say that make you feel good inside? Rotten inside?**

Group Rules

Review the group rules again this week.

"Talking Together in My Family" Scenarios

Before the session begins, prepare a poster board or overhead transparency by copying the following statements on it:

Talking Together in My Family

1. Say words that _____, not _____.
2. Say them in a _____ way; no _____ or _____.
3. Say what is _____.
4. Speak for _____.

Display the poster board or project the transparency where all can see it and you can write on it easily. Say:

> **What would you say is the single most important thing necessary to bring peace to your family, keep you out of trouble, and help you get the things you need and want most?** (*Let kids give ideas*) **You may not realize it, but good communication skills—how you talk to others in your family—is the key to making all those things happen. How we talk to each other is crucial to what life is like in our families. Let's illustrate this.**

Have two facilitators present the first scenario from the script. Then ask the kids to look at the first rule on the poster board and offer suggestions of what words go in the blanks. After a few guesses, fill in the words "help" and "hurt." Ask the kids how the scenario could be replayed, using this communication rule. Then have the facilitators replay the scene, using the kids' suggestions.

Repeat this process for all the rules on the chart, using the following information:

Rule #1

Missing Words: help and hurt

Main Point: It is very easy, almost natural, to hurt another person with our words. Hurting others with our words only makes life more difficult for everyone. It never brings peace and good feelings to our family.

Rule #2

Missing Words: kind, name-calling, and put-downs

Main Point: Tone of voice is very important to good communication. People will respond to our tone of voice rather than our words. The combination of harsh tone of voice with name-calling and cutting remarks is deadly!

Rule #3

Missing Word: true

Main Point: Many times we give distorted messages because the words we are using or hearing are not true. Restating messages so they say what is true allows us to have straight, clear communication.

Rule #4

Missing Word: yourself

Main Point: Speaking for yourself means you use "I" statements to own your own feelings and talk about your own experiences. You don't blame or attack the person with whom you are talking.

Keep this time moving as quickly as possible. When the chart is complete, dismiss to small groups. (*Note:* For the sake of time, Scenario #1 could be used to illustrate rules 1 and 2, and Scenario #3 could be used for both rules 3 and 4.)

Small Groups (40 Minutes)

Discussion of Session Theme

Note: If your small group is not meeting in a place where you can see the communication rules poster easily, use a copy of "Talking Together in My Family" (page 141) during this discussion time.

Use the following questions to discuss the session theme, "Let's talk."

Let's talk

Which of the rules we just talked about is the biggest problem in your family? *(Let kids respond)*

Which is the biggest problem for you, personally? *(Let kids respond)*

What's the best thing about the way your family communicates? *(Let kids respond)*

If you could change one thing about your family's communication, what would it be? *(Let kids respond)*

When we live with people as closely as we do our families, we will always have conflicts and times when we get on each other's nerves. Staying connected by communicating with each other—especially with our parents—is an important skill to learn now while we're still young. This is not an easy thing to do, since everyone has problems communicating, especially in families. But know this for sure—mastering these four principles for talking with others will make your life much better. Guaranteed!

For many kids, talking with parents gets harder as they get older. You are at a great age to learn how to talk with your parents in ways that will help your relationship. Let's think some more about that for a few minutes.

"Can We Talk?"

Distribute copies of the "Can We Talk?" worksheet (page 224) to the kids. Explain that kids usually have strong feelings about the subjects they want to—and don't want to—discuss with their parents. Ask kids to fill out this survey, ranking each subject as to whether they would like to talk to their parents more, less, or

not at all about each one. When complete, spend a few minutes reviewing the lists, taking particular note of the subjects kids indicate they would like to talk more about with their parents. Ask them to identify reasons why they don't talk more about these subjects. Brainstorm ways they might get into these subjects with their parents. If time allows, role-play a conversation between a child and her parent, using one of the topics the kids felt strongly they wanted to talk more about.

Prayer Time

Start your prayer time this week by referring to the goals the kids identified last week. Ask how they did with them.

> Setting goals for changing our behavior is hard work, and does not happen overnight! Keep working on them, and trust God to help.

Review and ask for other prayer requests.

Bible Focus (20 Minutes)

Regathering

Have one facilitator lead in a favorite song, game, or activity.

"Lifestyles of the Biblically Famous!"—V

Present the Bible skit (script is on pages 222 and 223).

Memory Verse

Introduce Ephesians 4:29 *(ICB)*:

> When you talk, do not say harmful things. But say what people need—words that will help others become stronger.

Then what you say will help those who listen to you.

Emphasize the importance God places on how we talk to and with each other. Then teach the verse using a "memory verse wave." Have kids sit in a circle. Display a poster of the verse and draw a line between each two or three words on the poster. Begin with one child and have him stand, raise his arms over his head as he reads the first segment of the verse, and then sit down. The next child repeats the same action for the second segment, and so on around the circle. (This simulates the wave done in sports stadiums.)

Closing Prayer Huddle

Close your meeting as in weeks past. In the prayer, ask God to give the kids continued wisdom and courage to follow through with their growth goals and to open up opportunities to talk with their parents about subjects of concern to them.

Snack (5 Minutes)

Distribute the snack the child brought. Before the kids leave, choose another child to take the snack tin home for next week.

Characters

- Two siblings

"Talking Together in My Family" Scenarios

Scenario 1: "Say Words That Help, Not Hurt"

Older Sibling   What's wrong with you?

Younger Sibling   *(Crying)* What do you think? You know I got two Ds on my report card. Mom grounded me for a whole month. I hate her!

Older Sibling   *(Laughs)* Good for her! You deserve to be grounded! You're probably too dumb to do anything but stay in your room anyway.

Younger Sibling   *(Hurt and angry)* Stop it! I hate you, too, and if you don't get out of my room right now, I'm telling Mom about how you stole those comic books and candy bars from the drug store last week!

Older Sibling   You do and you're dead! *(Leaves in a huff)*

Scenario 2: "Say Them in a Kind Way; No Name-calling or Put-downs"

Characters

- Jacob and his mother

Mom	Jacob, you didn't do the dishes yet.
Jacob	*(Staring at a TV; speaks sarcastically)* No kidding!
Mom	Don't use that tone of voice with me. Get into the kitchen and do those dishes—now!
Jacob	Can't you see I'm watching TV? I'll do it after this show. Better yet, why don't you tell my stupid sister to do it? She's so lazy she never does anything!
Mom	*(Angry)* Jacob, get off that couch now! And when the dishes are done, go straight to your room!

Scenario 3: "Say What Is True"

Characters

- A child and his (or her) father

Child   Hey, Dad, will you help me with my homework?

Dad   *(Reading something)* Not now, OK? Work was tiring today and I want to read for a while. Maybe later.

Child   You never help me with my homework! That's all you ever do is read, read, read! I'm going to flunk my math test tomorrow and it's all your fault!

Dad   *(Surprised)* Wait a minute! I helped you with your math homework three times this week already! And I helped you with your oral book report last week, and I believe I spent a lot of nights helping with a science project not too long ago! Tonight I want to read for a while and that will just have to be OK with you. If you fail your math test tomorrow, you can blame it on your bad attitude, not on me!

Child   *(Storms out of the room)* I'll bet if Brenda wanted your help, you'd stop reading and help her!

Scenario 4: "Speak for Yourself"

Mom	Charlene! You knocked the milk carton on the floor and it was almost full! How many times have I told you to stop hitting your sister at the table? Now get a towel and clean up this mess!
Charlene	Me? It's not my fault! She should clean it up! She's a big pest and she started it!
Mom	You started it and you knocked the milk carton over and you're going to clean it up!
Charlene	Well, how come you put the carton so close to the edge of the table? You should have known I'd knock it over if you put it there!
Mom	One more word and you're grounded for a week! Clean it up!

Characters

- Charlene and her mother

From

- Ephesians 4:29

Characters

- Adam, Eve, and Robin Church (program host)

Needed

- The same TV talk show set as last week (see last week for directions)
- Memory verse poster (Ephesians 4:29)

"Lifestyles of the Biblically Famous!"—V

As the theme music plays, Robin enters holding up the placard. He speaks energetically into the microphone.

Robin	Welcome to "Lifestyles of the Biblically Famous!" with your host—me—Robin Church! Let's bring out our guests! *(Applause)*

Adam and Eve enter, waving at the audience.

Robin	Well, we ended on quite a note last week. It's hard to imagine having one of your sons kill the other one!
Adam	It was the hardest thing we have ever lived through.
Eve	For sure!
Robin	Especially since you never saw it coming!
Eve	Well, that's not entirely true. There were signs.
Adam	You have to remember, Robin, we were the very first family and we didn't know much about what it meant to be a family in those days. We just did the best we could.
Eve	For instance, today parents understand that their children are different and need to be treated differently. One of the biggest mistakes we made was comparing Cain with Abel.
Adam	"Cain, why can't you listen like your brother?" "Cain, why don't you ever talk to us like Abel does?" "Cain, why are you always so angry and mean? Why can't you be cooperative like your brother?"
Eve	*(Shakes her head in agreement)* That happened all the time!

Robin	If it makes you feel any better, parents still do that today!
Eve	Well, the one thing I most want to say to all of you today is this—work hard to be good communicators! It's the most important part of having a good family!
Adam	I'll second that! And add one more thing. Read the Bible and learn from it.
Robin	The Bible? What does that have to do with communicating in our families?
Adam	The Bible? Why, it's a great book of instructions on how to make families the best they can be! Following all the teachings of the Bible is a sure-fire guaranteed way to improve your family!
Eve	Just think about it! God wrote the Bible to help people learn how to know Him and how to live as His people in the world. And He put all the instructions for living a healthy life right there in its pages!
Robin	You mean if I read the Bible, I'll have a happier family?
Adam	If you do what it says, you'll have a healthier family for sure!
Robin	I'm not sure I understand. I thought the Bible was just a bunch of stories and rules about church stuff.
Eve	*(To Adam)* Let's show them the verse poster we brought. *(Displays Ephesians 4:29 poster)* We've already talked about this verse as a rule for good family communication!
Robin	Wow! I thought that was a great rule, but I had no idea it came from the Bible! I think we need to talk more about this—next week. We're out of time for today. Until next week, this is Robin Church saying good-bye and see you next time on "Lifestyles of the Biblically Famous!"
They exit.	

"Can We Talk?"

Rate each topic, using this scale:

M = I want to talk to my parents more
L = I want to talk to my parents less
NOT = I don't want to talk to my parents at all!

I want to talk about

_____ My friends

_____ Something I'm afraid of

_____ Death (in general or someone who died)

_____ My future

_____ Help with my homework

_____ Other things about school

_____ My family's history

_____ Problems my parents are facing

_____ Something I'm worried about

_____ Questions about sex

_____ Mom (to my Dad)

_____ Dad (to my Mom)

_____ Why Mom _____

_____ Why Dad _____

_____ Other things:

One thing that would make communication in our family better:

Overall, I rank my communication with my parents as (check one):

____ Terrific

____ I'm happy the way it is

____ OK, but I wish it were better

____ We hardly communicate at all

Goals

- Discuss the importance of all family members caring for each other's needs

- Examine several families and identify how each one is caring—or not caring—for each other's needs

- Have the kids examine their own family and list three ways their family could improve its ability to care for one another

- Use Adam and Eve to affirm that God will never leave us

Needed

- Two indoor play balls or large bean bags
- Group rules poster
- Props for opening skit
- Five paper lunch bags for each small group, with a category label title from the "Create-a-Family" worksheets pasted on the front of each, and the rest of the cards cut apart and placed in the corresponding bags
- "What a Family!" worksheet (two copies per child)
- Prayer journal
- Items for regathering, if any
- Props for Bible skit
- Memory verse posters (Ephesians 4:29 and Romans 8:38, 39) and items for memory verse review games

"I Care About You!"
Preteen Session 6 Outline

Opening (25 Minutes)

"Patterns" Game

Group Rules

"When I Grow Up"

Small Groups (40 Minutes)

Discussion of Session Theme

"Create-a-Family"

Prayer Time

Bible Focus (20 Minutes)

Regathering

"Lifestyles of the Biblically Famous"—VI

Memory Verses

Closing Prayer Huddle

Snack (5 Minutes)

The snack can be served during the Bible Focus regathering.

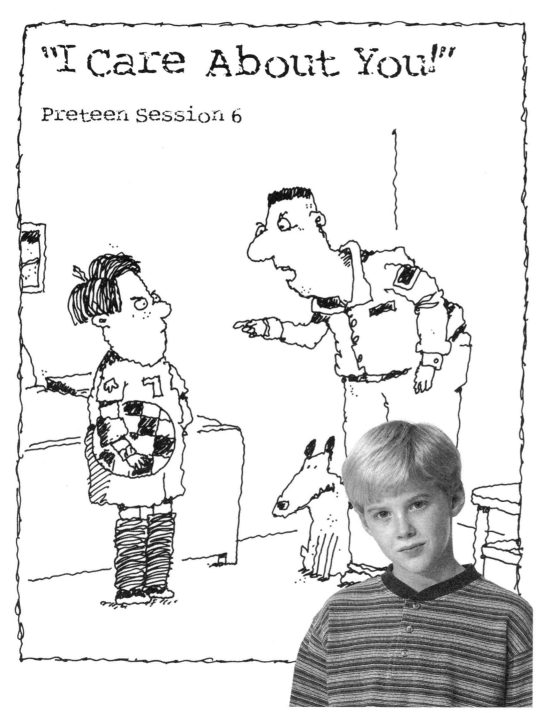

"I Care About You!"

Preteen Session 6

Opening (25 Minutes)

"Patterns" Game

"Patterns" is a cooperation game that reinforces the need for everyone to work together. You will need two indoor play balls or large bean bags. Have all the kids stand in a circle. Begin by establishing the pattern. To do this, tell the kids that you will throw the ball to one of them, who will in turn throw it to someone else in the circle. They must remember who threw them the ball, and to whom they are throwing it, because when everyone has had the ball once, they will have to throw it around the circle again in exactly the same order. This is called the pattern. Practice the pattern several times until the kids can throw it around easily, without having to stop and think who will throw it to them and to whom they will toss it.

When the pattern has been learned, add a second ball to the circle. After the first ball has been thrown to the third or fourth person, start the second ball at the beginning of the pattern. Encourage the kids to concentrate and help each other keep both balls moving smoothly through the pattern.

Group Rules

If necessary, review the group rules again this week.

"When I Grow Up"

Present the opening skit (script is on pages 229 and 230).

Small Groups (40 Minutes)

Discussion of Session Theme

Use the following questions to discuss the session theme, "Family members care for each other."

Have you ever thought about how you will run your family when you grow up? *(Let kids respond)* What would you do differently than your parents are doing? *(Let kids respond)*

In the skit, Bud said, "No one in this family understands my needs." What do you think he meant by that? *(Felt like his dad didn't understand how important the soccer game—or anything else in his life—was to him)* Have you ever felt like that in your family?

(Have kids share their ideas on the following) What do kids need from other family members? What do parents need from kids? Parents from parents? Kids from kids?

One of the most important aspects of being part of a family is learning how to care for each other! We care for each other in lots of ways. When family members are selfish and care only about their own needs and no one else's, the family is not a healthy one!

There are all kinds of needs in families. Those needs fall into several categories: *(Make a list of these as you talk about them for kids to refer to during the "Create-a-Family" activity)*

Physical Needs: Shelter, food, clothing, hugs

Safety Needs: Protection from anyone inside or outside the family who could hurt you

Belonging Needs: All family members feel included and wanted in the family

Self-Esteem Needs: Family members help each other feel good about themselves and do not tear each other down

Healthy families pay attention to what each family member needs and try their best to care for each other in all the categories listed above. But caring for each other's needs is a two-way street. That means sometimes you need people in your family to take care of you—but you need to pay attention to what others need, and help them out, too. It's hard work, but it makes a big difference in making our families good places to be. Let's look at some families and see which ones are meeting each other's needs and which ones are not.

"Create-a-Family"

For this activity you will need five paper lunch bags with a category title and label from the "Create-a-Family" activity sheets (pages 233 and 234) pasted on the front of each. Cut apart the cards from pages 234 and 235 and place them in the corresponding bags. You will also need two copies per child of "What a Family!" (page 236). To begin, place all the bags in the middle of the table and give everyone one copy of "What a Family!" Then follow these steps:

1. Have kids randomly take turns drawing cards from each bag and placing the cards in the appropriate columns on their sheets. When complete, talk about the family that each has created. Ask:

Family members care for each other

What are the strengths of this family? the weaknesses?

How is this family meeting each other's needs?

How are they not meeting each other's needs?

Is this a family you would like to live in? Why or why not?

2. Now place all the cards in the middle of the table, plus any cards still in the bags. Ask the kids to choose cards that would create a family they would want to live in. (They can write in the columns if there are not enough of certain cards for everyone.) When done, discuss how these families are different from the first ones.

3. Give kids a new copy of "What a Family!" and ask them to fill in the columns with descriptions of their own families. Then discuss ways in which their families are currently meeting each other's needs, and suggest ways their family can improve its ability to care for its members.

Prayer Time

Use your prayer journal to check up on past requests and add new ones.

Bible Focus (20 Minutes)

Regathering

Have one facilitator lead in a favorite song, game, or activity.

"Lifestyles of the Biblically Famous!"--VI

Present the Bible skit (script is on pages 231 and 232).

Memory Verses

Use the posters to review Romans 8:38, 39 and Ephesians 4:29 *(ICB)*. Then use a memory verse game to help kids memorize them. See Appendix B, "Resources," if you need suggestions.

Closing Prayer Huddle

Close your meeting as in weeks past. In the prayer, ask God to give the kids wisdom and courage to follow through with their growth goals to improve life in their families this week.

Snack (5 Minutes)

Distribute the snack the child brought. Before the kids leave, choose another child to take the snack tin home for next week.

Characters

- Dad, Jasmine, and Bud

Needed

- Simple props to create a kitchen scene and a boy's bedroom scene

"When I Grow Up"

Scene 1

Dad and Bud are having an argument in the kitchen.

Bud	*(Angry and sarcastic)* No way, Dad! Saturday's soccer game is really important to our team! You can't ground me on Saturday!
Dad	Don't use that tone of voice with me, young man! I can ground you any time I like, and there's nothing you can do about it!
Bud	But Dad!
Dad	If you say one more word to me, I'll ground you for the rest of the soccer season! Now go to your room! *(Exits)*
Bud	*(Turns and stomps toward his bedroom)* It's not fair! I don't deserve this much punishment!

Scene 2

Bud is sulking on his bed. His sister Jasmine enters.

Jasmine	*(Timidly)* Knock-knock! Can I come in?
Bud	What do you want? To gloat over my misfortune, I suppose!
Jasmine	Not this time, little brother. I heard the yelling all the way outside. What happened this time?
Bud	What do you think? I came home late from school again today and Dad over-reacted—as usual!

Jasmine	Where was your alarm watch? I thought you were going to set it so you'd know when to come home.
Bud	I did! I just forgot to come home when it went off. But that's not the point. Dad shouldn't ground me from soccer! It's the most important thing I do and I don't think coming home late again is reason enough to keep me from going to the big game this Saturday! I'll be letting the whole team down!
Jasmine	Well, I don't know, Bud. Dad really needs you to be home on time. He worries a lot when—
Bud	*(Interrupts)* And what about what I need! No one in this family understands my needs. I need to go to the game on Saturday! You know what, Jasmine? When I grow up, I'm never gonna treat my kids this way! I'm gonna run my family a lot different than Dad runs ours!
Jasmine	Like how?
Bud	Like I'll *never* ground my kid from something so important as a big soccer game. And I'll *never* send him to his room before he has a chance to tell his side of the story—that's how!
Jasmine	Yeah, and I'm going to make sure I *never* yell at my kids the way Dad just yelled at you. We'll just talk about things calmly.
Bud	Yeah! And I'm going to be sure I go to every single soccer game my kid plays in—and school programs, too.
Jasmine	Yeah, and I'm *never* going to get a divorce and make my kids have to live in two different houses all the time. I'm *never* even going to fight with my husband! Ever!
Bud	Yeah! *(Pauses)* You know what, Jasmine? Sometimes I wish we were all grown up right now.
They exit.	

Bible Focus

From

- Ephesians 4:29 and Romans 8:38, 39

Characters

- Adam, Eve, and Robin Church (program host)

Needed

- The same TV talk show set as last week (see last week for directions)
- Memory verse posters (Ephesians 4:29 and Romans 8:38, 39)

"Lifestyles of the Biblically Famous!"—VI

As the theme music plays, Robin enters holding up the placard. He speaks energetically into the microphone.

Robin   Welcome to "Lifestyles of the Biblically Famous!" with your host—me—Robin Church! Let's bring out our guests! *(Applause)*

Adam and Eve enter, waving at the audience.

Robin   This is our guests' last appearance, and I still have one question. You are the ones who named all the animals, right?

Eve   Oh, Adam did that job before I came along! But, uh, this is kind of a touchy subject for Adam.

Robin   It is? Why?

Adam   I just prefer not to talk about that part of my life, OK?

Eve   This happens every time this subject comes up. And just try getting him to go to a zoo! Well, I tell you, he carries on so!

Robin   Adam, millions of people enjoy going to zoos all over our world every day! What problem could you possibly have with that? Oh, I know! You don't like to see them in cages, is that it?

Adam   No, that's not it! It's—well, it's seeing their names on the cages that bothers me.

Robin   Their names?

Adam   Have you ever been to a zoo and seen a platypus? Don't you think that's a pretty silly name for an animal?

Robin   I never thought about it. Besides, you named all the animals.

Adam	That's what I mean. I got to thinking about what a rotten job I did of it, too. I mean, platypus. What a dumb name. And how about rhinoceros? Or, hippopotamus?
Eve	*(Giggling)* I always thought cow was pretty stupid. *(Looks at Adam)* Oh, I forgot—that's one of your favorites. But naming all those animals was a huge job, Adam, and you did it well! I couldn't have done it.
Adam	*(Brightens)* Really? You know, you've never said that to me before!
Eve	Well, I should have! I've thought it lots of times. In fact, I think you do lots of wonderful things. But you know that!
Adam	Whether I know it or not isn't important. What's important is that I needed to hear you say that to me just now. You really helped me feel better. Thanks!
Robin	Well, that's exactly what we've been talking about today—meeting each other's needs. You've just shown us Ephesians 4:29 at work! *(Displays poster)*
Eve	You know, Robin, since this is our last week on the show, Adam and I want to be sure the kids know that there will be times for them—as there were for us—when their families will not meet their needs.
Adam	But the one thing they can count on is that God's love and care for them will never change and will never go away. *(Displays Romans 8:38, 39 poster)* There were times we couldn't feel God's love, but we always came to realize that no matter what had happened, His love never left us; He had always been there taking care of us. And we want the kids to know that He's always there taking care of them, too!
Robin	What an excellent way to end our time together. It certainly has been a great experience having you two with us these weeks. I know I've learned a great deal! But now we must say good-bye. Thank you for joining us on "Lifestyles of the Biblically Famous!" *(Applause)*
They exit.	

Jobs/Roles

Family
Rules

Family
Relationships

Family Members

Create
a
Family!

Family

Family Members	Jobs/Roles of Family Members	Family Rules	Favorite Family Activities	Family Relationships
(Draw one card)	(Draw three cards)	(Draw three cards)	(Draw three cards)	(Draw three cards)
This family has • A father • A mother • One brother (12) • One sister (10)	In this family No adults work; the family is on welfare.	A rule in this family is Parent(s) can get angry and fight with each other or kids, but kids can never get angry and fight with anyone.	This family likes to Go to movies and out for ice cream sundaes together.	Family relationships Kids get yelled at for doing any little thing wrong.
This family has • A mother • A brother (7) • A brother (9) • A grandmother	In this family The kids have chores they must do every Saturday.	A rule in this family is Kids must do all their homework before they can watch TV. They can watch only programs the parent(s) allow.	This family likes to Have many friends and relatives visit on holidays.	Family relationships Parent(s) give lots of praise for doing a good job and lots of help and encouragement to do better.
This family has • A father • A stepmother • A sister (10) • A stepsister (10) • A stepbrother (14)	In this family The kids must do all the laundry, fix supper on weeknights, and clean up the kitchen after every meal.	A rule in this family is Everyone's opinion on important family matters is valuable and should be taken seriously.	This family Never does any fun activities together.	Family relationships The parent(s) fight all the time.

Create-a-Family Labels and Cards

This family has Two sisters (ages 8 and 12) who live with their aunt, uncle, and their cousin (6)	In this family Parent(s) earn money and kids get paid for doing work around the house.	A rule in this family is Parent(s) make all the rules and kids do not get any say in these decisions.	This family likes to Play games and walk in the park together.	Family relationships The oldest child constantly teases the younger kid(s) in a mean and hurtful way.
	In this family Kids must pay for their own clothes and special activities (Little League, camp, etc.)	A rule in this family is Kids must be home for dinner every night so the whole family can eat together.	This family likes to Work on projects, like building or baking something together.	Family relationships Kids feel comfortable talking to the parent(s) about anything and know the parent(s) will listen.
	In this family The parent(s) do all the housework and the kids never have to do anything.	A rule in this family is Parent(s) go to all games and programs in which their kids participate.	In this family Parents do adult things and kids do kid things but they only do family things on holidays.	Family relationships The kids are afraid of one parent, who is an alcoholic.
	In this family Family members take turns helping fix dinner and cleaning up.	A rule in this family is Everyone has a room or private space that no one else can enter or violate.	In this family Dad plays with the kids, but Mom never joins in.	Family relationships This family has many relatives who see each other often and enjoy being together.

What a Family!

Family Members	Jobs/Roles	Family Rules	Favorite Activities	Family Relationships

What a Family!

Goals

- Present God's invitation to join His family
- Identify barriers to accepting God's invitation and a means for overcoming them
- Give kids an opportunity to respond to God's invitation
- Prepare the parable of the Lost Son (Luke 15:11–24) as a play to present on Family Night

Needed

- Family night invitations
- Five small containers (boxes or cans with a slit in the top, or paper lunch bags)
- Agree/Disagree worksheet, cut apart and individual cards stacked so all 1s are together, all 2s, etc. (one set per child)
- Group rules poster
- Items that can be stacked to form a barrier (blocks, cans, empty milk cartons, or plastic storage boxes) (two items per child)
- Five or six red paper hearts. *Optional:* Small treats or prizes to attach to the hearts)
- Prayer journal
- "Becoming a Member of God's Family" prayer
- "The Parable of the Lost Son" scripture sheet (one copy per child)
- Memory verse poster (2 Corinthians 6:18)
- Copies of "Affirmation Balloons" and unit certificates from Appendix A (pages 371 and 373)

I Can Belong to God's Family, Too

Preteen Session 7 Outline

Opening (25 Minutes)

Family Night Invitations and "Agree/Disagree" Activity

Group Rules

"The New Family"

Small Groups (40 Minutes)

Discussion of Session Theme

"Barriers/Benefits of Belonging to God's Family"

Prayer Time

Bible Focus (20 Minutes)

Regathering

Dramatizing "The Parable of the Lost Son"

Memory Verse

Closing Prayer Huddle

Snack (5 Minutes)

The snack can be served during the Bible Focus regathering.

I Can Belong to God's Family, Too

Preteen Session 7

Opening (25 Minutes)

Family Night Invitations

Next week is the final session of this unit, which is a Family Night. Tell the kids that next week you will host a party, and they can invite their parents to come with them. Talk about the party enthusiastically to build a sense of excitement for sharing the group with their parents. Have the kids make invitations (page 244) or use purchased party invitations.

"Agree/Disagree" Activity

Before kids arrive today, place five containers (boxes or cans with a slit in the top, or paper lunch bags) on small tables around the room. Cut apart the cards from copies (one sheet per kid) of the Agree/Disagree worksheet (page 245). Place all the 1s next to one container, all the 2s with the next container, etc. Direct kids to visit all the stations (they don't have to do them in any order), take a slip of paper at each one, read the statement, circle if they agree or disagree, and then place the slip in the container. *Note:* When all are finished, have one facilitator tally the results and fill out one tally sheet for each facilitator to use during the small group time.

Group Rules

If necessary, review the group rules again this week.

"The New Family"

Present the opening skit (script is on pages 242 and 243).

Small Groups (40 Minutes)

Discussion of Session Theme

Use the following questions to discuss the session theme, "God invites me to belong to His family."

> Why do you think Larry didn't want to be adopted by the Davis family? *(He was scared of the unknown)*
>
> How would life be different for Larry and Carrie in a family than in a children's home? *(Refer to the things Carrie talked about: a real family to love them, Christmas presents, their own rooms, etc.)*
>
> Even though the Davises were eager to adopt Larry, what did he have to do before that could happen? *(Agree to it, make a commitment by signing the release paper)*
>
> Have you ever wished a family other than your own would adopt you? *(Let kids respond)* Why? *(Let kids respond)*

Because our families are imperfect, they cannot meet our needs all of the time. There will be times in your family when others mess up, let you down, or hurt you. During those times, it is easy to look around and wish we could find a different family. Sometimes we may wish we could be adopted by other families we know, or we make up a perfect family in our minds and pretend we belong to it. Unfortunately, neither of these options helps us get through the times when our families are not meeting our needs. But there is another family we can belong to that will help us in ways our own family cannot. There is a family with a loving Father who wants to adopt us and take care of us. This family has lots of people in it who care for one another in special ways. That Father is God, and His family is the church. We can belong to God's family at the same time we belong to our own family. In fact, we very much need both families!

Barriers and Benefits of Belonging to God's Family

You will need to bring with you today two stacking items per child (such as blocks, cans, or empty milk cartons), slips of paper cut to fit on the face of those items, and red paper hearts cut out and lettered with one of the following phrases on each.

- God's constant presence with us
- The Holy Spirit living inside us to give us power
- Other Christians become our family, too
- The Bible to teach us how to live a healthy life

Add more benefits to being a member of God's family that are important to you, writing one on each heart.

Optional: Attach a small treat or prize to these hearts to make them more "valuable" from the kids' perspective. Keep all the items in a bag or box until directed to bring them out.

Introduce the activity as follows:

> In a way, we are all like Carrie and Larry in the skit. Each of us is invited to become a member of God's family. But being a member of God's family is not automatic. We are not born into God's family the way we are born into our own families. We are invited to become a member of God's family, just like Carrie and Larry were invited to join the Davis family. And, just like Carrie and Larry, we have to decide if we will accept God's invitation. No one can do that for us. We

God invites me to belong to His family

have to decide on our own. But that decision can be hard to make. Lots of things can get in the way and keep us from choosing to join God's family. Larry had his reasons for hesitating to go with the Davises. Now let's look at what some of our reasons might be for hesitating to join God's family.

Distribute the stacking items and slips of papers to kids at this time. Ask them to think of barriers to knowing God. Refer to the tally sheet from the "Agree/Disagree" activity to get an idea of what barriers the kids are feeling. Have the kids write their barriers on slips of paper and attach them to the stacking items. Decide as a group which barriers each child will write so that all the stacking items display a different barrier. Now stack all the items to form a wall. When it is complete, take the red hearts and place them behind the wall so that they are inaccessible to the kids.

There are many benefits to knowing God and being a part of His family. But those benefits are only available to us when we know Him personally. So, how do we get through the barriers and get to know God? We do so by believing in God and placing our trust in Him. As we trust Him, the barriers fall away.

Take the barriers away and then use the hearts to talk about the benefits of belonging to God's family.

Prayer Time

Since this is the last small group of the unit, be sure to spend a few minutes reviewing the answers to prayer that have happened during the last few weeks. Encourage kids to keep praying for the requests that are still current. As you close in prayer, give each child a prayer scroll (page 246). Give kids an opportunity to read the prayer on their scroll. Help them understand the concept of commiting their lives to Jesus. To avoid

peer pressure, give them time to pray silently and invite them to tell you what they prayed when the group is dismissed.

Bible Focus (20 Minutes)

Regathering

Have one facilitator lead in a favorite game, song, or activity.

Dramatizing "The Parable of the Lost Son"

Introduce the skit:

Jesus told a story that helps us understand how much God wants us to belong to His family. It's called, "The Parable of the Lost Son." Next week, we may act this story out for your parents. Let's get ready for that by reading the story together and thinking about the parts of it.

Distribute copies of "The Parable of the Lost Son" (page 247). Read the parable and discuss the following:

In what ways is the father in the story like God? (God loves us as we are, He waits anxiously for us to come to Him, He cares for our needs)

What can we learn from the son? (We don't have to be afraid to go to God with our feelings, even when we feel guilty or unlovable; living with God is better than living without Him)

Now organize the kids to act out the parable. The simplest way to do this is through pantomime. Have one child act as the narrator while the others act out what is being read. Assign a part to everyone in the group. This will include the father, the two sons, servants, pigs, and townspeople. Talk through the play, helping kids think of what they can do to depict the action. For example, in the first verses, the father can put his arms around his son's shoulders to show his affection; the son can pretend he is drinking and laughing hysterically with townspeople to show "wild living," etc. Ask the kids:

What can you do to help those watching understand this part of the story?

When all the actions have been established, practice going through the play until the kids are comfortable with their parts.

Memory Verse

Use 2 Corinthians 6:18 (*ICB*) as your final affirmation of the relationship we can have with God.

"I will be your father, and you will be my sons and daughters, says the Lord All-Powerful."

Closing Prayer Huddle

Close your meeting as in weeks past.

Snack (5 Minutes)

Distribute the snack. Thank all of the children who brought snacks during this unit.

Characters

- Carrie and Larry, Mr. and Mrs. Davis

The New Family

Carrie and Larry are getting ready to be adopted out of a children's home. They enter, arguing.

Carrie	*(Very upset)* What do you mean, you don't want to do it?
Larry	Read my lips— *(Slowly and deliberately)* I don't want to do it!
Carrie	You are such a noodle brain! This is what we've wanted for years! This is our big chance to have a real family!
Larry	Then you go!
Carrie	I intend to! *(Pauses; softens)* But I don't want to go without you, Larry. We've been together in this children's home for three years. Besides being my brother, you're my best friend.
Larry	Well, what's so bad about this place anyway? Let's just stay here.
Carrie	*(Upset again)* What? You were the one who kept talking about getting adopted! You said being with a real family is better than being alone! You said we'd get more stuff at Christmastime! You said you wanted your own room! You said you wanted a real mom to hug you after school! You said—
Larry	All right! I get the idea! So I changed my mind.
Carrie	*(Ready to burst)* Why? The Davises really want us and they'd give us plenty of stuff at Christmas! We'd even have our own rooms! What kind of wiggly worm has gotten into your brain?
Larry	Maybe they don't want us! Maybe they'd give us back someday! Maybe they'd give us stuff at Christmas we don't want! Maybe they'd put snakes in our bed!
Carrie	Oh, gross! Only you could think of something so dumb!
Larry	And they'd probably have all kinds of rules and chores and stuff we'd have to do!

Carrie	Of course they do! That's part of being in a family. We'll all have to work together and that means sometimes doing stuff we don't like, but we have to because that's just the way it is. Look, Larry, you can stay here and be afraid if you want, but I'm going to have a new family. A real family with real parents and—

Mr. and Mrs. Davis enter.

Mr. Davis	There you are! We are so excited about having you two come to live with us! Your rooms are all ready and waiting.
Mrs. Davis	You know, we looked at fifteen different children's homes, and thought about asking twenty different children to become a part of our family. But when we saw both of you, we knew you were just the kids we were looking for. We loved you from the first.
Mr. Davis	There's only one thing left to do. You have to sign the papers saying you want to join our family. Are you ready to do that?
Carrie	*(Excited)* Yes! *(Looks at Larry)* Well, at least I am. How about you, Larry?

They exit.

An Invitation

To _____

From _____

Please Come!
To Family Night at Confident Kids

A Ministry of Confident Kids

Date _____

Time _____

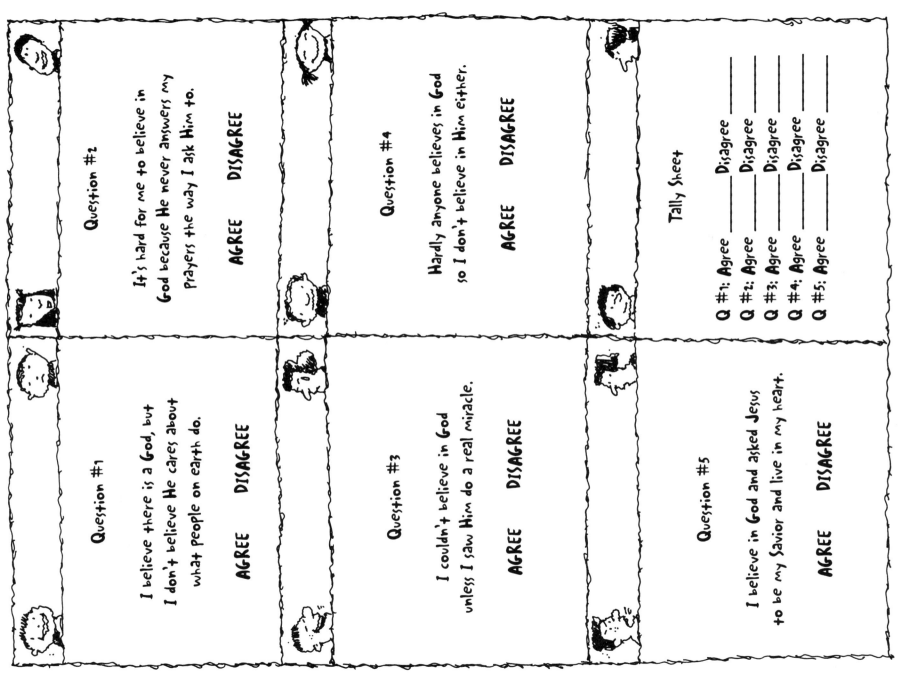

Question #2

It's hard for me to believe in God because He never answers my prayers the way I ask Him to.

AGREE   DISAGREE

Question #4

Hardly anyone believes in God so I don't believe in Him either.

AGREE   DISAGREE

Tally Sheet

Q #1: Agree _____ Disagree _____
Q #2: Agree _____ Disagree _____
Q #3: Agree _____ Disagree _____
Q #4: Agree _____ Disagree _____
Q #5: Agree _____ Disagree _____

Question #1

I believe there is a God, but I don't believe He cares about what people on earth do.

AGREE   DISAGREE

Question #3

I couldn't believe in God unless I saw Him do a real miracle.

AGREE   DISAGREE

Question #5

I believe in God and asked Jesus to be my Savior and live in my heart.

AGREE   DISAGREE

Agree/Disagree Cards

Dear God,

Thank You for wanting me to join
Your family! I want to accept Your
invitation. I believe in You and that
Your Son, Jesus, died on the
cross for me. I invite You to live in
my heart and teach me how to live
as Your child for the rest of my life.
And someday, I know we will live
together in Heaven because I
belong to Your family!

Signed,

Will You Accept God's Invitation?

Dear God,

Thank You for wanting me to join
Your family! I want to accept Your
invitation. I believe in You and that
Your Son, Jesus, died on the
cross for me. I invite You to live in
my heart and teach me how to live
as Your child for the rest of my life.
And someday, I know we will live
together in Heaven because I
belong to Your family!

Signed,

Will You Accept God's Invitation?

The Parable of the Lost Son

From Luke 15:11-24 (ICB)

A man had two sons. The younger son said to his father, "Give me my share of the property." So the father divided the property between his two sons.

Then the younger son gathered up all that was his and left. He traveled far away to another country. There he wasted his money in foolish living. He spent everything that he had.

Soon after that, the land became very dry, and there was no rain. There was not enough food to eat anywhere in the country. The son was hungry and needed money. So he got a job with one of the citizens there. The man sent the son into the fields to feed pigs. The son was so hungry that he was willing to eat the food the pigs were eating. But no one gave him anything.

The son realized that he had been very foolish. He thought, "All of my father's servants have plenty of food. But I am here, almost dying with hunger. I will leave and return to my father. I'll say to him: Father, I have sinned against God and have done wrong to you. I am not good enough to be called your son. But let me be like one of your servants." So the son left and went to his father.

While the son was still a long way off, his father saw him coming. He felt sorry for his son. So the father ran to him, and hugged and kissed him. The son said, "Father, I have sinned against God and have done wrong to you. I am not good enough to be called your son."

But the father said to his servants, "Hurry! Bring the best clothes and put them on him. Also, put a ring on his finger and sandals on his feet. And get our fat calf and kill it. Then we can have a feast and celebrate! My son was dead, but now he is alive again! He was lost, but now he is found!" So they began to celebrate.

PARENT SESSIONS

TIPS FOR WORKING WITH PARENTS
IN A SUPPORT-GROUP SETTING   250

1   THERE ARE NO PERFECT FAMILIES   253

2   WHAT'S A FAMILY FOR, ANYWAY?   261

3   CHANGES CAN UPSET MY FAMILY   271

4   MY ACTIONS CAN HELP—OR HURT—MY FAMILY   285

5   MY WORDS CAN HELP—OR HURT—MY FAMILY   295

6   "I CARE ABOUT YOU!"   305

7   I CAN BELONG TO GOD'S FAMILY, TOO   315

8   FAMILY NIGHT   325

Tips for Working With Parents in a Support-Group Setting

Understanding Confident Kids Parents

As you begin the parent group, it is important for you to understand a few key points about working with parents of high-stress kids.

- **Stressed-out kids have stressed-out parents.**

    Many of the parents who come to your group will be feeling desperate about their lives, with little idea of where to turn for help or how to make their family a healthier place. They will see Confident Kids as a lifeline, a place where they can bring their kids to get some help in ways they seem unable to provide themselves.

    As the parent group leader, your job will be to reassure parents that there is hope for their families, and that you see them as capable of managing their own stress levels and the stress of their children. Let them know that being a part of Confident Kids was a great step for them to take toward improving the quality of their family life.

- Confident Kids **parents typically carry a lot of guilt and shame about their children.**

    "It's my fault my kids are having these problems," or, "If I were a better parent, we wouldn't be in this mess," or, "I'm terrified that my kids will grow up to be totally screwed up," are some of the statements we've heard in parent groups. Although guilt and shame about their kids is what brings parents to Confident Kids, an even deeper issue is the guilt, shame, and sense of failure parents have about their own lives. Parents who are struggling to manage a painful, unwanted divorce; the financial pressures of being unemployed; or the challenges of raising a child with attention-deficit hyperactivity disorder or other kind of disability have all they can do to

manage their *own* feelings of grief, revenge, or anxiety. Their children's emotional pain becomes an added burden they feel ill-equipped to handle.

As the parent group leader, your task will be to make Confident Kids as stress-free and shame-free as possible. This means we do not chastise parents for missing sessions, or not doing at-home activities, or asking "dumb" questions. Rather, *we do encourage parents* to realize they are doing the best they can, given their present circumstances and past experiences. Here again, we offer hope that by sharing their life journeys with each other, and learning some new, healthy living skills, their families can make progress toward effective stress management and improved relationships.

- **Most of the parents will have little or no idea of what a healthy family is, let alone how to make their family a healthy place.**

Many parents today are reaping the results of having grown up in dysfunctional families. Many have no models of effective parenting to guide them. Since the natural response is to parent as they were parented, today's parents are simply reproducing the dysfunction they learned in their families of origin, and they are confused as to why things keep getting messed up.

As the parent group leader, it is your job to help the parents learn to identify destructive behavior patterns learned in childhood, and how to replace them with healthy living skills. This is the function of the teaching time and the weekly "Reflection" sheets. Remember that the material you will be covering is new to most of the parents who will be coming to your group; therefore, you must keep your teaching simple, cover the basics, and have patience with those who seem to be resistant to change!

- **Stressed-out parents feel isolated and alone.**

Many times we hear parents say, "I thought I was the only one in the whole world who was having such awful problems with their children!" As ridiculous as this may sound to those of us who work with families in today's culture, it is indicative of the nature of pain. No matter what the source of our emotional pain, it is true that we feel isolated and alone when dealing with our issues.

As the parent group leader, your job will be to facilitate open sharing among group members. As valuable as the teaching about healthy life skills is, many parents will receive the most benefit from hearing other parents share their experiences. This lets the parents know they are not alone and gives them the opportunity to have others who understand their feelings listen to them as they tell their stories. There is tremendous power in this support-group dynamic.

- **Parents come to the parent group expecting to hear about how to help their children, not how to work on their own issues.**

Parents who place their kids in Confident Kids groups are concerned only with the problems their children are having and how they can help them. Most of the parents will not be thinking about how their own personal growth—or lack of growth— directly affects their kids. They will be expecting to hear about what their kids are learning in the group, and how they can reinforce those concepts at home.

As the parent group leader, it is your job to respect this basic expectation the parents have in coming to the group. It is also your job to guide the parents into their own personal growth by helping them discover the following truth:

- **Parents cannot take their children any further in the journey of life than they have come themselves!**

Parents cannot expect their children to learn how to grieve, express their feelings, or make wise choices if they cannot do these things themselves. This becomes the leverage by which you can get the parents working on their own growth issues.

Once parents realize that the best thing they can do for their children is to grow themselves, they will work much harder on their own issues.

Expectations and Limitations of the Parent Group

As you begin the parent group, it is important to think through exactly what you are expecting to happen as a result of this experience. This is a two-sided coin; what can happen in the group (expectations), and what cannot happen in the group (limitations). Expectations of what *can* happen in the group include:

- Parents receive encouragement as they realize they are not alone in their pain.
- Parents receive hope as they realize they can learn new living skills.
- The entire family system of relationships improves as parents and kids work on the same issues at the same time.
- Families that need additional help can be guided to appropriate places for professional help.

Limitations, or what *cannot* happen in the group, are:

- Confident Kids is a support group, not a therapy group. We do not offer therapy in any way, nor do we want to!
- We cannot fix anyone's problems for them, or "save" them from difficult life circumstances. We can offer a supportive, caring environment; teaching; and insights aimed at the goal of personal growth, but we cannot do the parents' work for them!
- We will not be able to help all the families that come to us. Some families are simply not able to benefit from the support-group experience.
- It is not our goal to encourage parents to stay in the support-group setting forever. Parents need to know up front that Confident Kids is a limited program. Parents will need to set new goals on how to care for their families' continued growth.

Referring to Other Sources for Help

In a program such as Confident Kids, you will be working with many families who may need more help than the support-group setting can provide. Before you begin your first group, be sure you know what to do when parents say or do things that concern you. If you are not the Confident Kids program administrator, your first step is to go to the person who is responsible for the Confident Kids program at your location, who will have a clearly defined procedure for dealing with such cases. This procedure should have been discussed during your training time. If not, be sure to ask about the procedure you are to follow for making referrals and/or reporting abuse (page 10).

OVERVIEW

Many of the parents who bring their kids to Confident Kids feel shame and failure about their current family situation. This session will seek to neutralize some of those feelings by giving parents a more realistic perspective about the nature of family life, i.e., there are no perfect families.

NEEDED

- Letters of welcome from page 337 for new parents (if you did not use the "Welcome to Confident Kids" session) last week
- SKILL handout (page 339)
- Topic overview (page 341)
- Session Summary for Parents (page 343)
- "Reflections" worksheet
- "Building on God's Word" worksheet
- Prayer journal

Parent sessions were planned by Gail VanderWal.

THERE ARE NO PERFECT FAMILIES
PARENT SESSION 1 OUTLINE

Getting Started (20 Minutes)

    Check-In

    Group Rules

    Review Session Summary for Parents

Teaching Time (20 Minutes)

    "How Does My Family Measure Up?"

Making It Personal (35 Minutes)

    Reflections: "Get Real About Your Family"

    Group Sharing

Building on God's Word (15 Minutes)

    Bible Focus

    Prayer Time

THERE ARE NO PERFECT FAMILIES

PARENT SESSION 1

CHECK-IN

Form a circle of chairs and have everyone introduce themselves. Distribute and review the welcome letter and the SKILL handout, if you did not use the introductory session last week. Then distribute the unit overview to everyone and use it to introduce the unit theme.

GROUP RULES

Review the three basic rules of Confident Kids parent groups. Be sure everyone understands them. (See "Getting Started" on page 15 for information about group rules.)

1. Confidentiality
2. No advice giving
3. The right to pass

REVIEW SESSION SUMMARY FOR PARENTS

Read through the "Session Summary for Parents" (page 343) together. Be sure parents understand that this handout summarizes what their children will learn in their session today.

TEACHING TIME (20 MINUTES)

HOW DOES MY FAMILY MEASURE UP?

Introduce the session theme, "How does my family measure up?"

> Did you ever have your child come home and say something like, "I wish I lived at Joey's house! His family has so much fun all the time." And, of course, this is not

HOW DOES MY FAMILY MEASURE UP?

an isolated remark! After a while, you probably want to go to Joey's house and yell at his parents!

It is natural for kids (especially those around the ages of 9–12) to compare their family with other families; this is a part of separating from home and moving out into the world. But that doesn't make it any easier for you to hear! And if there have been problems in the family, it can quickly stir up feelings that you are, indeed, a rotten parent! Although these feelings are unpleasant, it can be very dangerous if you don't openly talk about the kids' statements. That's what this unit is all about— sorting out what it really means to live in a family versus what we may think it means. Let's begin this journey by taking a look at where we get our expectations of what our family "should" be.

Unrealistic Expectations Can Come From Looking at Only the Outward Appearances of Other Families Around Us

Share the following experience from Gail VanderWal, or a similar one from your own life.

"When I was a young child, I looked at the 'outside' of other people's family life. I found myself constantly comparing other family's 'outsides' to my family's 'insides.' I would say, '[The other family] always has fun together, but I have to entertain myself.' I would say, '[The other family] always hugs each other, but I am never touched in a loving way.'

"As an adult, I continued to compare the quality of my family life against what other people had, or appeared to have. It created in me an emptiness, a loneliness, that could not be satisfied. Consequently, subconsciously I set out to find that perfect relationship, that perfect family, that stability that had never been mine. It had never once occurred to me in all those years that the 'outside' of those families was not the entire picture. That those other families had problems, difficulties, pain in their lives, was beyond my comprehension. Despair became my middle name."

This is a common experience for many. The first step to overcoming our unrealistic expectations about our family is to understand that all families do have problems of one sort or another. Comparing my family's "insides" to other families' "outsides" is like comparing apples and oranges. It is OK to look at other families and see things we like about them. But it hurts us when we convince ourselves that "all those families out there have great families, and I am the only one who is having problems with my family." Intellectually we may know that is not true, but emotionally many of us discover that that is exactly how we feel inside.

Unrealistic Expectations Come From Our Own Distorted Images of What a Family "Should" Be

All of us have these images, but most of us never think about where those images came from. What do you think a family should be? (Ask parents to brainstorm their images/expectations about family life; list these on a board or a flip chart)

Whether we realize it or not, we all have long lists of expectations. We form those expectations in many ways, but most of them come from two sources, both going back to our childhood: We want our families to be just like all the good things we had when we were growing up; and we want our families to be all the things we never had when we were growing up!

If we can see these expectations as qualities we desire in our family, we can move through our lives understanding that some of these expectations will be met and others will not—and that's okay. More often, however, we turn these qualities into statements of what our family *should* be, thereby setting ourselves up for failure when an expectation is not met. As a result, we begin to long for the life that could have been:

- If only my spouse didn't work so much.

- If only I hadn't gotten a divorce.

- If only we had more money.

- If only my kids were better behaved.

- If only Grandma didn't live with us.

- If only I had the right person in my life.

"If only's" are deadly. They allow us to get stuck in despair and keep us from seeing our family as a real family! To overcome this, we must realize that although all families have areas that are difficult and painful, all families have areas of strengths, too—including yours! You can overcome unrealistic expectations by identifying your family's areas of strengths *and* weaknesses.

Realistic Expectations Come From Looking at God's Plan for Family Relationships

This unit is built on the biblical principle that God's blueprint for us includes living in families. We can have realistic expectations for our family when we look at the Bible's account of what it means to live in a family, beginning with Adam and Eve. Here are a few of the Bible's expectations:

- *Families are made up of imperfect human beings.* Even the first family suffered from the imperfection of being human; lack of communication, blame, jealousy, disregard for authority, sibling rivalry, and more has plagued families from the start! Expect your family to struggle with these problems, too.

- *The foundation for a healthy family is in a restored relationship with God.* In the beginning, Adam and Eve lived in perfect relationship to God and each other. But that relationship was broken when they became convinced their way was better than God's, became self-conscious and hid, and tried to excuse and defend themselves.

  To restore our relationship with God, we must drop our excuses and self-defenses, stop trying to hide from God, and become convinced that God's way is better than our way.

- *God's instruction book for living in our families is the Bible.* A restored relationship to God is the first step; living according to His instructions is the second step. In the Bible we not only learn about the effects of human nature on our family relationships, but how to deal with them, too. Over the next few weeks, we will see how living according to God's principles can improve the quality of our family life.

So remember, even though your family has things about it you don't like and wish you could change, it is your family! Even if you are struggling with seemingly insurmountable problems, you can take your family and improve the quality of your life together. That's what this unit seeks to help us all do.

MAKING IT PERSONAL (35 MINUTES)

GET REAL ABOUT YOUR FAMILY

Distribute copies of the "Reflections" worksheet (pages 258 and 259) to all participants and give them a few minutes to fill them out.

GROUP SHARING

After everyone is finished, share responses around the circle. Remind everyone of the "Right to Pass" rule before starting. *Optional:* If you have more than eight parents in your group, you may want to divide them into groups of four or five.

BUILDING ON GOD'S WORD (15 MINUTES)

BIBLE FOCUS

Distribute copies of the "Building on God's Word" worksheet (page 260) and discuss it together. Encourage parents to use this sheet at home during the coming week as a means of spiritual encouragement and connecting to God.

PRAYER TIME

Ask parents to fill in the prayer request line on their "Building on God's Word" worksheet. Give opportunity for parents to share these requests with the rest of the group. As the leader, you can keep a journal of these requests for your own prayer time during the week, and help the group track the requests shared each week. End the session with a time of open prayer.

REFLECTIONS

GET REAL ABOUT YOUR FAMILY

1. My present expectations about what my family "should" be are

2. Things about my family of origin I liked that are included in the above list are

3. Things I did not get from my family of origin that are included in the above list are

4. One thing I would have changed about my family of origin is

5. One thing I would change about my current family is

GET REAL ABOUT YOUR FAMILY

6. Would you say your expectations are realistic or unrealistic?

7. If your child(ren) could change one thing about your family, what do you think they would change?

   Child #1:

   Child #2:

8. **Check below any statements you have heard yourself say about your family:**

   ___ Other families always have enough money to buy anything they need, and they never worry about anything. I have to save every penny just to survive, and I have to worry about everything.

   ___ Her/his spouse cherishes the ground s/he walks on. My spouse is too busy to know I exist.

   ___ Other families never fight. They talk.

   ___ Our house is a mess. No one cares or helps clean up.

   ___ There are happy couples in church or going to movies, walking hand in hand. Everyone has someone! I'm all alone. I have to raise these children by myself.

   Others:

BUILDING ON GOD'S WORD

ROMANS 8:1, 2

One of the biggest obstacles to having a healthy family is that our families are made up of imperfect human beings who suffer the effects of living in a sin-dominated world. As sin pervades the culture, it gets more ingrained in our family life. Blaming, jealousy, lack of communication, disregard for authority, sibling rivalry, and other issues that have plagued families from the very beginning of family life are even more problematic in our contemporary culture! Sometimes we fear we will never be able to break these destructive behavior patterns. If that is how you are feeling today, here is a word of hope from the book of Romans:

> **Therefore, there is now no condemnation for those who are in Christ Jesus, because through Christ Jesus the law of the Spirit of life set me free from the law of sin and death.**
>
> **Romans 8:1, 2** (*NIV*)

Jesus' death on the cross broke the power of sin's hold over us. That means God's power within you, through Jesus, can break the power of any destructive behavior pattern that may be hurting your family—no matter how discouraged or hopeless you may feel about it. Place your trust in Him today!

Write out your prayer to God as you and your children begin this unit of Confident Kids.

Your #1 prayer request for this week:

OVERVIEW

This session looks more closely at the things families are designed to do for each other. It also affirms that no family is perfect; thus, no family provides completely for the family members. Understanding this, we can then be free to accept our family as a special place for us, and begin to work to make it the best place it can be—humanly speaking.

NEEDED

- Session Summary for Parents (page 345)
- "Reflections" worksheet
- "Building on God's Word" worksheet
- "Traits of a Healthy Family" handout
- Prayer journal

WHAT'S A FAMILY FOR, ANYWAY?
PARENT SESSION 2 OUTLINE

Getting Started (20 Minutes)
> Check-In
>
> Group Rules
>
> Review Session Summary for Parents

Teaching Time (20 Minutes)
> "What's a Family For, Anyway?"

Making It Personal (35 Minutes)
> Reflections: "My Family—For Better or for Worse"
>
> Group Sharing

Building on God's Word (15 Minutes)
> Bible Focus
>
> Prayer Time

WHAT'S A FAMILY FOR, ANYWAY?

PARENT SESSION 2

GETTING STARTED (20 MINUTES)

CHECK-IN

Ask parents if anyone has a question or follow-up to last week's session. Then go around the circle and ask everyone to answer this question:

> **In your opinion, what are the two most important functions of a family?**

GROUP RULES

Review the three basic rules of Confident Kids parent sessions. Be sure everyone understands them:

1. Confidentiality
2. No advice giving
3. The right to pass

REVIEW SESSION SUMMARY FOR PARENTS

Read through the "Session Summary for Parents" (page 345 together. Be sure parents understand that this handout summarizes what their children will learn in their session today.

TEACHING TIME (20 MINUTES)

WHAT'S A FAMILY FOR, ANYWAY?

Begin with the following story or choose one of your own that illustrates the theme of today's session, "What's a family for, anyway?"

> "Hello?" I answered the phone, unaware of what I was about to hear. It was my oldest and dearest friend, calling from halfway across the country. She was sobbing. "What's wrong?" I asked,

WHAT'S A FAMILY FOR, ANYWAY?

knowing the answer without having to be told—marriage problems. Her words, however, shocked me. "It's my worst nightmare come true," she cried. "I woke up this morning and my only prayer was, 'Dear God, please let me be single again!' I always thought being married and having a family would be so much better than being single. But right now, all I want is to have the relief of being alone. This family stuff is not all it's cracked up to be!"

For countless numbers of people in our country today, "family" brings more feelings of disappointment than fulfillment. In fact, most of the pain in our society today is the result of broken family relationships. This has led to a lot of discussion about the nature of family life. The bottom line, though, is this: Family is still held as the central means by which people in our culture find security and belonging in the world. That being the case, we are left with a few questions that deserve discussion:

What Is a Family For, Anyway?

If broken family relationships are the cause of so much pain, why have families? Why not just forget the whole institution and let everyone make his own way in the world? Of course, that's what many people are saying and doing today. If you don't like the way things are going in a marriage—leave. If the responsibility of being a parent is too much—leave the kids, too. Let them all fend for themselves; they're probably better off without you, anyway. Get a new family; marry someone, anyone; don't marry at all, just live with someone (and his/her kids?) until you feel like moving on. After all, the pursuit of happiness is our right! Right?

The Bible teaches about this kind of approach to life, and says that the end result is destruction. As we look around us today, we can see that the Bible is right. People are suffering from distorted and broken relationships more than ever before. What's the answer? Embrace family as God's ordained way for people to live in the world. Why? What does a family provide that is so important? *(Ask parents to brainstorm the positive aspects of living in a family and write these on a board or a flip chart)*

Distribute copies of the "Traits of a Healthy Family" handout (page 266) and look at it together. How many of these items are on the list your group generated? What did you miss?

Healthy families provide for each other's needs. All of us have the same basic needs. When our families are working properly, most of the time (not all!) the members will have these basic needs met at home. The basic needs provided for by families are:

- Physical Needs: This includes food; shelter; clothes; proper diet, rest, and exercise; healthy, nurturing touch, etc.

- Safety Needs: Family members need to feel protected from threatening circumstances and outside influences. Children in particular need to know that they will be cared for, especially when a family crisis occurs. Appropriate rules and a shared value system provide an important safety net. And commitment to the family by all family members is essential to eliminate the fear of abandonment.

- **Belonging Needs:** Every family member needs to feel that they are an important part of this family. "You are wanted and needed" is the message that must come through loud and clear. Also, there needs to be some connections for the family in the broader community (church, community organizations, etc.) and in the extended family (a shared family history is important).

- **Self-Esteem Needs:** Self-esteem is a two-sided coin. Family members must receive nurturing (warmth and caring) and guidance (learning how to survive in the world). When these are provided, family members come to see themselves as lovable (they have a warm, nurturing side) and capable (they know they can do some things well).

What If My Family Doesn't Meet All Those Needs?

Here is a difficult truth: It won't! It can't! Because no family is perfect. But our goal is this: Let's build on our strengths (those traits of a healthy family that we currently possess) and strengthen our weaknesses (those traits we do not currently possess). Your family is not providing all the needs mentioned above—no one's is. But it is meeting some of them. Use those strengths to motivate you to work on those areas in which your family needs improvement!

Why Is Family Life So Much Work?

> We get into trouble when we look at our family and see all the imperfections, then think the solution is to scrap this family and look for another one. We are setting ourselves up for failure if we think that the perfect family is out there somewhere, and our job is to find it! Healthy, functioning

families are the result of hard work and wise choices. If you want a healthy family, don't expect to find it "out there somewhere!" Be willing to do the hard work necessary to make your family the best place it can be, and you'll find your healthy family at home.

Special Note: Abusive relationships must never be allowed to continue. The goal of this session is to motivate families to work hard at their family life issues, not to encourage participants to remain in abusive and destructive relationships!

Making It Personal (35 Minutes)

My Family—For Better or for Worse

Distribute copies of the "Reflections" worksheet (pages 267 and 268) to all participants and give them a few minutes to fill them out.

Group Sharing

After everyone is finished, share responses around the circle or divide into smaller groups. Remind everyone of the "Right to Pass" rule before starting.

Building on God's Word (15 Minutes)

Bible Focus

Distribute copies of the "Building on God's Word" worksheet (pages 269 and 270) and discuss it together. Encourage parents to use this sheet at home during the coming week as a means of spiritual encouragement and connecting to God.

Prayer Time

Ask parents to fill in the prayer request line on their "Building on God's Word" worksheet and share these requests with the rest of the group. Add these to your journal for your own prayer time during the week, as well as to help the group track the requests shared each week. End the session with a time of open prayer.

TRAITS OF A HEALTHY FAMILY

Taken from "Traits of a Healthy Family" by Dolores Curran

A healthy family is one that:

- communicates and listens
- affirms and supports one another
- teaches respect for others
- develops a sense of trust
- has a sense of play and humor
- exhibits a sense of shared responsibility
- teaches a sense of right and wrong
- has a strong sense of family in which rituals and traditions abound
- has a balance of interaction among members
- has a shared religious core
- respects the privacy of one another
- values service to others
- fosters family table time and conversation
- shares leisure time
- admits to and seeks help for problems

Confident Kids © 1997 Linda Kondracki Sibley. Permission granted to photocopy. The Standard Publishing Co.

REFLECTIONS

MY FAMILY—FOR BETTER OR FOR WORSE

1. Looking at the "Traits of a Healthy Family" handout, which traits do you feel were strengths in your family of origin?

   In your family today?

   Which were weaknesses in your family of origin?

   In your family today?

2. How did you feel in your family of origin?

   ___ I didn't belong
   ___ I fit perfectly
   ___ I sometimes belonged

   How do you feel in your present family?

   How would you say each of your children feels?

MY FAMILY— FOR BETTER OR FOR WORSE

3. **Finish these sentences:**

   I wish my family were more

   I'm glad my family

   I wish my family would

   My family thinks I am

   One thing I wish I could change is

   One thing I would never change is

4. **When you are disappointed with your family, what do you believe? (Check all that apply)**

   My family would be just about perfect if
   ___ I were married to someone else.
   ___ We just had more money.
   ___ I were not a single parent.
   ___ My parents had been different.
   ___ Other:

BUILDING ON GOD'S WORD

2 CORINTHIANS 6:18

As parents, we are often so consumed with meeting our children's needs that we neglect our own. God intends for all family members to get their needs met through the family—including you! But He did not leave our need for fulfillment just to our earthly families. He promises to personally care for each one of His children:

> **"I will be a Father to you, and you will be my sons and daughters, says the Lord Almighty."**
>
> 2 Corinthians 6:18 (*NIV*)

Write your initial response to this verse:

Talk to God this week about each specific need you have. As your heavenly Father, you can ask Him to provide for your:

Physical Needs

Safety Needs

Belonging Needs

Self-Esteem Needs

Your #1 prayer request for this week:

OVERVIEW

Many families that have functioned well in the past find their stability seriously threatened when a major change occurs. It is not uncommon for a family to break apart as they struggle to adjust to a crisis or change of some kind. Families need to find healthy ways to get through the disruption of major change in order to remain intact. This session addresses some skills for coping with significant changes in families.

NEEDED

- Session Summary for Parents (page 347)
- "Responding to Change" role play scenarios
- "Reflections" worksheet
- "Building on God's Word" worksheet
- Prayer journal

CHANGES CAN UPSET MY FAMILY
PARENT SESSION 3 OUTLINE

Getting Started (20 Minutes)
>Check-In

>Group Rules

>Review Session Summary for Parents

Teaching Time (20 Minutes)
>"Why Did This Have to Happen to Us?"

Making It Personal (35 Minutes)
>"Responding to Change" Scenarios

>Reflections: "Weathering the Storms of Life"

Building on God's Word (15 Minutes)
>Bible Focus

>Prayer Time

CHANGES CAN UPSET MY FAMILY

PARENT SESSION 3

GETTING STARTED (20 MINUTES)

CHECK-IN

Ask if anyone has a question or follow-up to last week's session. Then ask parents to share the most difficult family change they remember facing as a child.

GROUP RULES

Review the three basic rules of Confident Kids parent sessions. Be sure everyone understands them:

1. Confidentiality
2. No advice giving
3. The right to pass

REVIEW SESSION SUMMARY FOR PARENTS

Read through the "Session Summary for Parents" (page 347) together. Be sure parents understand that this handout summarizes what their children will learn in their session today.

TEACHING TIME (20 MINUTES)

WHY DID THIS HAVE TO HAPPEN TO US?

Introduce the session theme, "Why did this have to happen to us?"

> Have you ever heard yourself saying something like: "Everything was going along just fine until . . ." my husband left, my dad died, I was diagnosed with cancer, I lost my job, I got pregnant, etc. What all these phrases have in common is one thing—change! We are not always aware of it, but we are creatures of habit; we like our world to be structured and

ordered. We organize our lives so things run comfortably, providing a net of safety and security. The one thing we dislike most is chaos. We will do anything to avoid feeling out of control. Therein lies the problem with changes; they disrupt our well-ordered life and send us, at least temporarily, into a state of confusion. Dealing with changes is a major issue in families. Many families are so disrupted by changes that they actually break apart as they struggle to face them. Let's look at some ways to deal with changes in a healthier way.

Change Is a Fact of Life—It Will Happen!

"Nothing stays the same forever" is a true statement. God has designed our world so that things change. *(Ask parents to brainstorm a list of changes that occur within our lives. Make a lengthy list and include both positive and negative changes. Write these on a board or a flip chart. Then ask parents to look at the list and sort out the different kinds of changes we face in our families.)* Here are some examples:

- Crisis: Unexpected, disastrous changes

- Lifestage: Changes that occur naturally throughout our lives, such as leaving home, marrying, having babies, mid-life, empty nest, etc.

- Planned: Changes that we intentionally plan and prepare for, such as moving up in a career path, going back to school, starting a family, etc.

- Serendipity. Unexpected, happy changes, such as a job promotion or developing a close friendship with new neighbors

Change Disturbs Our Security and Causes Us to Adapt

The point to remember here is that all changes, even ones we might categorize as wanted or happy, put pressure on the family and cause it to adapt to a new way of living. Getting through a disruption will be easier if the change was wanted and planned for, but it will still take a time of adjustment. *It is this time of adjustment that is the most dangerous for the family.* Since families are made up of individuals, every family member will respond differently to the change. For instance, a new baby may elicit different responses from each of the parents and from its siblings. Even if a pregnancy is planned, all members of the family will have to adjust to different things when the baby is born. Mom's adjustment (physical drain, tied down to home, managing more than one child, etc.) is different from Dad's (more mouths to feed, loss of sleep, loss of attention from wife, etc.), which is different from the oldest child's (feels more responsible, gets even less attention from parents, etc.), which is different still from the youngest child's (loss of status as the baby of the family, etc.).

Ask parents to discuss other life changes, naming specific differences in the adjustments called for by different members of the family. Ideas include: Mom goes back to work, Dad loses his job, serious illness of a parent, serious illness of a child, grandparent moving in, etc.

When we think it all through, it is no wonder families struggle to adapt to changes; it is hard work for the family unit to be sensitive to and meet the different levels of needs generated by all

WHY DID THIS HAVE TO HAPPEN TO US?

Confident Kids © 1997 Linda Kondracki Sibley. Permission granted to photocopy. The Standard Publishing Co.

the different members! Healthy families have enough strength to get through this time and settle down into a new way of life. Families with problems may not have the communication skills and other traits *(Refer to last week's session)* needed to make all those changes; the family unit may be damaged, or may not survive.

Change Can Bring Great Growth or Devastating Destruction—It's Our Choice!

Change is not always "bad news." Many changes are good, and times of change are often the times when people go through significant personal growth. *(Ask parents to think about the times in their lives when they have grown the most, and to connect it to precipitating events. These will almost always be times of major change.)* But positive growth does not happen automatically; it stems from the choices we make when we face changes.

Our first reaction to change is often to protect ourselves by doing something that is not healthy. This is a natural response, particularly when the change takes us by surprise. However, we must choose to make wise choices when dealing with changes! What are some examples of healthy and unhealthy ways of dealing with changes?

- Unhealthy: Lash out and hurt someone, run away, get sick, get drunk, blame someone or yourself.

- Healthy: Talk out feelings, get help from a friend or support group, express feelings in appropriate ways, expect other family members to be hurting, too.

If we want our family to grow from the change points in our lives, we can follow these principles:

- Uncover our true feelings about what happened. Avoid denial, blaming, hiding, etc. and express our feelings in appropriate ways. As parents, we can model this for our children, giving them permission to express their feelings, too.

- Discover the points of growth that can come from this situation. It's healthier to ask, "What do I need to learn from this divorce?" than it is to blame everything on the errant spouse. You may discover the need to learn to let go of destructive behaviors, improve your communication skills, or learn more about parenting.

- Discard negative attitudes and behavior patterns that have hurt you in the past. Statements such as, "This is all my fault! I can't ever do anything right!" or "I just can't deal with this," are self-defeating. We must not only discover areas of growth, we must also avoid feeling paralyzed by making specific choices and following through with them!

- Ask for help. Realize that you cannot cope with everything or grow in isolation. Be willing to ask for and accept help from other people and from God.

MAKING IT PERSONAL (35 MINUTES)

"RESPONDING TO CHANGE" SCENARIOS

Divide parents into groups of four, and give each group one of the "Responding to Change" scenarios (pages 276–279). If your group is large, you can give more than one group the same scenario. Give them time to work through the scenario, following the directions on the sheet. Then reassemble the group and have each group give their report.

WEATHERING THE STORMS OF LIFE

Distribute copies of the "Reflections" worksheet (pages 280 and 281). Since time will be short, assign these as homework this week.

BUILDING ON GOD'S WORD (15 MINUTES)

BIBLE FOCUS

Distribute copies of the "Building on God's Word" worksheet (pages 282 and 283) and discuss it together.

Encourage parents to use this sheet at home during the coming week as a means of spiritual encouragement and connecting to God.

PRAYER TIME

Ask parents to fill in the prayer request line on their "Building on God's Word" worksheet and share these requests with the rest of the group. Refer to your prayer journal to check up on past requests. End the session with a time of open prayer.

REFLECTIONS

DIRECTIONS

- Read the scenario and discuss the answers to each of the questions.
- Decide how you will share your discussion with the rest of the group. You could present a skit, write a news report, create a commercial promoting healthy ways of responding to change, etc.

RESPONDING TO CHANGE

SCENARIO 1

Bill arrives home from court. His wife Susan has just divorced him. It was not his idea. He wanted to stay married. Now he faces an empty house. His children will visit him on weekends, every other week.

1.   **What feelings is Bill experiencing?**

2.   **What are some unhealthy ways Bill could handle this change?**

     Possible results of these actions:

3.   **What are some healthy ways Bill could handle this change?**

     Possible results of these actions:

Design your presentation for the group.

REFLECTIONS

DIRECTIONS

- Read the scenario and discuss the answers to each of the questions.
- Decide how you will share your discussion with the rest of the group. You could present a skit, write a news report, create a commercial promoting healthy ways of responding to change, etc.

RESPONDING TO CHANGE

SCENARIO 2

Marcia gets a call in the middle of the night. One of her parents has died unexpectedly. Her children love their grandparents very much and have had a close relationship with them.

1. What feelings is Marcia experiencing?

2. What are some unhealthy ways Marcia could handle this change?

    Possible results of these actions:

3. What are some healthy ways Marcia could handle this change?

    Possible results of these actions:

Design your presentation for the group.

Confident Kids © 1997 Linda Kondracki Sibley. Permission granted to photocopy. The Standard Publishing Co.

DIRECTIONS

- Read the scenario and discuss the answers to each of the questions.
- Decide how you will share your discussion with the rest of the group. You could present a skit, write a news report, create a commercial promoting healthy ways of responding to change, etc.

RESPONDING TO CHANGE

SCENARIO 3

Betty knows that her husband Phil is drinking a lot. When he drinks, he sometimes gets violent and, on occasion, he disappears. Now this erratic behavior is accelerating and is affecting every member of the family.

1. What feelings is Betty experiencing?

2. What are some unhealthy ways Betty could handle this change?

    Possible results of these actions:

3. What are some healthy ways Betty could handle this change?

    Possible results of these actions:

Design your presentation for the group.

REFLECTIONS

DIRECTIONS

- Read the scenario and discuss the answers to each of the questions.
- Decide how you will share your discussion with the rest of the group. You could present a skit, write a news report, create a commercial promoting healthy ways of responding to change, etc.

RESPONDING TO CHANGE

SCENARIO 4

Fred came home from work and informed his wife, Maria, that he just lost his job. They have three children, and Maria's mom lives with them. This is the third job Fred has lost in the last five years.

1. **What feelings are Fred and Maria experiencing?**

2. **What are some unhealthy ways they could handle this change?**

    Possible results of these actions:

3. **What are some healthy ways they could handle this change?**

    Possible results of these actions:

Design your presentation for the group.

REFLECTIONS

WEATHERING THE STORMS OF LIFE

1. What changes occurred in your family of origin that were difficult for the family unit to handle?

    ___ Divorce
    ___ Remarriage
    ___ Death
    ___ Long-distance move
    ___ New baby
    ___ Serious illness
    ___ Discovery of abuse (drug, physical, sexual, or emotional)
    ___ Others:

    What unhealthy behaviors (if any) did the family use to handle these changes?

    Healthy behaviors?

2. **Describe a recent or current change that has or is occurring in your family.**

    What unhealthy behaviors (if any) did you use to deal with it?

WEATHERING THE STORMS OF LIFE

Healthy behaviors?

3. What patterns do you see as you observe your children dealing with these changes?

4. Check all the statements that describe the feelings present in this situation:

    I felt   I am feeling   My child felt   My child is feeling

    _____   _____   _____   _____   Angry

    _____   _____   _____   _____   Depressed

    _____   _____   _____   _____   Vengeful

    _____   _____   _____   _____   Afraid

    _____   _____   _____   _____   Confused

    _____   _____   _____   _____   _____

5. List specific steps you can take to help your family deal with the change in healthier ways.

BUILDING ON GOD'S WORD

ROMANS 8:38, 39

When your family must face changes, particularly unwanted changes, your relationship to God may be called into question. "Why did God let this happen to me?" "What terrible thing did I do to deserve this?" "God has stopped caring for us." If you are prone to self-blame, you may even stop praying, feeling that "God couldn't possibly listen to someone who messes up as I did." If you are having any of those feelings today, let these verses from Romans reassure you. Can you grasp the awesome truth that no matter what has happened in your family's life, no matter what part you played in what happened, God will not stop loving and caring for you?

> **For I am convinced that neither death nor life, neither angels nor demons, neither the present nor the future, nor any powers, neither height nor depth, nor anything else in all creation, will be able to separate us from the love of God that is in Christ Jesus our Lord.**
>
> **Romans 8:38, 39 (*NIV*)**

In prayer this week, ask God to help you get through any current changes, or past changes you have not yet let go of. In the spaces below, write out any insights God reveals to you during your time alone with Him:

Uncover your true feelings about anything that is still unresolved:

Discover the points of growth that can come from this situation:

Discard negative attitudes and behavior patterns that have hurt you in the past:

Ask for help. Realize you cannot grow by yourself.

Your #1 prayer request for this week:

Living in families means that there will be good times and hard times. This session explores how our actions and reactions in various situations affect the overall feeling tone of the family. Session 4 encourages parents to improve the quality of their family life by discovering and minimizing actions that are causing difficult feelings in their families, while discovering and increasing the actions that are strengthening the family.

NEEDED

- Session Summary for Parents (page 349)
- "It Started Out to Be Such a Nice Day!" script
- "Reflections" worksheet
- "Building on God's Word" worksheet
- Bibles
- Prayer journal

MY ACTIONS CAN HELP—OR HURT—MY FAMILY

PARENT SESSION 4 OUTLINE

Getting Started (20 Minutes)
> Check-In
>
> Group Rules
>
> Review Session Summary for Parents

Teaching Time (20 Minutes)
> "Stop That!"

Making It Personal (35 Minutes)
> Reflections: "Increasing the Good Feelings in My Family"
>
> Group Sharing

Building on God's Word (15 Minutes)
> Bible Focus
>
> Prayer Time

My Actions Can Help—Or Hurt—My Family

Parent Session 4

Check-In

Ask if anyone has any feedback or questions from last week's session. Then ask parents to briefly share a high or low point from the week.

Group Rules

Review the three basic rules of Confident Kids parent sessions. Be sure everyone understands them:

1. Confidentiality
2. No advice giving
3. The right to pass

Review Session Summary for Parents

Read through the "Session Summary for Parents" (page 349) together. Be sure parents understand that this handout summarizes what their children will learn in their session today.

Teaching Time (20 Minutes)

Stop That!

Ahead of time, ask four people to prepare the skit (script is on pages 289–291) for presentation. If the actors are from the parent group, send scripts to them in advance. Another alternative would be to ask a family to come and present the skit for the group. After the skit is presented, begin discussion of the session theme, "Stop that!"

> How would you answer these two questions?
>
> 1. Is it fun to live in our family?

2. Overall, do we have more fun times in our family, or unpleasant times?

How would you say your children would answer these two questions?

Every family has what we might call a feeling tone. A feeling tone is the overall feeling one gets from being with the family for any length of time. Can you think of families you have been with that left you feeling warm, loving, or caring? Cold, angry, or tense? Neutral or unconnected?

How would you say people feel after spending time with your family?

Every family, of course, has different moods. But the feeling tone of the family is the overall feeling generated by the most fundamental interactions between the family members. We may or may not be aware of the feeling tone of our family; it is usually taken as a matter of course. For example, one person may feel their family is a safe haven and they would rather be home than anywhere else. Another person might avoid coming home because of the underlying tension that is always present. The most important point for us to consider today is that the feeling tone of our families is determined by our actions—how we treat each other. A feeling tone should never be taken as "just the way our family is." It can change! Here are a few points for us to consider about the feeling tone of our families.

STOP THAT!

Negative Actions in the Family Produce Negative Feelings

Let's look at the relationship between negative actions and our family's feeling tone.

Ask parents to brainstorm a list such as the following. Record their responses on a board or flip chart.

Action		Feeling
Alcoholism	→	Fear, confusion
Absent parent	→	Abandoned
Abusive actions	→	Fear, anger, self-hatred
Constant fighting	→	Sadness, fear, withdrawal
Verbal put-downs	→	Shame, self-blame
Comparing to another	→	Hopelessness, pressure to be perfect

If it is true that negative actions produce negative feelings, then the opposite must also be true.

Positive Actions in the Family Produce Positive Feelings

Brainstorm another list, such as the following, and write it on a board or flip chart.

Action		Feeling
Active listening	→	Valued
Affirmations	→	Empowered
Play together	→	Loved, bonded
Set boundaries	→	Safe, protected

Based on the above, we can come up with a simple formula for improving the feeling tone of our family:

Discover and minimize the negative behaviors in the family, and discover and increase the positive behaviors.

Sounds simple, doesn't it? But as we all know, it is not as simple as it sounds. The reason is that so much of the way we treat others in our family is automatic; we don't think about what we are doing. If we grew up in a home where we learned to relate to others in negative ways, we will bring those behaviors to our current family.

Confident Kids © 1997 Linda Kondracki Sibley. Permission granted to photocopy. The Standard Publishing Co.

Much of the time, we just react, instead of carefully choosing our responses. But it is possible to change our behaviors.

We Can Choose Positive Actions

You have heard people say, "This is just the way I am. You'll have to learn to live with it!" Those words come from a person who is stuck in negative behavior patterns. If we want to improve the quality of our family's life together, we must let go of those kinds of attitudes and be willing to take an honest look at how we treat the other family members. And we must never forget that we choose how we treat others! We choose our actions—positive or negative. If we allow our reactions to choose us, we become victims to our negative behavior patterns, and the end of that road is always destroyed relationships.

Changing negative behavior patterns and replacing them with positive ones is one of the hardest things we must do in life. But it is the best way to improve our relationships with everyone—children, spouses, bosses, etc. Although what we are describing here is a lifelong process, here are a few tips to help get started:

- Change your negative behavior patterns one small step at a time.

- Ask for help from trusted friends, a support group, or counselor.

- Be willing to risk new behaviors, even if they feel uncomfortable.

- Stay with it! Change takes time and intentional work.

- Rely on the greatest change agent of all—the power of God's Spirit within you!

MAKING IT PERSONAL (35 MINUTES)

INCREASING THE GOOD FEELINGS IN MY FAMILY

Distribute copies of the "Reflections" worksheet (pages 292 and 293) to all participants and give them a few minutes to fill them out.

GROUP SHARING

After everyone is finished, share responses around the circle or divide into smaller groups. Remind everyone of the "Right to Pass" rule before starting.

BUILDING ON GOD'S WORD (15 MINUTES)

BIBLE FOCUS

Distribute copies of the "Building on God's Word" worksheet (page 294) and discuss it together. *(Note: Because of the length of this passage, it is not printed on the handout. Be sure Bibles are available.)* Encourage parents to use this sheet at home during the coming week as a means of spiritual encouragement and connecting to God. Give a Bible as a gift to any parent who may not have one.

PRAYER TIME

Ask parents to fill in the prayer request line on their "Building on God's Word" worksheet and share their request with the rest of the group. Use your prayer journal to check on past requests. End the session with a time of open prayer, with a particular focus on asking for God's Spirit to help each parent decrease the negative, destructive behaviors in their family, and grow the fruit of the Spirit in their place!

REFLECTIONS

CHARACTERS

- A family: Mom, Dad, Rodney (10), and Josie (8)

NEEDED

- Four chairs arranged to look like the seats of a car
- A sound effect of an alarm clock ringing
- A bathrobe

"It Started Out to Be Such a Nice Day!"

Scene 1

The family is in the car, headed for a family outing. Everyone is smiling and has an angelic glow on their faces.

Mom	Isn't this great? We're finally getting a day together. We're going to have such a great time at *[Fill in the name of a favorite family activity in your community]*!
Dad	You bet! I've been looking forward to this all week!
Kids	*(Together)* Us, too!
Josie	Rodney, give me back my doll! You didn't ask if you could touch her!
Rodney	Oh, you're right. I'm sorry for violating your rights. You know, you have a very pretty doll.
Josie	*(Smiling)* Thanks! I think she's the best!
Dad	Hey, kids, how was your week? I haven't had time to ask.
Kids	*(Together)* Great, Dad! No problems this week!
Mom	They're right. They've been angels all week. We have such great kids! Oh, look! There's the entrance to the *[Name of place they are going to]*. We just passed it.
Dad	*(Laughs)* So we did! I guess I was so interested in what everyone was saying, I missed it. No problem! I'll just turn around. I'm so excited! Aren't you, kids?
Kids	*(Together)* Yeah!

Everyone exits. From offstage an alarm clock rings loudly.

Confident Kids © 1997 Linda Kondracki Sibley. Permission granted to photocopy. The Standard Publishing Co.

SCENE 2

The family kitchen.

Mom   *(Enters in a bathrobe, yawning)* Wow! What a dream! Hmmm. Maybe it's a sign! Maybe our family outing today will set a new record for the Smith family nice days! Well, I'd better get the troops up and running. *(Exits, still yawning)*

SCENE 3

The family is back in the car.

Mom   Isn't this great? We're finally getting a day together. And we started out so well; no fights at breakfast. We're going to have such a great time at *[Fill in the name of a favorite family activity in your community]*!

Dad   *(Sarcastically)* Yeah, right! Just like the last family fun day!

Mom   Don't start that again today, OK?

Josie   Rodney, give me back my doll! Mom!

Rodney   I'll give her back when I'm ready. What are you going to do about it, runt? *(Holds the doll out of Josephine's reach as she tries to grab it)*

Josie   *(Cries)* Stop calling me that! Now give her back!

Dad   Here we go again. If you two don't stop it, I'm turning this car around and we're going home! Josie, if you didn't cry when he calls you runt, he wouldn't do it! Rodney, give her the doll back—now!

Rodney   *(Throws doll at her)* Oh, sure, like it's all my fault! Here's your stupid doll!

Josie   Thanks. *(Pauses, then reaches over and punches him)*

Rodney	Hey! Mom, she hit me for no reason! I get to hit her back!
Dad	OK! That's it! I'm not putting up with this. We're going home!
Kids	*(Together)* No, Dad—please!
Mom	*(Sighs)* And it started out to be such a nice day!

REFLECTIONS

INCREASING THE GOOD FEELINGS IN MY FAMILY

1. What was the overall feeling tone of your family of origin?

    ___ Warm, caring, loving
    ___ Angry, cold, tense
    ___ Uncommitted, detached, no one cared about each other
    ___ Other:

2. **What specific actions, positive and/or negative, do you remember as a child that produced that feeling tone?** (Examples: Parents never listened, just lectured us; screaming and namecalling; lots of hugs; parents always took an interest in my activities)

3. **What would you say is the feeling tone of your family now?**

    What do you think your kids would say?

INCREASING THE GOOD FEELINGS IN MY FAMILY

4. What specific actions, positive and/or negative, are producing the feeling tone in your family now?

Are any of these the same as the ones from your childhood family? Describe them.

5. List two negative behaviors you would like to change in your family.

1.

2.

6. **What can you do to bring about change in this area?** (Remember, you can only change you. You cannot control the actions of another person; they may change in response to the changes you make.)

1. I will

2. I will

GALATIANS 5:14-26

The Bible offers clear instruction about the relationship between our human (sinful) nature and our lives when God's Spirit lives in us. These verses in Galatians 5 are particularly helpful on the subject of today's session. Find them in a Bible and read them now.

What destructive behaviors are listed as characteristic of our human, sinful nature?

What behaviors does God's Spirit produce in us when we give the control of our lives to Him?

Looking at the list of the fruits of the Spirit, which one in particular "jumps off the page" as a need for you to cultivate in your life?

The best part about being a Christian is that we have the full power of God's Spirit to help us make changes in our lives! You can have the fruit of the Spirit growing in your life; all you have to do is ask! Write a prayer. Give God control of your life and ask His Spirit to grow His fruit in your life.

Your #1 prayer request for this week:

Communication is one of the most basic foundations for building a healthy family. When family communication is open, the foundation is solid and the family can withstand many storms. When communication is poor, however, the opposite will be true. This session briefly introduces this important subject.

NEEDED

- Session Summary for Parents (page 351)
- "Talking Together in My Family" worksheet
- "Reflections" worksheet
- "Building on God's Word" worksheet
- Prayer journal

MY WORDS CAN HELP—OR HURT—MY FAMILY

PARENT SESSION 5 OUTLINE

Getting Started (20 Minutes)
  Check-In

  Group Rules

  Review Session Summary for Parents

Teaching Time (20 Minutes)
  "What Did You Say?"

Making It Personal (35 Minutes)
  Reflections: "Let's Talk About It"

  Group Sharing

Building on God's Word (15 Minutes)
  Bible Focus

  Prayer Time

MY WORDS CAN HELP—OR HURT—MY FAMILY

PARENT SESSION 5

GETTING STARTED (20 MINUTES)

CHECK-IN

Ask if anyone has any feedback or questions from last week's session. If there are none, ask parents to share a feeling word describing how they are feeling as they come to this session.

GROUP RULES

Review the three basic rules of Confident Kids parent sessions. Be sure everyone understands them:

1. Confidentiality
2. No advice giving
3. The right to pass

SESSION SUMMARY REVIEW

Read through the "Session Summary for Parents" (page 351) together. Be sure parents understand that this handout summarizes what their children will learn in their session today.

TEACHING TIME (20 MINUTES)

WHAT DID YOU SAY?

Introduce the session theme, "What did you say?"

> As children, we all used little ditties to either verbally attack another kid or defend ourselves from being attacked. Can you remember any of them? *(Let parents respond)* Here are some more examples:
>
> "Your mother wears combat boots!" *(Attack another)*

WHAT DID YOU SAY?

"Liar, liar pants on fire!" *(Attack another)*

"Sticks and stones may break my bones, but words can never hurt me." *(Defend against verbal attacks)*

"I'm rubber, you're glue; whatever you say bounces off me and sticks on you!" *(Defend against verbal attacks)*

What we really wanted to believe when we said those ditties was that nothing anyone said to us could possibly affect us at all—and words we said to others would not seriously affect them, either. But as we all know, words have tremendous power. We can be seriously wounded by what others say to us, and we can wound others just as deeply by what we say to them!

In our families, communication is the single most important factor in building relationships. When a family has good communication skills, it is built on a solid foundation that can withstand many storms. However, when the communication skills are poor, the opposite will be true. Virginia Satir, founder of the modern family therapy movement and a leading pioneer in family systems theory, has this to say:

"Once a human being has arrived on this earth, communication is the largest single factor determining what kinds of relationships she or he makes with others and what happens to each in the world."[1]

Communication is, of course, a very complex subject. In this session, we will be able to raise only a few issues concerning this important family dynamic. Here are just two issues for us to discuss.

Communication Happens at Many Levels

Let's consider three questions about your current communication styles.

1. **What Messages Do Others Receive When They Look at Me?**

    The first message people receive is sent by your facial expressions and body language. Ask yourself, "Overall, what does my face communicate to my children? my spouse? my friends?" (e.g., melancholy, joy, anger, confidence, misery, faith, self-pity, happiness, fear, enthusiasm, pride, curiosity, jealousy, determination, envy).

Communication Experiment 1. Ask two group members (one male, one female) to come forward. Ask one to clench his teeth and fists and look angry. Then, while maintaining this stance and without looking at his partner, he is to say "I care about you" to her. Afterward, ask the partner if she was convinced. Which message was stronger, the body language or the words?

> Nonverbal communication, or body language, is much more powerful than words. People will believe what they see in us before they will believe the words we say. Therefore, in order for others to believe our words, we must make our body language match our words.

2. **What Messages Do Others Receive When They Hear My Words?**

    Words are powerful things. They can be constructive, build others up (affirming); destroy or tear others down (put-downs, name-calling); or confuse, so the other person has no idea how to respond.

---

[1]Virginia Satir, *The New Peoplemaking* (Mountain View, CA: Science and Behavior Books, Inc., 1988), 51.

Communication Experiment 2. Invite another group member to come forward. Set the scenario by telling the person that she is a ten-year-old child who has just come in twenty minutes late for dinner. You are the mother, and you say in an angry tone:

> **"You make me so mad I want to scream! If you do that again, you'll be sorry!"**

Now ask the volunteer to describe what she is feeling, and to tell you exactly what Mom meant by what she said.

> **What did the child do? Was it coming home late, or something else? What will happen if she does whatever it is she did wrong again? What does Mom want from her?** *(We can't really know because we don't know what she's talking about; we can only guess)*

Now repeat the experience, only this time say:

> **"You are late for dinner again! When you are late and don't call me, I feel angry and worried. If you do it one more time, you will be grounded for a week."**

Repeat the same questions as above:

> **What did the child do? What will happen if she does it again? What does Mom want from her?**

Notice how much easier the questions are to answer in the second dialog.

> **It is our job to be sure our words are helpful, not hurtful, and that we are sending clear, accurate statements so others will know exactly what we mean. Our words must communicate these three things:**

- **What we want to say (facts)**
- **What we are feeling about what we're saying**
- **What we need from the other person**

Ask for volunteers to give an example from their own families of unclear communication, and how it can be changed to include the three items listed above.

3. **What Messages Do Others Receive by the Way I Listen to Them?**

> **An important communication skill is how we listen to others. Remember that listening is about much more than being in the same room with someone who is talking. Listening involves letting the other person know that they have our full attention, that we care about what they are saying, and that we are trying hard to understand their point of view.**

Communication Experiment 3. Ask parents to pair off. Then have one partner stand on a chair, and the other kneel down in front of them. Instruct the one on the chair to look straight ahead throughout the experiment, maintain a blank stare, and use only one-word responses. Now instruct the one kneeling to tell their partner about a particularly difficult thing that happened this week. Give a minute or so for this conversation. Then have everyone return to their chairs and ask group members to respond to what they observed.

> **There were a number of important listening techniques ignored in this experiment! To listen well, we must give our full attention, be on the same level and maintain eye contact, use facial expressions and body language to communicate interest, and respond appropriately.**

> **When it comes to our children, one of**

the most valuable lessons we can learn is that it is OK for us to let go of our parenting role and just listen to our kids! Many children do not talk with their parents because anytime they try to do so, they are not listened to, but preached at or scolded. Identify the person you most want to talk to when you have problems. Does this person:

- Cut you off to express displeasure at what you did?

- Say "I told you so" when you make a mistake?

- Lecture you on the way you should have done something?

- Give you unwanted advice?

Ask parents to list other qualities of the people they seek out to listen to them.

The point, of course, is clear. As adults, we seek out people who will know when to listen and be supportive, are warm and empathetic, and offer advice only when it is asked for or needed. Our children want the same kind of listening from us!

A Few Basic Skills Can Improve Your Family's Communication

Distribute copies of the "Talking Together in My Family" handout (page 304). Discuss each point, sharing the following information. If possible, include illustrations of these principles from your own life to make them come alive.

Rule #1

Missing Words: help, hurt

Main Point: It is very easy, almost natural, to hurt another person with our words. Hurting others with our words only makes life more difficult for everyone. It never brings peace and good feelings to our family.

Rule #2

Missing Words: kind, name-calling, put-downs

Main Point: Tone of voice is very important to good communication. People will respond to our tone of voice rather than our words. The combination of harsh tone of voice with name-calling and cutting remarks is deadly!

Rule #3

Missing Word: true

Main Point: Many times we give distorted messages because the words we are using or hearing are exaggerated or global (e.g., "You never do what I tell you!" "I hate you!"). They simply are not true. Restating messages so they say what is true allows us to have straight, clear communication.

Rule #4

Missing Word: yourself

Main Point: Speaking for yourself means you use "I" statements so that you own your own feelings and talk about your own experiences. You don't blame or attack the person with whom you are talking.

MAKING IT PERSONAL (35 MINUTES)

LET'S TALK ABOUT IT!

Distribute copies of the "Reflections" worksheet (pages 301 and 302). Ask them to fill them out.

Group Sharing

After everyone is finished, share responses around the circle or divide into smaller groups. Remind everyone of the "Right to Pass" rule before starting.

Building on God's Word (15 Minutes)

Bible Focus

Distribute copies of the "Building on God's Word" worksheet (page 303) and discuss it together. Encourage parents to use this sheet at home during the coming week as a means of spiritual encouragement and connecting to God.

Prayer Time

Ask parents to fill in the prayer request line on their "Building on God's Word" worksheet and share their requests with the rest of the group. Check up on past requests. End the session with a time of open prayer.

REFLECTIONS

"LET'S TALK ABOUT IT!"

1. Describe the kind of communication that took place in your family as you were growing up.

    ___ We were always yelling at each other; no one ever listened to me.

    ___ My parents yelled at each other a lot, but not at the kids.

    ___ I never talked to my parents because they always lectured and nagged me when I tried to open up.

    ___ There were a lot of family secrets; no one ever talked about certain people or events.

    ___ I always felt listened to and supported; I could talk about anything.

    ___ Other:

2. **How do you feel your children would answer the above questions about your family today?**

    ___ We are always yelling at each other; no one ever listens to me.

    ___ My parents yell at each other a lot, but not at the kids.

    ___ I never talk to my parents because they always lecture and nag me.

    ___ There are a lot of family secrets; no one ever talks about certain people or events.

    ___ I always feel listened to and supported; I can talk about anything.

    ___ Other:

3. **What messages do others get when they look at you (most of the time)?**
    Examples of nonverbal communication: I am depressed and withdrawn—don't talk to me;
    I am angry and hard—don't expect any sympathy or warmth from me; I am fun to be with—
    let's play; I am interested in what you have to say—let's talk; I am super-spiritual—let's
    pray; etc.

    Family members

Work associates

People at church

Friends

Other friends

4. List two specific changes you can make to improve your family's communication:

1.

2.

BUILDING ON GOD'S WORD

EPHESIANS 4:29

The Bible is full of instruction about how we communicate with each other! Here are just a few examples for you to read during the week:

1. James 3:1–12 contains strong teaching about the destructive powers of our words and the need to keep a constant watch over what we say!

2. The whole book of Proverbs offers wisdom about many aspects of communicating with each other. Make a point of skimming six chapters of Proverbs each day, looking just for words of wisdom about communicating with others. Write down the ones that feel particularly helpful for you.

3. Ephesians 4:29 contains a good summary that is particularly helpful for families:

    Do not let any unwholesome talk come out of your mouths, but only what is helpful for building others up according to their needs, that it may benefit those who listen.
    Ephesians 4:29 (*NIV*)

This is a key verse for this unit. You can reinforce it for you and your kids by memorizing it together as a family.

Your #1 prayer request for this week:

Talking Together in My Family

1. Say words that _____, not _____.

2. Say them in a _____ way; no _____ or _____.

3. Say what is _____.

4. Speak for _____.

OVERVIEW

Caring for each other in the family essentially means we look out for and try to meet each other's needs. This session focuses on just one aspect of this broad subject—the need to encourage and affirm each other. This skill is not very hard to learn; it just takes practice!

NEEDED

- Session Summary for Parents (page 353)
- "Reflections" worksheet
- "Building on God's Word" worksheet
- Note cards, envelopes, and stamps
- Prayer journal

"I CARE ABOUT YOU!"

PARENT SESSION 6 OUTLINE

Getting Started (20 Minutes)
> Check-In
>
> Group Rules
>
> Review Session Summary for Parents

Teaching Time (20 Minutes)
> "You Are Important to Me!"

Making It Personal (35 Minutes)
> Reflections: "Affirmations in My Life"
>
> Group Sharing
>
> Writing Notes of Affirmation

Building on God's Word (15 Minutes)
> Bible Focus
>
> Prayer Time

"I Care About You!"

Parent Session 6

Getting Started (20 Minutes)

Check-In

Ask parents to share the nicest thing they remember anyone ever saying to them. If time allows, go around the circle again, asking them to share the nicest thing someone said to them this week.

Group Rules

Review the three basic rules of Confident Kids parent sessions. Be sure everyone understands them:

1. Confidentiality
2. No advice giving
3. The right to pass

Review Session Summary for Parents

Read through the "Session Summary for Parents" (page 353) together. Be sure parents understand that this handout summarizes what their children will learn in their session today.

Teaching Time (20 Minutes)

You Are Important to Me

Introduce the session theme, "You are important to me."

> One of the functions of a family is that the members take care of each other by looking out for each other's needs. As we said earlier in this unit, all of us have various levels of needs. To review, they are:

Level 1—Physical Needs: food; shelter; clothes; proper diet, rest, and exercise; healthy, nurturing touch; etc.

Level 2—Safety Needs: Family members need to feel protected from threatening circumstances and outside influences.

Level 3—Belonging Needs: All family members need to feel they are an important part of the family, and there needs to be connections for the family in the broader community (church, community organizations, etc.) and in the extended family (a shared family history is important).

Level 4—Self-Esteem Needs: Self-esteem is a two-sided coin. Family members must receive nurturing (warmth and caring) and guidance (learning how to survive in the world). When provided, family members come to see themselves as lovable (they have a warm, nurturing side) and capable (they know they can do some things well).

To the extent that the family is meeting these needs, the family members will feel cared for at home. Although there is much we could say about meeting each of these needs, we are going to focus our attention on the last one: how building self-esteem gives family members the feeling of being cared for.

As a parent, you know that the development of healthy self-esteem in your children is part of your responsibility. But you must also realize that you give no higher self-esteem than you have yourself! So, as we look at the following points, keep in mind that you must apply these to your own life, as well as to the parenting

of your children. How you were treated as a child and how you care for your own self-esteem needs today has a direct bearing on how much self-esteem develops in your child.

Self-Esteem Is Not Our First Priority

That sounds pretty strange, doesn't it? But it is important to note that the levels of needs mentioned above build on each other. That is to say, we cannot worry about our self-esteem needs if we are cold and hungry, or preoccupied with staying safe. We must not have to worry about issues of basic survival. So, the first step to raising our self-esteem, or our children's self-esteem, is to give attention to the three lower levels of need fulfillment. This point cannot be over-emphasized! However, it is also true that even when the basic needs of life are provided, high self-esteem does not happen automatically. All family members must be encouraged into high self-esteem.

High Self-Esteem Results in a Person Being Encouraged Into Life

Note the make up of that word: En-*courage*-d. Essentially, a person (even a child) with high self-esteem has the courage to face whatever life brings. Let's think of some words or phrases to describe this state of high self-esteem. *(Write parents' suggestions on the board)* Here are some examples:

I am confident in what I can do.

I am aware of the difference I make in the world.

YOU ARE
IMPORTANT
TO ME

I see myself as loved.

I believe others will help me if I need help.

Notice that each of these phrases begins with a word that describes how I feel about me. In other words, self-esteem is based on what I believe to be true about me. These beliefs are the result of the messages I have been given throughout my life about who I am and what I do; i.e., how lovable and capable I am. When I receive many positive messages, I grow in my ability to see myself as lovable and capable, and my actions will reflect this. Let's think about what encourages us to have high self-esteem. *(Involve parents in brainstorming a list such as the one that follows)*

Lovable (I have worth and value just because of who I am)

- Being treated with warmth and tenderness

- Receive hugs, smiles

- Verbal messages of "I'm glad you're here" or "I'm glad you're my kid"

- Time taken to talk with me or to listen carefully to me

- Active interest taken in my interests and activities

Capable (I am gifted and can accomplish something in the world)

- Encouraged to try new things

- Verbal affirmation of jobs well done

- Do not do for others what they can (should) do for themselves

- Given help and support to improve skills, take risks, keep going

- Given permission to try and fail; encouraged to try again

As adults, we can help increase self-esteem by giving these messages to ourselves, and surrounding ourselves with friends and support people who will give them to us. As parents, we must work hard to give our kids a steady diet of these positive affirmations!

Low Self-Esteem Results in a Person Being Discouraged Out of Life

Just as a person with high self-esteem has the courage to face whatever life brings, a person with low self-esteem is robbed of courage to face the challenges of life. Let's think of some words or phrases to describe this state. *(Write these on a board as parents suggest them)*

"No one wants me around."

"I can't do anything right."

"Everything that goes wrong is my fault."

"Why try?"

Let's think about messages that encourage low self-esteem. *(Involve parents in brainstorming a list such as the one that follows)*

Lovable

- Being treated with coldness, detachment, or abandonment

- Never touched, or touched abusively

- Verbal slams, name-calling ("You're worthless")
- No time taken to talk to or listen to me

Capable

- No encouragement to try new things
- Verbal messages of "You can't"
- Do for others what they can (should) do for themselves
- No time or interest taken in anything I do

Living with a steady diet of these kinds of negative messages has the effect of paralyzing us. We become convinced that we are not lovable, touchable, or capable of succeeding in life, so why try? People with low self-esteem generally have no courage to face life's challenges.

One Negative Message Destroys Many Positive Affirmations

Sound incredible? We receive negative messages at a deep level in our souls, and these messages overshadow positive ones. Think of every negative message you receive as a shotgun blast; it takes out many positive messages with each shot. Say, for example, one negative message destroys twenty-five positive ones. If a person receives five negative messages a day, he must receive 125 positive ones to counteract them!

We are not suggesting this as a scientific formula, but as an illustration of a very important principle: To build self-esteem in our family members, we must make it our practice to offer them a rich smorgasbord of affirmations. In as many

ways as we can find, we must tell others—and ourselves—that they are valuable, wanted, and important to us, and that we believe in them and expect them to become all that they are capable of becoming.

How do we offer positive affirmations? Here are a few tips:

- We need to see our family members with new eyes.
- We need to seek out the positive qualities and abilities of each one.
- We need to speak our affirmations. They don't do the other person any good unless that person hears them.

MAKING IT PERSONAL (35 MINUTES)

AFFIRMATIONS IN MY LIFE

Distribute copies of the "Reflections" worksheet (pages 311 and 312) to all participants and give them a few minutes to fill them out.

GROUP SHARING

After everyone is finished, share responses around the circle or divide into smaller groups. Remind everyone of the "Right to Pass" rule before starting.

WRITING NOTES OF AFFIRMATION

Bring with you today a supply of note cards, stationery, envelopes, and stamps. Distribute them to parents at this time. Ask parents to reflect on this session and choose one person to write a note of affirmation to. It can be for anyone—even be a note of positive affirmation to themselves! Collect these when done and mail them during the week.

BUILDING ON GOD'S WORD (15 MINUTES)

BIBLE FOCUS

Distribute copies of the "Building on God's Word" worksheet (page 313) and discuss it together. Encourage parents to use this sheet at home during the coming week as a means of spiritual encouragement and connecting to God.

PRAYER TIME

Ask parents to fill in the prayer request line on their "Building on God's Word" worksheet and share these requests with the rest of the group. Review past requests; end the session with a time of open prayer.

REFLECTIONS

AFFIRMATIONS IN MY LIFE

1. **Growing up, which messages did you receive most often?**

   __ "You will never amount to anything! You can't do anything right!"
   __ "We'll always be here for you."
   __ "You were a mistake; we never wanted another child."
   __ "That's not good enough. Do it better. You're lazy!"
   __ "You are a beautiful child and I'm so glad you're mine!"
   __ "You're dumb, stupid, clumsy, ugly," etc.
   __ "You can do it! It's okay to try; so what if you don't make it?"
   __ Other:

   Who gave you these messages?

   __ My parents
   __ My teachers, particularly:
   __ People at church, particularly:
   __ A grandparent
   __ Other family member(s), particularly:

2. **In your life today, who gives you positive messages that you are loved and capable?**
   (List specific people and what they say or do)

   Who gives you negative messages? (Be specific)

AFFIRMATIONS IN MY LIFE

3. Do you see your children acting in ways that show they feel lovable and capable, or are they paralyzed in dealing with life issues?

4. Thinking about your parenting style, do you give your children more positive or negative messages?

    In which area do you need the most improvement?

    ___ Seeing my family members with new eyes
    ___ Seeking out the positive qualities of my family members
    ___ Speaking positive messages to my family members

BUILDING ON GOD'S WORD

JOHN 3:16, 17

Many people grow up with the belief that God is a vindictive God who is out to get us for any little thing we do wrong; that He is most often displeased with us. Actually, the Bible tells us just the opposite. It is full of positive affirmations from God. Here is the most powerful—and most commonly quoted—of all of God's affirmations to us:

> **For God so loved the world that he gave his one and only Son, that whoever believes in him shall not perish but have eternal life. For God did not send his Son into the world to condemn the world, but to save the world through him.**
>
> **John 3:16, 17 (*NIV*)**

God expressed how much He loves and values us by sending His own Son to die in our place, thereby making it possible for all of us to be reconciled to Him. This is just one place in the Bible that speaks of this. There are countless others!

If you are struggling with your own feeling of worth, or feeling like there is nothing you could ever do right, come to God in prayer right now and ask Him to make His love very real to you. If you have never done so, ask God to take control of your life, making you His own dear son or daughter.

Write your prayer here:

Remember, when we are secure in God's love for us and we depend on the power of the Holy Spirit within us, there is nothing in life we cannot face and get through!

Your #1 prayer request for this week:

OVERVIEW

One of the fundamental principles of Confident Kids is that our relationship with God is the most important element for living a healthy life. Through Him, not only are we caring for our spiritual needs, but we are given power to change destructive behavior patterns into healthy, life-giving family relationships. This session is dedicated to helping parents strengthen their relationship with God and the family of God.

NEEDED

- Session Summary for Parents (page 355)
- "Reflections" worksheet
- "Building on God's Word" worksheet
- "The New Family" script
- Bibles
- Prayer journal

I CAN BELONG TO GOD'S FAMILY, TOO
PARENT SESSION 7 OUTLINE

Getting Started (20 Minutes)
> Check-In
>
> Group Rules
>
> Review Session Summary for Parents

Teaching Time (20 Minutes)
> "God Invites Us to Belong to His Family"

Making It Personal (35 Minutes)
> Reflections: "Responding to God's Invitation"
>
> Group Sharing

Building on God's Word (15 Minutes)
> Bible Focus
>
> Prayer Time

I Can Belong to God's Family, Too

Parent Session 7

Getting Started (20 Minutes)

Check-In

Remind parents that next week is the last week of the unit, and give them any special instructions for that session, such as where to meet and if you want them to bring snacks. If you are planning to continue beyond this unit, give them a preview of the next unit, and tell them how to sign up for it.

Group Rules

Review the three basic rules of Confident Kids parent sessions. Be sure everyone understands them:

1. Confidentiality
2. No advice giving
3. The right to pass

Review Session Summary for Parents

Read through the "Session Summary for Parents" (page 355) together. Be sure parents understand that this handout summarizes what their children will learn in their session today.

Teaching Time (20 Minutes)

God Invites Us to Belong to His Family

The skit that is being presented to the kids today, "The New Family," is an excellent opening for this session on belonging to God's family. You'll find the script on pages 323 and 324. Invite someone to prepare it in advance for presentation at this time. After the skit is presented, begin discussion of the session theme, "God invites us to belong to His family."

GOD INVITES US TO BELONG TO HIS FAMILY

As a child, you probably looked around at some point and wished you could live in another family. For some of you in this room, the pain of living in your family gave you good reason to want to live somewhere else; for others, it was a simply part of growing up. Comparing our family with another, and wishing another family would adopt us is a common experience for children. However, when as adults we find ourselves desperately wanting to escape the pain and pressures of our family by looking longingly at other families, we are in trouble. As we discussed earlier in this unit, we may become trapped in the "If only's." "If only my life were more like theirs, everything would be OK."

Some of you may be feeling a great deal of hopelessness and even despair at the way your family life has turned out so far. There may be circumstances in your life that seem overwhelming, or even impossible to overcome: an alcoholic partner, a debilitating divorce, an uncontrollable child, perhaps an addiction of your own. You may feel trapped, hopeless. The important first step you must take is to realize your family is not hopeless, then make a conscious commitment to work on making your family the healthiest, best place it can be. But where do you start? Where does the confidence, strength, and wisdom to accomplish this seemingly impossible task come from? It is our firm belief in Confident Kids that the power to change in our families comes from a personal relationship with God, through our Lord Jesus Christ. Let's take a closer look at how this works.

God's Invitation to Us

It is true that in this life, none of us will ever have a perfect family. But as we are telling the kids today, there is another family we can belong to that will help us in ways our own family cannot. There is a family with a loving Father who wants to adopt us and take care of us. The people in this family care for each other in special ways. That Father is God, and His family is the church.

When you read the Bible carefully, you will notice that it contains a record of God's relationship to His people throughout history. What is most significant about this record is that it tells of a God who initiates a relationship with His people. He reaches out to us and makes a way for us to be in relationship with Him. This is a major difference between Christianity and the rest of the world's religions. In most religions, man must work hard to be good enough, or find a way to appease the gods, just to gain the hope that he will reach Heaven one day. Not so with God. The Bible speaks clearly of God as a loving Father who continually seeks His children, pays their debts, offers forgiveness for their rebellion, and longs to have a close, loving relationship with them. The Davises sought out the children and wanted them so much they were willing to sign a legal document making a lifelong commitment to love and care for them, give them a place in their home, pay their bills—in short, to make them a son and a daughter. Each would have all the legal rights, privileges, and responsibilities thereof! We can understand that God comes to us, and invites us to become His sons and daughters!

The Benefits of God's Invitation to Us

Being a part of the family of God has a set of rights, privileges, and responsibilities, too. What are they? *(Ask parents to share their thoughts about this; if selected verses have been particularly meaningful to them in their walk with God, they can share these as well. As part of the sharing, ask parents to read the following verses to be sure these items are highlighted in your discussion. Make a list of all items on a board or flip chart.)*

- God's presence in every detail of our lives (Matthew 6:25–34)
- God's availability to us in prayer (Jeremiah 33:2, 3; Romans 8:26, 27)
- Power to break destructive behavior patterns in our lives (Romans 7:14–25; Ephesians 6:10, 11)
- God's joy and peace in the midst of life's circumstances (Philippians 4:4–7; John 14:27; John 15:11)
- The Bible, to teach us how to live the best way possible. (2 Timothy 3:16, 17)
- The family of God to be our family (John 17:20–23)
- Certainty of going to Heaven when we die (Romans 6:23)

Can you think of any others?

Our Response to God's Invitation

The Bible makes it clear that there is nothing we can do to earn God's love and gift of eternal life. However, membership in God's family is not automatic; we must respond to God's invitation. God will never force His way into our lives. Rather, He seeks us and makes His gift available, and then waits for our response. Look up the following verses:

- Revelation 3:20—God knocks at the door of our heart; He doesn't bust down the door!
- Romans 10:9, 10—This verse describes our heartfelt response to God's invitation; believing in our hearts and making our belief known to others.

We can sum up God's invitation to us and our response to Him by looking at the parable of the lost son in Luke 15:11–24. *(Read this story to the group; then discuss the following questions)*

What can we learn about how to respond to God's invitation from the son? *(We must want to come home, we must want to change our lifestyle, we must be willing to ask forgiveness from God)*

What can we learn about God's response to us from the father in the story? *(He waits patiently for us to come home, He accepts our expression of repentance and gladly grants forgiveness, He is filled with love and rejoices when we come to Him!)*

What excuses might the son have given to keep him from going home to his father? *(His father would not accept him or let him come home, he would rather starve with the pigs than take any help from his father, he believed he should be able to take care of himself without any help from anyone)*

How would his life have been different if he had stubbornly refused to go home? *(He'd still have been eating with the pigs)*

What excuses do people have today that keep them from having a personal relationship with God? *(Hard to believe in a God you can't see, afraid of having to give up things or how life will change, don't feel they could ever be good enough to be accepted by God, etc.)*

Your heavenly Father is waiting for you, just as the lost son's father was waiting for him. God offers you a personal relationship with Him, and an honored place as His son or daughter. The question is, will you let your excuses keep you away from God? Or will you run to Him and accept His invitation to become a member of His family?

MAKING IT PERSONAL (35 MINUTES)

RESPONDING TO GOD'S INVITATION

Distribute copies of the "Reflections" worksheet (pages 320 and 321) to all participants and give them a few minutes to fill them out.

BUILDING ON GOD'S WORD (15 MINUTES)

BIBLE FOCUS

Distribute copies of the "Building on God's Word" worksheet (page 322) and discuss it together. Encourage parents to use this sheet at home during the coming week as a means of spiritual encouragement and connecting to God.

PRAYER TIME

Use your prayer time to give parents who may have never done so an opportunity to ask Jesus to come into their lives. Give all parents an opportunity to pray quietly about becoming a member of God's family. Close with a prayer for all the parents, and ask God to be particularly close to those having a hard time feeling His presence in their lives at this time. Affirm anyone who has turned his or her life over to Jesus, making Him Lord and Savior.

REFLECTIONS

RESPONDING TO GOD'S INVITATION

1. **Describe your present relationship to God.**

    ___ God is my source of strength and comfort.

    ___ I am a member of God's family, but I don't feel very close to Him right now.

    ___ I am living in the pig sty, but I don't think I could ever be good enough to go home to God; He'd never accept me.

    ___ I don't know God personally, but I really want to!

2. **If you have never established a relationship with God, what keeps you from doing so?**

    ___ I can't believe that God really exists, or if He does, that He could care about me.

    ___ God could never love or accept me into His presence after all the things I've done!

    ___ I cannot face all the changes I would have to make if I made a commitment to God.

    ___ I would like to know God, but the church is full of hypocrites who do not live what they preach! I couldn't be one of them.

3. **What do you most want for your children in terms of a relationship to God?**

    How is this different from what you have (or want) for your own relationship to God?

RESPONDING TO GOD'S INVITATION

4. If you have never responded to God's invitation to become a member of His family, are you now willing to turn your life over to Him? Personalize this prayer of commitment.

Dear God, I want to belong to Your family. I understand that, like the son in the story, I have gone off on my own and departed from Your plan for me. Please forgive me for all the things I have done wrong to hurt You, others in my life, and myself. I understand that I cannot earn a relationship with You, but that You will come into my life, fill me with Your Holy Spirit, and give me eternal life—if I ask You! I'm asking now. Please come into my life, fill me with Your Holy Spirit, and make all things in my life new. Thank you, in Jesus' name! Amen!

BUILDING ON GOD'S WORD

2 CORINTHIANS 6:18; ROMANS 6:23

God's promise is true and can be trusted completely. As we finish this unit, remember that God invites you to be His son or daughter, with all the rights, privileges, and love that goes with it!

"I will be a Father to you, and you will be my sons and daughters, says the Lord Almighty."

2 Corinthians 6:18 (*NIV*)

Remember, too, that we cannot earn this relationship; it is a gift God offers to us.

For the wages of sin is death, but the gift of God is eternal life in Christ Jesus our Lord.
Romans 6:23 (*NIV*)

Finally, remember that beginning this relationship with God happens when we accept this gift by offering our lives to Him and asking Him to come into our lives, for all eternity!

Here I am! I stand at the door and knock. If anyone hears my voice and opens the door, I will come in and eat with him, and he with me.
Revelation 3:20 (*NIV*)

Will you accept His gift to you? Talk to Him about it today!

Your #1 prayer request for this week:

REFLECTIONS

CHARACTERS

- Carrie and Larry, Mr. and Mrs. Davis

THE NEW FAMILY

Carrie and Larry are getting ready to be adopted out of a children's home. They enter, arguing.

Carrie	*(Very upset)* What do you mean, you don't want to do it?
Larry	Read my lips— *(Slowly and deliberately)* I don't want to do it!
Carrie	You are such a noodle brain! This is what we've wanted for years! This is our big chance to have a real family!
Larry	Then you go!
Carrie	I intend to! *(Pauses; softens)* But I don't want to go without you, Larry. We've been together in this children's home for three years. Besides being my brother, you're my best friend.
Larry	Well, what's so bad about this place anyway? Let's just stay here.
Carrie	*(Upset again)* What? You were the one who kept talking about getting adopted! You said being with a real family is better than being alone! You said we'd get more stuff at Christmastime! You said you wanted your own room! You said you wanted a real mom to hug you after school! You said—
Larry	All right! I get the idea! So I changed my mind.
Carrie	*(Ready to burst)* Why? The Davises really want us and they'd give us plenty of stuff at Christmas! We'd even have our own rooms! What kind of wiggly worm has gotten into your brain?
Larry	Maybe they don't want us! Maybe they'd give us back someday! Maybe they'd give us stuff at Christmas we don't want! Maybe they'd put snakes in our bed!
Carrie	Oh, gross! Only you could think of something so dumb!
Larry	And they'd probably have all kinds of rules and chores and stuff we'd have to do!

Carrie	Of course they do! That's part of being in a family. We'll all have to work together and that means sometimes doing stuff we don't like, but we have to because that's just the way it is. Look, Larry, you can stay here and be afraid if you want, but I'm going to have a new family. A real family with real parents and—

Mr. and Mrs. Davis enter.

Mr. Davis	There you are! We are so excited about having you two come to live with us! Your rooms are all ready and waiting.
Mrs. Davis	You know, we looked at fifteen different children's homes, and thought about asking twenty different children to become a part of our family. But when we saw both of you, we knew you were just the kids we were looking for. We loved you from the first.
Mr. Davis	There's only one thing left to do. You have to sign the papers saying you want to join our family. Are you ready to do that?
Carrie	*(Excited)* Yes! *(Looks at Larry)* Well, at least I am. How about you, Larry?

They exit.

GOALS

- Have kids and parents share the *Confident Kids* group experience
- Have kids and parents play together
- Give opportunity for kids and parents to evaluate the group and enroll for the next unit (if you are having one)
- Bring closure to this unit.

NEEDED

- Name tags and a variety of rubber stamps, stickers, and other materials to decorate them
- Poster boards cut into four pieces, one piece per family
- Items for family games, if any
- Props for Bible story
- Unit verse posters
- Unit verse cards, copied onto card stock and cut apart
- Evaluation sheets for parents and kids (pages 369 and 371)
- Affirmation balloons, filled out in advance (page 375)
- Completion certificates, filled out in advance (page 377)
- Snacks

FAMILY NIGHT
SESSION 8 OUTLINE

Getting Started (20 Minutes)
> Name Tags
>
> Family Puzzles
>
> Introduction of the Parents by the Kids

Family Games (15 Minutes)

Split Session (20 Minutes)
> Bring Closure to the Unit (Parents)
>
> Prepare for Presentations (Kids)

Closing Program (20 Minutes)
> Songs
>
> "The Parable of the Lost Son"
>
> Memory Verses
>
> Awarding of Certificates and Affirmation Balloon Sheets

Snacks and Evaluations (10 Minutes)
> Snack Table
>
> Evaluations and Enrollment Time

Family Night

Family Session 8

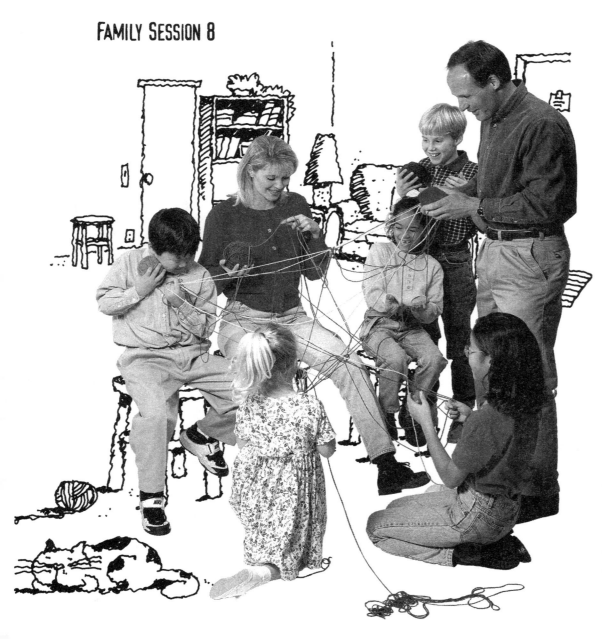

Gathering Activity (25 Minutes)

Name Tags

As participants arrive, direct kids and parents to make name tags for themselves. Have available a variety of rubber stamps and stickers to personalize the tags. Be sure everyone, including facilitators, makes one.

Family Puzzles

Direct families to make a family puzzle by having all family members create a design on a quarter of a piece of poster board. They can decide as a family how to design it. Ideas would include making a family portrait, picturing the family doing a favorite activity together, having family members sign their names (include paw prints for pets), creating a family crest, etc. When the design is complete, have each family cut the picture apart into puzzle pieces. Complete the activity by having families pair up with another family, exchange and assemble the puzzles, and introduce themselves to each other by talking about the pictures they drew on their puzzles.

Introduction of the Parents by the Kids

Have everyone sit in a circle and ask the kids to introduce their parents to the rest of the group by giving their name(s) and one special thing about them (e.g., a character quality, a favorite food, something they like to do).

Family Games (15 Minutes)

Prepare several games the children and adults can play together. It doesn't matter what the games are, as long as everyone can play. Choose some of your favorite games, or some of the games from past sessions that the kids particularly enjoyed. Also, Appendix B, "Resources," contains some ideas. *Important:* Choose games that will encourage families to work together or are not too competitive. We don't want family members trying to win against each other during this time!

SPLIT SESSION (20 MINUTES)

Send the parents to their meeting room with the parent group facilitator to do the following:

- Ask for any last questions parents may still have.
- Have parents share the most helpful part of the unit for them personally.
- Give an overview of the next unit, if you are planning to do one, including starting date, unit theme, and any special instructions.

Meanwhile, have the kids meet in their room(s) to prepare for the closing program. *Note:* If you have multiple age groups in your program, you might assign responsibilities for the program as follows:

- Preschoolers: Say one or two of the verses using their picture posters or motions.
- Elementary: Do the play "The Parable of the Lost Son" led by Adam and Eve. The script is on pages 329 and 330.
- Preteens: Use the verse posters to teach the verses to the parents, then pass out the Unit Scripture verse cards.

CLOSING PROGRAM (20 MINUTES)

SONGS

Choose an energetic song leader to lead families in some action songs, as well as favorite songs the kids have been singing in their groups throughout the unit.

"THE PARABLE OF THE LOST SON"

Have Adam and Eve introduce themselves to the parents and help the kids present their play.

MEMORY VERSES

Invite preschoolers to say their verses to the parents. Then invite older kids to use the memory verse posters to lead the parents in saying the unit verses together. Involve as many kids as possible in this activity.

AWARDING OF CERTIFICATES AND AFFIRMATION BALLOON SHEETS

Before the meeting, be sure facilitators have already completed a certificate and an affirmation balloons sheet (pages 371 and 373) for each child in their group. (Rolling them up together and tying with a ribbon is a nice way to present them. Real balloons would be fun, too!) Have each facilitator award these to their kids. Allow time for the facilitators to give a brief verbal affirmation to each child as well. Affirming kids in front of their parents is a powerful experience for the kids.

SNACKS AND EVALUATIONS (15 MINUTES)

SNACK TABLE

For this special event, create a special party table for families to enjoy. The facilitators can bring the treats, or you might have a potluck snacks table. Be sure to include this information on the party invitations, or have facilitators write a special note to each of their kids this week inviting them to bring snacks.

Note: Before dismissing to the snack table, set a rule that kids must go through the line with their parents! This will prevent a stampede, and will keep the families together so they can fill out the evaluations.

EVALUATIONS AND ENROLLMENT TIME

Place the unit evaluations for both parents and kids (pages 365 and 367) on the snack table. Be sure all participants take one to complete before leaving. Notice that kids and parents have different forms. Also, if you are planning to host another Confident Kids unit, invite parents to reenroll by signing the statement on the bottom of their evaluation sheet.

Allow families to "hang around" and visit as long as they like!

THE PARABLE OF THE LOST SON

Adam and Eve enter and greet the families. They introduce themselves as Adam and Eve.

Adam	It has been a great pleasure for us to be here with your kids during this Confident Kids unit. You know, we were the very first family that God created. And when you read about us in the Bible, you—
Eve	*(Interrupts)* We're in the very first book! Who can tell us the name of the Bible book that tells our story? *(Let kids respond)* Right!
Adam	*(Stares at Eve)* Ahem!
Eve	Oh! I'm sorry, I guess I interrupted you. Please continue!
Adam	As I was saying, when you read about us in the Bible—in the book of Genesis—you discover that from the very beginning, families were not perfect. We made a lot of mistakes and had hurts in our family, too!
Eve	But in spite of that, God saw that family was good, and would be the best way for human beings to live on our earth. We have had families ever since!
Adam	We also learned during this unit that as humans, we can belong to two families! Not only does God give us a human family to meet our needs, but He invites us to be a part of His family, too. We even learned a little play that talks about that, and we want to do it for you today.
Eve	This play is a story that Jesus told about how much God loves us and wants us to be in His family!

Present the parable of the lost son (Luke 15:11-31).

Eve	Well, that's about it for this unit.
Adam	Eve, aren't you forgetting something?
Eve	What do you mean?

FROM

- Luke 15:11-31

CHARACTERS

- Adam and Eve

NEEDED

- Unit Scripture verse cards
- *Note:* The text of the parable is on pages 161 and 162, Elementary Session 7.

Adam	I mean these! *(Invite older kids to pass out unit Scripture verse cards to everyone)* We want you to take these home as a gift from us to remind you of some of the very important truths from God's Word we talked about during this unit.
Eve	*(Looks at Adam)* Now?
Adam	Now.
Adam and Eve	*(Together)* It was great to be with you! Good-bye!

They exit.

2 Corinthians 6:18

"I will be your father, and you will be my sons and daughters, says the Lord All-Powerful."

(ICB)

2 Corinthians 6:18

"I will be your father, and you will be my sons and daughters, says the Lord All-Powerful."

(ICB)

Romans 8:38, 39

Yes, I am sure that nothing can separate us from the love God has for us. Not death, not life, not angels, not ruling spirits, nothing now, nothing in the future, no powers, nothing above us, nothing below us, or anything else in the whole world will ever be able to separate us from the love of God that is in Christ Jesus our Lord.

(ICB)

Romans 8:38, 39

Yes, I am sure that nothing can separate us from the love God has for us. Not death, not life, not angels, not ruling spirits, nothing now, nothing in the future, no powers, nothing above us, nothing below us, or anything else in the whole world will ever be able to separate us from the love of God that is in Christ Jesus our Lord.

(ICB)

Ephesians 4:29

When you talk, do not say harmful things. But say what people need— words that will help others become stronger. Then what you say will help those who listen to you.

(ICB)

Ephesians 4:29

When you talk, do not say harmful things. But say what people need— words that will help others become stronger. Then what you say will help those who listen to you.

(ICB)

PARENT INFORMATION HANDOUTS

Confident Kids

GETTING INFORMATION TO THE PARENTS	335
WELCOME TO CONFIDENT KIDS!	337
LET'S LEARN HEALTHY LIVING SKILLS	339
LIVING IN MY FAMILY TOPIC OVERVIEW	341
WEEKLY SESSION SUMMARIES	343

GETTING INFORMATION TO THE PARENTS

Parent Information Handouts are helpful for many reasons, but particularly because of the *Confident Kids* confidentiality rule. Elementary kids will have difficulty sorting out what is OK to talk about and what should be kept confidential. Therefore, they will typically tell their parents that their leaders told them *not* to talk about what they are doing in the group. These handouts will allay parents' fears and answer many of their questions about the program.

Parent Information Handouts will keep parents well informed about the *Confident Kids* program by including the following handouts:

- **Welcome to** *Confident Kids*! **Information for Parents**

  This letter gives an overview of the program, and should include the name and telephone number of the person parents can contact if they have any questions about their kids' experience during the sessions.

  - **Let's Learn Healthy Living Skills**

    Much of the *Confident Kids* material is designed to teach families healthy living skills. For many families, this material will be new, and the skill being taught will feel awkward and uncomfortable. Review this handout periodically to encourage parents to work hard at replacing old, unhealthy behavior patterns with new, healthy living skills.

- **Topic Overview**

  This piece summarizes the theme for the entire set of sessions.

- **Weekly Session Summaries**

  Each week a session summary details each week's theme and key verse, plus gives a suggested follow-up activity parents can do throughout the week.

Distribute the Session Summaries in one of these ways:

- **During the Parent Sessions**

  The best way to keep parents informed, of course, is to involve them in the parents sessions. Parents who participate will receive and review the Session Summaries as part of their meeting.

- **In the Kids' Rooms or a Central Location**

  Place the handouts where parents can pick them up when they drop off or pick up their kids each week.

- **Through the Mail**

  By mailing them each week, you will ensure every parent receives one.

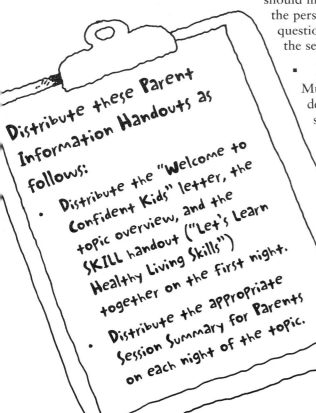

Distribute these Parent Information Handouts as follows:

- Distribute the "Welcome to Confident Kids" letter, the topic overview, and the SKILL handout ("Let's Learn Healthy Living Skills") together on the first night.
- Distribute the appropriate Session Summary for Parents on each night of the topic.

Welcome to Confident Kids!

Dear Parent or Sponsor,

Welcome to Confident Kids Support Groups. I am delighted you have chosen to involve your child in this experience. Please take a moment to read the information with this letter about the group, and be sure to keep my name and phone number close by in the coming weeks. I will be glad to talk with you about your child's experience at any time.

Our Goals

In our changing society, children are having a harder and harder time growing up. There are so many stressful things for all of us to manage, and our kids are approaching overload! Confident Kids is designed to help both you and your children learn to deal with these high-stress situations in healthy and growing ways. We hope to:

- Teach children how to talk about their experiences and provide a loving and safe environment in which to do so
- Teach children skills to cope with their life experiences in healthy and positive ways
- Build self-esteem and a sense of trust through relationships with caring adults (facilitators)
- Guide children into a relationship with God and show them how prayer and the Bible are resources for dealing with their life circumstances

The Curriculum

Confident Kids is taught through a series of topics, each of which is eight weeks long and designed to teach a specific life skill. An outline of the topic you and your children are about to begin is enclosed. Each session plan uses stories, games, learning activities, and discussion questions to communicate with the children. In addition, each child is assigned to a small group, led by a carefully trained facilitator. These small groups will give your children an opportunity to build a relationship with a caring adult who will be their guide through the program.

Your Role

We ask you to take an active interest in what the children are learning. You will receive a summary of each session's theme, including an activity you can do at home to reinforce what kids are learning. If you are attending a parents group, the summaries will be distributed there. If not, they will be sent home with each child each week. Be sure to look for them.

Snacks are an important part of the Confident Kids meetings. Children will take turns bringing the snack for the group each week. When the "snack tin" comes home with your child, instructions concerning what to send will be listed on the lid. Also, if there are restrictions on the snacks your child can have, be sure to call me immediately.

The last night of each unit is Family Night. You will be invited to come and share the group experience with the children. This is an important time; it brings closure to the unit, and provides an opportunity for you to meet your child's facilitator(s). Please plan to come to the party!

Deal with high-stress situations

Tested curriculum and trained facilitators

The Parent Group helps you, too!

The *Confident Kids* experience is most effective when you experience the program, too. To make this possible, we have a Parent Group that meets while the kids are meeting. The time is spent discussing the same topic the kids are learning, with emphasis on how to incorporate the skills at home, and time for personal sharing and prayer support. We would love for you to come.

Finally, please be aware that the information any child shares in the group will be respected as confidential. Children will be told not to share at home what others have said in the group setting; only information about themselves, if they wish to do so. Also, each facilitator has been instructed to treat every child's personal sharing as confidential, so please do not ask facilitators for detailed information. We don't want our program facilitators to be caught in the middle between you and your child. However, be assured that as the program administrator, I will monitor your child's participation carefully. If issues arise concerning your child that you need to know about, I will be sure to get you that information.

Once again, I am thrilled to have your family join us in the *Confident Kids* program. If I can help you in the weeks ahead, please do not hesitate to call me.

Sincerely,

Program Administrator

Phone Number

P.S. Much of the material in *Confident Kids* is designed to teach you and your family healthy living skills. If the material is new to you, you may feel awkward and uncomfortable using it at first. Let me encourage you that working at learning new life skills is worth the effort it takes to do it! I've included a copy of the SKILL Handout, "Let's Learn Healthy Living Skills," to encourage you along these lines.

Let's Learn Healthy Living Skills!

Learning new skills takes time and feels uncomfortable at first!

Remember when you were first learning to ride a bicycle or play a musical instrument or hit a baseball? It took time to perfect the skills you needed to accomplish those tasks, and much of that time was spent in boring practice sessions. You probably went through periods of discouragement and thought you would never improve. But persistence and practice eventually paid off, especially if the learning process was a group experience that took place in a friendly environment where everyone's efforts were treated with respect. It helped even more if you were guided by someone who had already mastered the skill and encouraged your every sign of progress.

Developing healthy life skills in a family setting is like that. Learning to live together in new ways will take time and commitment and patience on the part of every family member. Both you and your children will sometimes feel awkward and uncomfortable, as if things will never change for the better. There are no shortcuts to making healthy life skills a reality in your home, but knowing what to expect can keep you going. New skills normally develop in five stages, as the following acrostic illustrates:

S = **Stage 1: Seeing the Need.** All change begins here. It is only when we are motivated by the need for change that we will go through the hard work of learning a new skill.

K = **Stage 2: Keeping On.** As you start practicing a new skill, it is natural to feel awkward, so you may want to revert to behavior patterns that are familiar and comfortable. At this point, you will need lots of encouragement and the determination to keep going. This is the stage of greatest discouragement and the point at which many people give up.

I = **Stage 3: Increasing Confidence.** Over time, you will begin to see changes, and the ability to use the new skill will take root. Learning to recognize and celebrate small steps of growth will build your confidence and keep you going.

L = **Stage 4: Letting Go.** As your skill level improves, more and more you will find yourself letting go of past behavior patterns and replacing them with the new and healthier ones.

L = **Stage 5: Living It!** In this last stage, the new skill has become so integrated into your life that it becomes almost automatic. When you find yourself using it easily, you realize that the hard work of the earlier stages has paid off!

Living in My Family
Topic Overview

Unit Slogan

There Are No Perfect Families!

Bible Lessons

The first family, Adam and Eve (Genesis 1-4) and The Prodigal Son (Luke 15:11-24)

Key Verses

2 Corinthians 6:18
"I will be your father, and you will be my sons and daughters, says the Lord All-Powerful." *(ICB)*

Romans 8:38, 39
Yes, I am sure that nothing can separate us from the love God has for us. Not death, not life, not angels, not ruling spirits, nothing now, nothing in the future, no powers, nothing above us, nothing below us, or anything else in the whole world will ever be able to separate us from the love of God that is in Christ Jesus our Lord. *(ICB)*

Ephesians 4:29
When you talk, do not say harmful things. But say what people need—words that will help others become stronger. Then what you say will help those who listen to you. *(ICB)*

Key Concepts

- Every family is special and unique, and every family has weaknesses and problems!
- Changes in family life disrupt our sense of security and force us to adapt.
- There will always be times when our family won't—or can't—meet all our needs.
- Good communication skills are the primary building blocks of a strong family.
- Families grow when all members take responsibility to act and speak in ways that help—not hurt—the family unit.
- Belonging to God's family gives us the strength and security we need to face whatever life brings our way.

Session Titles

1 There Are No Perfect Families!
2 What's a Family For, Anyway?
3 Changes Can Upset My Family
4 My Actions Can Help—Or Hurt—My Family
5 My Words Can Help—Or Hurt—My Family
6 "I Care About You!"
7 I Can Belong to God's Family, Too!
8 Family Night

Living in My Family

From the beginning of time, God's design has been for people to live in families. But in our world today, the family is often a confusing and even hurtful place, especially for children. Divorce, absent parents, adjusting to blended families, abusive relationships, and kids left home alone have become family norms in many of our communities. Even intact families suffer the effects of trying to survive in our increasingly fast-paced, morally decaying world. It is unlikely that family life has ever been more challenging than it is at this time in our history.

For children, the center of the universe is their family. It is not only their primary source of belonging and caring, but also the place where they learn who they are and what it means to live in the world. To the degree that the family functions in healthy ways, children grow up feeling valued, secure, and empowered to take their place in the world. When families experience high amounts of stress, however, the likelihood of children growing up feeling valued and secure is dangerously threatened. In fact the opposite can easily be true: If the family cannot find a sense of balance and relief from the stress, the children may grow up feeling hopeless and ill-equipped to lead a healthy, fulfilling life.

In this unit, we will address what it means to live in and be part of a family. Our goal is to help both you and your children realize that living in families is not always easy and that in order to be successful, family members must learn how to work together. We also want you and your children to see that all families change, make mistakes and sometimes fail to meet each others' needs. But it is also true that your ties to your family are the most powerful bonds you will ever have and it is possible for everyone in your family to learn to work together to make it the best place possible for all the members!

SESSION 1 SUMMARY FOR PARENTS

THERE ARE NO PERFECT FAMILIES!

MAIN POINTS YOUR CHILD LEARNED TODAY

As the title of this session indicates, we began this unit on family with a simple premise: Every family has some things that are irritating, less than ideal, and even hurtful. In fact, almost everyone wishes from time to time that they could live in a different family! But in this first session we also made the point that every family has some things about it that are unique and special, too! The kids were asked to identify a few of these qualities as they introduced their families to each other.

In spite of the ways in which family life has changed in our culture today, most kids still believe that "family" equals mom, dad, and kids all living together in close relationship. Therefore, they see many family configurations—possibly even their own—as not a real family at all. Our goal today was simply to set the foundation for this unit by saying to the kids that no matter what may have happened—or is happening—in their family, or who lives in their house, their family is a "real" family and for them it is a special and important place! No one (except maybe a TV character) gets to live in a perfect family. With that understanding, we can move on to talk about how to make each family the best it can be for everyone who is part of it.

BIBLE EMPHASIS

We introduced Adam and Eve as the first family, and affirmed that God created people to live in families from the very beginning of time. But as the kids will see as we move through the unit, even that first family had problems and was not by any means perfect!

We also started talking about what it means to belong to God's family by introducing our first memory verse, 2 Corinthians 6:18 *(ICB):*

> "I will be your father, and you will be my sons and daughters, says the Lord All-Powerful."

DO-AT-HOME ACTIVITY

CELEBRATE YOUR FAMILY

Use one or more of the following ideas to strengthen family cohesion:

1. *Share family stories.* Part of belonging in families comes from feeling connected to history. Get out old photo albums, scrapbooks, and movies or videos and gather the family together. Share stories from your own childhood, as well as stories about grandparents and other relatives.
2. *Celebrate your ethnic background.* Learn a song or Bible verse in your ethnic language, if it is different from what is spoken at home. Choose a cultural tradition common to your ethnic background and make it a part of your home, or at least practice it for the evening.
3. *Discover your family's greatest strength.* Ask each family member to share what they think is most special about your family. (These are your family strengths.) Then negotiate a family consensus about the most special thing about your family. (Consensus means everyone must agree with the final choice!)

SESSION 2 SUMMARY FOR PARENTS

WHAT'S A FAMILY FOR, ANYWAY?

MAIN POINTS YOUR CHILD LEARNED TODAY

In today's session, your kids spent time thinking about the many things our families do for us. Our list included things such as:

Physical Needs

Food
Shelter
Clothes
Care when sick

Emotional Needs

Love
Listen to each other
Stick up for each other
Have fun together

From a general description of what families do for us, we moved the kids to thinking about their own families—naming both things they value and things they wish they could change in their families. Our goal once again was to affirm to the kids that all families have both strengths (things we would never want to change about our families) and weaknesses (things we wish we could change)! They can value their family, weaknesses and all, as the place they can find care, love, and belonging.

BIBLE EMPHASIS

Adam described how God provided Eve as a wife and companion, and how his loneliness disappeared when they established a family.

We continued memorizing 2 Corinthians 6:18. We reminded the kids that no matter what their earthly family may be like, God is a heavenly Father who is always available to care for us.

DO-AT-HOME ACTIVITY

TALK ABOUT YOUR FAMILY

You can use the same questions at home that we used in the group today to identify what each family member considers to be the strengths and weaknesses of your family. You may be surprised by some of the discussions you can generate with your children by talking about these questions:

1. I wish my family were more _____.
2. I'm glad my family _____.
3. I wish my family would _____.
4. My family thinks I am _____.
5. The one thing about my family I wish I could change is _____.
6. The one thing about my family I would never change is _____.

SESSION 3 SUMMARY FOR PARENTS

CHANGES CAN UPSET MY FAMILY

Main Points Your Child Learned Today

Today we discussed the disruption that can occur in families when a significant change takes place. Of course, most of us would rather that things never changed. But changes happen in families all the time, threatening our sense of security and forcing us to adapt. The main point we tried to communicate to your child today is that they can't stop change from happening; change is simply a fact of life.

We listed the following examples of disruptive family changes: divorce, birth of a baby, death of a family member, long-distance move, serious illness, parent goes to work, stepfamily established, grandparent moves in, or alcohol or drug abuse.

We also helped your child see that when changes occur, everyone in the family is likely to respond in a different way. If a person has been hurt by the change, they may instinctively respond in a way that is unhealthy, and in the long run only makes matters worse. We listed the following examples of unhealthy responses to change:

- Anger
- Running away
- Blaming yourself
- Taking it out on someone else
- Silence/withdrawal
- Fear
- Pretending it didn't happen

Finally, we talked with your child about making wise choices when things change. They, and all family members, can learn healthy ways to cope with change when it occurs. Some of the healthy ways we discussed include:

- Talking about how they feel to parents, friends, and other trusted adults
- Talking to other family members about what they are feeling

- Feeling angry for awhile, but expressing it in a healthy way (no destructive actions)
- Crying and feeling sad for awhile
- Asking someone for help
- Asking for a hug or to be held
- Talking to God
- Coming to Confident Kids!

As a parent, you need to be aware that when a significant change happens in your family, your kids will most likely respond in an unhealthy way at first. You can help them grieve and adjust to the change by helping them choose—and choosing for yourself—healthy responses. It's hard work, but you can do it! (And don't forget a primary Confident Kids rule: Ask for help, if you need it!)

Bible Emphasis

Adam and Eve discussed the big changes in their lives when they disobeyed God and were removed from the garden. They also affirmed that as difficult as that change was, God never stopped loving and caring for them in the midst of it. They then introduced a new memory verse (Romans 8:38, 39, *ICB*) to let the kids know that no matter what changes happen in their lives, God continues to love and care for them:

> **Yes, I am sure that nothing can separate us from the love God has for us. Not death, not life, not angels, not ruling spirits, nothing now, nothing in the future, no powers, nothing above us, nothing below us, or anything else in the whole world will ever be able to separate us from the love of God that is in Christ Jesus our Lord.**

Do-at-Home Activity

How Does Our Family Handle Changes?

People respond to change in different ways. Knowing how each member of the family reacts in times of change can help you understand and help each other during those times. Around the dinner table, discuss how each person in your family reacts when things change. Are their responses primarily healthy or unhealthy? Choose and practice healthy ways of responding so that your family will be better prepared to deal with change when it comes.

Please note: There is a Confident Kids unit available on dealing with significant change. If your family is currently dealing with a major change, ask your Confident Kids leaders if they will be offering *Growing Through Changes* in the future.

SESSION 4 SUMMARY FOR PARENTS

MY ACTIONS CAN HELP— OR HURT—MY FAMILY

MAIN POINTS YOUR CHILD LEARNED TODAY

Our goal in today's session was to help the kids see a relationship between the actions they (and other family members) choose and the overall tone of the family. We said that every family will have both good times when there is lots of warmth and good feelings, and difficult times when there is conflict and hurt feelings. However, what we don't often think about is that the family members bring about these feelings by how they choose to act. Therefore, it is possible for a family to change the feeling tone of the family by learning to choose their actions carefully—choosing more actions that result in positive feelings in the family, and fewer actions that upset the family.

To help the kids understand this concept, we had them make a list of various actions common in families and then identify the feelings each one generates. These were then sorted into actions that produce positive feelings, and actions that produce negative feelings. Examples:

Some Actions That Produce Positive Feelings
- Whole family playing a game together
- Talking together without yelling or blaming
- Doing chores without being told
- Apologizing

Some Actions That Produce Negative Feelings
- Name-calling and put-downs
- Blaming
- Hitting, kicking, etc.
- Not doing chores or homework and getting yelled at
- Temper tantrums or screaming

By identifying *specific* actions, we could then talk with the kids about targeting certain behaviors they could work on eliminating, thereby doing their part to bring more positive feelings to their family.

As a parent, it is important for you to understand that your child is only responsible for his own behavior. Increasing the positive feelings in a family's overall feeling tone requires that *all* family members take responsibility for their own actions. The "Do-at-Home Activity" will help you take steps toward this end.

BIBLE EMPHASIS

Adam and Eve talked about their son Cain and how his jealousy and anger led him to kill his brother. Kids were encouraged to make better choices by talking through their powerful feelings rather than acting on them.

We also continued to work on Romans 8:38, 39 as the memory verse.

DO-AT-HOME ACTIVITY

MAKE YOUR OWN "ACTIONS/FEELINGS" LIST

Your whole family can make a list similar to the one included here. Making the list will help to identify key behaviors that could increase the positive feelings in your family. Involve as many family members as possible as you clearly identify behaviors that are sabotaging family peace. Make an action plan to eliminate—or at least minimize—those behaviors, as you increase the ones that bring positive feelings.

Please be aware that in order for this to be most effective, all family members must be willing to do the hard work necessary to change their behaviors. However, if some or all of your family is unwilling to get involved in this way, you can begin with yourself. Make a personal list about just your actions in the family. What goals can you set for yourself? For instance, you might identify the need to no longer get into power struggles with your children, or to stop enabling a family member to abuse alcohol or drugs, or to learn better skills of listening to your children without blaming or criticizing. As you work to change your actions, you will begin to see corresponding changes in others. This is hard work, but you can do it! And don't forget to ask for help when you need it.

SESSION 5 SUMMARY FOR PARENTS

MY WORDS CAN HELP— OR HURT—MY FAMILY

MAIN POINTS YOUR CHILD LEARNED TODAY

Last session we talked with your child about how the actions they choose can help make their family a good or a hurtful place to be. Today we talked about how the *words* they choose can either help or hurt others in their family. Although similar to last week's concept, this session gives some basic communication principles because it is a fact that we hurt each other with words in our families more than we realize!

The central point of the session was that when others talk to us with kind, helpful, loving words, we can handle whatever happens to us. Unfortunately, people who live together in families are not always careful about the way they talk to each other. Many families have lots of yelling and hurtful words that make living there difficult. But we can work to make our family a better place by learning to choose our words carefully. Here are some rules about using words that we shared with your kids. You can apply these to your parenting style.

1. *Say words that help, not hurt.* As a parent, realize that you have great power to encourage or discourage your children by what you say. Your words do make a difference!
2. *Say them in a kind way; no name-calling or put-downs.* Parents often don't realize that their sarcastic, angry tone of voice is as hurtful to a child as the words themselves. And, of course, name-calling and put-downs are some of the most destructive forms of communication ever devised! They should never be allowed in your family— spoken by you or your children!
3. *Say what is true.* Calling someone stupid, saying "I hate you" or "I'm going to ground you for a year!" is not truthful. "I'm really angry," "I don't like what you are doing," or "There will be no TV privileges tonight!" are examples of true, realistic statements.
4. *Speak for yourself.* The skill to be learned is to use "I" statements: "I'm really angry" or "I don't like what you are doing." "I" statements allow you to own your feelings. "You make me so mad" or "You're driving me crazy" are blaming and shaming statements that shut down communication and wound the other person.

BIBLE EMPHASIS

We introduced a new memory verse today, Ephesians 4:29 (*ICB*). Ask God to help you make this verse a basic rule in your family's life!

> **When you talk, do not say harmful things. But say what people need—words that will help others become stronger. Then what you say will help those who listen to you.**

DO-AT-HOME ACTIVITY

ESTABLISH LISTENING TIMES WITH EACH OF YOUR CHILDREN

Parents often have trouble communicating with their children because they cannot listen without criticizing, blaming, or giving advice. If you want your children to talk with you about the matters that really concern them, learn to set aside times for nonjudgmental listening. You might take a child out for dinner or an ice cream cone or take a few minutes at bedtime. The point is to let them talk about anything they want, while you simply listen. You may have to bite your tongue occasionally, but the rewards of increased communication with your child are worth it!

What do you talk about with your children? Here are some subjects kids say they would like more time to talk about with you: friends, things they fear or worry about, death (in general or someone who died), their future, help with my homework or other things about school, family's history, problems you (parents) are facing, questions about sex, "Why Mom _____," and "Why Dad _____."

SESSION 6 SUMMARY FOR PARENTS

"I CARE ABOUT YOU!"

MAIN POINTS YOUR CHILD LEARNED TODAY

Today we talked with the kids about the greatest value of living in families: Having others in our lives who care about, and for us. Family members care for each other in lots of ways. When family members are selfish and care only about their own needs and no one else's, no one feels cared for and the family is not a healthy one! We also talked with your children about the fact that caring for each others' needs is a two-way street—sometimes we need people in our family to take care of us, but we need to pay attention to what others need and help them out, too. It's hard work but it makes a big difference in making families good places to be!

The starting place to make this work in our families is to answer the question: "What do our family members need from each other to feel loved and cared for?" Although each family will answer this a little differently, a basic list would look something like this:

- *Kids from parents:* Provide food, shelter, clothing; listen to their concerns; spend time with them; encourage them in things they can do well; tell them "I love you," etc.
- *Parents from kids:* Cooperation, honesty, hugs, tell them "I love you," take responsibility for actions, minimal fighting with siblings, etc.
- *Parent from parent:* Support, tell them "I love you," acts of kindness, willingness to compromise in areas of disagreement, etc.
- *Siblings from each other:* Play together, don't use put-downs or name-calling, treat them in ways they would want to be treated, etc.

Finally, we talked with the kids about the power of affirmations, which are positive statements or actions that communicate to others "I care about you!" For instance, saying "I love you" or "Good job!" or bringing an unexpected gift are ways to communicate how much we care. One characteristic of healthy families is that they give and receive lots of positive affirmations expressing how much they mean to each other!

BIBLE EMPHASIS

We used Ephesians 4:29 (*ICB*) as a foundation for the need to affirm each other:

> When you talk, do not say harmful things. But say what people need—words that will help others become stronger. Then what you say will help those who listen to you.

We also presented Romans 8:38, 39 (*ICB*) as a powerful affirmation that God gives to us; there is nothing that could ever stop Him from loving us!

> Yes, I am sure that nothing can separate us from the love God has for us. Not death, not life, not angels, not ruling spirits, nothing now, nothing in the future, no powers, nothing above us, nothing below us, or anything else in the whole world will ever be able to separate us from the love of God that is in Christ Jesus our Lord.

DO-AT-HOME ACTIVITY

HOW DO I CARE FOR YOU? LET ME COUNT THE WAYS!

Help your family create your own list of what family members need from each other to feel loved and cared for. Set it up with the categories listed above (kids from parents, parents from kids, etc.) and then ask each family member to answer these two questions:

When in our family do you feel loved and cared for? What happens that makes you feel that way?

Are there times in our family when you don't feel loved and cared for? What happens that makes you feel that way?

Use your list as a guideline for setting goals to improve the quality of your lives together.

SESSION 7
SUMMARY
FOR
PARENTS

GOD'S SPECIAL PLAN FOR ME

MAIN POINTS YOUR CHILD LEARNED TODAY

The final session of this unit is perhaps the most important of all. We talked with the kids today about the greatest resource they can have to deal with whatever life brings their way: a relationship to God. We wanted them to know that it is a fact of life that families are imperfect, and therefore cannot meet our needs all of the time. There will be times in their family—as there are in everyone's family—when others mess up, let them down, or hurt them. During those times, they may be tempted to feel discouraged or even hopeless and may emotionally "go looking for a different family." Children often wish they could be adopted by other families they know, or make up a perfect family in their minds and pretend they belong to it. Unfortunately, none of these options will help their families meet all their needs.

Our central goal in this session was to offer the kids a means for dealing with this problem. The first step is to recognize that all families have hard times and therefore everyone needs to find resources to help meet their needs in ways their own family cannot. It is a central belief in Confident Kids that we find our most important resource in our relationship to God. So, we talked with your children about a family with a loving Father who wants to adopt them into His family and take care of them; a family that also has many people in it who care for one another in special ways. Of course, that Father is God, and His family is the church. We can belong to God's family at the same time we belong to our own family; in fact, we very much need both families!

But being a member of God's family is not automatic. We are not born into God's family the way we are born into our own families. We are all invited to become a member of God's family and every person must decide individually to accept or refuse God's invitation. No one can do that for us. We have to decide on our own.

As a parent, this invitation is open to you, too. If you have not already done so, you can accept God's invitation and begin your new life in his family. We shared a prayer similar to this one with your kids today:

> Dear God,
>
> Thank you for wanting me to join your family! I want to accept your invitation. I believe in you and that your Son, Jesus, died on the cross for me. I invite you into my life to lead me and teach me how to live as your child for the rest of my life. And some day, I know we will live together in Heaven because I belong to your family! Amen.

God's Word assures us that when we open our hearts to God, He will enter our lives and make us His children. From then on, we can count on His presence to be with us, His wisdom to guide us, and His people to give us help and support when we need it.

BIBLE EMPHASIS

Our Bible story today was one Jesus told in Luke 15:11-24, "The Parable of the Lost (or Prodigal) Son." This story clearly presents God's great desire to welcome us into His family, no matter who we are or what past mistakes we've made!

Our verse today was 2 Corinthians 6:18:

> "I will be your father, and you will be my sons and daughters, says the Lord All-Powerful."

Do-at-Home Activity

Make God's Family Your Family, Too

To seal your commitment to God and to gain the most from the resources for living He provides, you will need to make church attendance, Bible study, and prayer a regular part of your family's life. If it currently is not, take steps to make it so today. Begin by attending a church with active children's and adult activities. Help your kids find friends there, and attend children's activities regularly. Get involved in some Bible studies yourself, and if you need it, find a church that offers divorce recovery or a single parent ministry.

If you need help with any barriers that are keeping you from having a personal relationship to God and becoming a member of His family, find a spiritual advisor you can talk to. Don't let unanswered questions or past issues keep you from the most important relationship and life resource you could ever have! Do it for you—and for your kids!

APPENDIX A

FORMS

You will need the following forms as you conduct your Confident Kids unit:

- Facilitator Application   359
- Family Enrollment Form   361
- Parent Phone Interview   363
- Children's Evaluation Form   365
- Parent's Evaluation Form   367
- Postcards   369
- Affirmation Balloons   371
- Unit Certificate   373

Confident Kids Facilitator Application Form

Sponsoring Church/Organization: _____

Name: _____

Address: _____

City: _____ State: _____ Zip: _____

Home phone: (_____)_____

Work phone: (_____)_____

Are you a church member?_____ Regular attender?_____

For how long?_____

What other ministries have you been involved with, for how long, and what was your role?

Please write a brief statement describing your Christian experience, including your understanding of what it means to be a Christian and significant personal experiences that have shaped your faith:

Please tell us why you are interested in working in the Confident Kids program:

Briefly describe your childhood, including any significant issues directly relating to your work in the Confident Kids program (e.g., parental divorce, relationship to parents). Include any personal counseling or recovery process relating to your past that you have worked through as an adult:

Which areas of Confident Kids are you most interested in? Please rank in order, with 1 indicating the area of greatest interest:

_____ Facilitating a small group of children
       _____ Preschool _____ Grades 1–4 _____ Grades 5, 6

_____ Facilitating a parent group

_____ Drama team

_____ Leading music

_____ Organizing and preparing materials and supplies

_____ Other:

(continued)

Background Information

Have you at any time been accused, rightly or wrongly, of child abuse, sexual molestation or neglect? _____

If yes, please explain fully:

Have you ever been arrested/convicted for anything more serious than a traffic violation? _____

If yes, please explain fully:

Have you ever been treated for any nervous or mental illness? _____

If yes, please explain fully:

I, the undersigned, authorize the Confident Kids program administrators or its representatives to verify the information on this form. Confident Kids administrators may contact my references and appropriate government agencies as deemed necessary in order to verify my suitability as a Confident Kids facilitator. I verify that the above information is completely true.

Signature: _____ Date:_____

Personal References

Please attach the names, addresses, and phone numbers of three persons who are not related to you, and have known you for more than five years.

Confident Kids Family Enrollment Form

Sponsoring Church/Organization: _____

Unit Title:_____

Unit Dates:_____

Name: _____

Address:_____

City: _____ State: _____ Zip: _____

Home phone: (_____)_____

Work phone: (_____)_____

Your relationship to the child(ren) listed below: _____

List all children you would like to enroll (age four years through sixth grade), *and* younger children for child care:

_____Age/Grade: _____ Birthdate: _____

_____Age/Grade: _____ Birthdate: _____

_____Age/Grade: _____ Birthdate: _____

Child(ren)'s mailing address/phone if different from yours:

Address:_____

Phone: (_____) _____

If this is your first unit, please tell us why you want to place your child(ren) in the Confident Kids program:

If you are continuing in the program, please tell us any new information about your child(ren) or family that we should know:

Will you attend the Confident Kids parents group (meets at the same time as the kids' meeting)?

(continued)

Release Statement

Please be advised that the Confident Kids program is a support group program only. It is not therapy, nor a substitute for therapy in any way. Our leaders are volunteers, not trained counselors. (If at any time you feel your child is in need of professional counseling services, we will be happy to talk with you about a referral.) All information given by both parents and children will be held in strict confidence. Information shared by children in confidence will not be passed on to adults outside the leadership of the Confident Kids program, except as deemed necessary by the Confident Kids program administrators to ensure the health and safety of the child.

Having read the above and understanding it fully, I hereby authorize my child(ren) to be enrolled in the Confident Kids program.

Signature: _____ Date: _____

Confident Kids **Parent Phone Interview**

Interviewed By: _____

Parent's Name:_____

Address:_____

City: _____ State: _____ Zip: _____

Home phone: (_____)_____

Work phone: (_____)_____

Relationship to the child(ren) listed below: _____

Children in the family (list *all,* including children for child care and teen siblings):

_____Age/Grade: _____ Birthdate: _____

_____Age/Grade: _____ Birthdate: _____

_____Age/Grade: _____ Birthdate: _____

Child(ren)'s mailing address/phone if different from yours:

Address:_____

Phone: (____) _____

Why do you want to place your child(ren) in the Confident Kids program?

What, if any, behaviors are you seeing in your child(ren) that are of concern to you? (e.g., unexpressed feelings, aggressive behavior, withdrawal):

(continued)

When did these behaviors start? If recently, were they *un*characteristic of your child(ren) before that time?

What help, if any, are you getting (or have gotten in the past) for you and/or your child(ren)? (Include counseling, divorce recovery or other support groups, school counselors/teachers, professional diagnosis of ADHD or other learning disability, medications, etc.)

Are you currently married? _____

If yes, tell your spouse's name and briefly describe your relationship, particularly as it affects your kids (e.g., loving and close, strained, dad's never around, mom's an alcoholic):

If no, describe your ex-spouse's relationship to you and your children (e.g., friendly/hostile, sees or does not see the kids regularly):

Do you understand the participation expected of you (i.e., participation in a Confident Kids parents group or other requirements)? _____

Are you willing to participate in this way? _____

Other information:

Do you (the parent) have any questions you would like to ask of me (the interviewer)?

If you are enrolling the family into Confident Kids, give the parent all necessary details. If you believe they should be referred to other sources of help rather than or in addition to enrolling them (e.g., counseling for past sexual abuse, ADHD evaluation), do so at this time. In either case, be sure to end your conversation with words of encouragement and hope.

Confident Kids **Children's Evaluation Form**

Unit Title:_____

Unit Dates:_____

Your Name:_____

In what ways has Confident Kids helped you in this unit?

What things did you like best during this unit?

What didn't you like about this unit?

What things would you like to do that we didn't do?

How could we make Confident Kids better?

Confident Kids **Parent's Evaluation Form**

Unit Title:_____

Unit Dates:_____

Your Child(ren)'s Name(s): _____

Your Name: _____

In what ways has Confident Kids been helpful to your child(ren)?

To you?

What, if any, changes have you seen in your child?

In you?

How could Confident Kids be more helpful to you and/or your children?

Re-enrollment Request

_____ Yes, please enroll us in the next eight-week session

_____ No, we will not be returning for the next session.

_____ Please keep our name on file for a future eight-week unit.

Copy these CONFIDENT KIDS POSTCARDS onto
8.5" x 11" card stock.

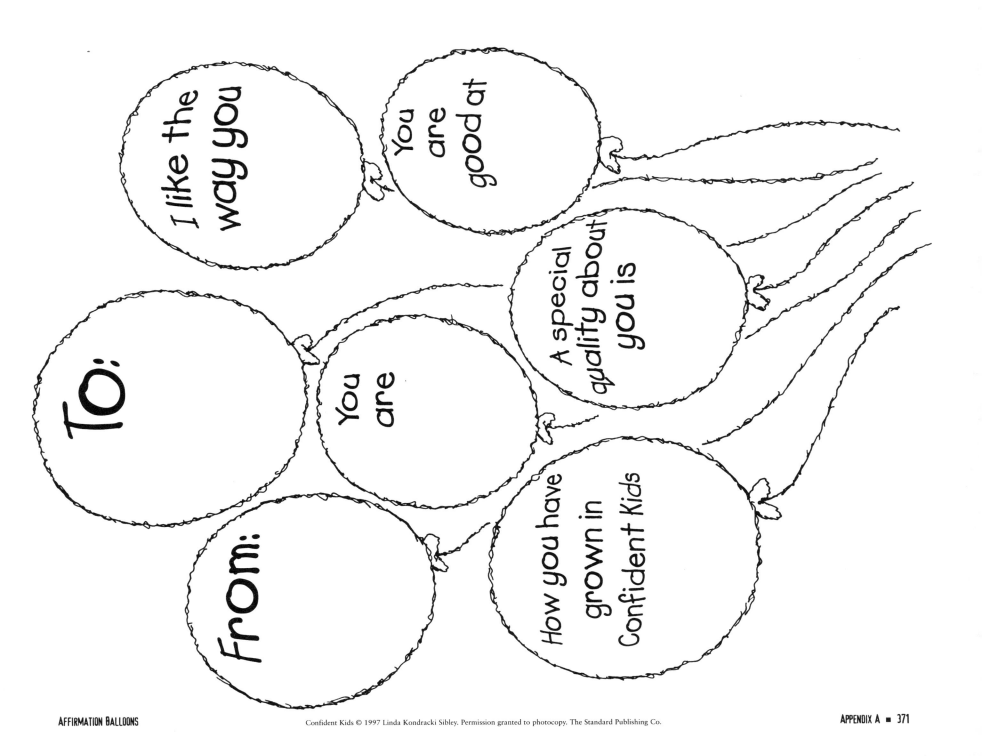

I like the way you

You are good at

A special quality about you is

To:

You are

How you have grown in Confident Kids

From:

This is to certify that

_____

has completed

Living in My Family

on this, the   day of

Congratulations!

Confident Kids

_____

Signed

APPENDIX B

RESOURCES

Use resources listed here to supplement the Confident Kids curriculum.

Games and Activities

Memory Verse Games

The Wave

This activity simulates "The Wave," which is popular at sporting events. Have the kids sit in a straight line or in a circle. Have one child quickly stand, raise his arms over his head, say the first word of the verse, and then sit down. Ask the next child to immediately stand and do the same thing. Continue around the group. After the kids have practiced with the memory verse poster, take the poster away and repeat the wave until the whole verse, reference included, has been said. Begin again if a mistake is made.

Popcorn Verse

In advance, write out the verse, including the reference, on slips of paper. Place one word on each slip and number the slips consecutively. Have the kids sit in a long line or in a circle, and randomly pass out the slips of paper. Keep going until all the slips are distributed, even if some kids get more than one. Then have the kids read the verse by standing, saying their word, and then sitting down again. They will know their turn by the number on their slip of paper. Keep this moving as quickly as possible, like popcorn popping!

Memory Verse Puzzles

Cut 3" x 5" cards in half and print one word of the verse on each card, including the reference. Scramble the cards and then work together to put them in the right order. Increase the fun by making two or more sets, dividing the kids into teams, and having the team race to see who can assemble the verse first.

For younger children, print the verse on a larger piece of paper and cut it into pieces, like a jigsaw puzzle. Let kids assemble the verse and then read it together.

One Word at a Time

Review the verse using the verse poster, then put the poster aside. Have the kids sit in a circle and ask one of them to say the first word of the verse. Ask the next person to say the second word, and so on around the circle. If someone makes a mistake, begin again. See how quickly the group can say the entire verse without a mistake.

Memory Verse Scramble

Print the verse on half sheets of paper, placing one or two words on each sheet. Scramble the sheets and distribute them randomly to the kids. Have the kids place themselves in order so the verse can be read. Add interest for the older kids by timing them the first time, and then seeing if they can improve their speed.

Regathering Activities

The purpose of the regathering time is to engage kids who have completed their small group work in a short activity until the other small groups finish. The Bible story follows the regathering activity, so decide if your kids need to settle down with quiet activities, or burn some energy with active activities. Choose activities that a few kids can begin and the other kids can easily participate in as they arrive. Ask the kids for suggestions, or try some of the ideas below.

Songs

This is a great time for music! You can teach the kids new songs or stick to their favorites from Sunday school. If one of your leaders plays guitar or another musical instrument, have that person play and sing quietly as the kids come together. Music can be very calming to high-stress kids.

Memory Verse Games

Use the regathering time to work on memorizing unit verses.

Games and Activities for Younger Children

Younger children like these games and activities:

- Simon Says
- Duck, Duck Goose
- Follow the Leader
- Simple bending and stretching exercises
- Telling Bible stories, using a flannel board

Games and Activities for Older Children

Older children enjoy these games and activities:

- Charades, using one word or a simple phrase
- Guessing a word or phrase one letter at a time (similar to Wheel or Fortune™)
- Artist, in which one child begins drawing a simple object and continues until someone guesses what it is

Past Gathering Activities

Some of the gathering activities suggested for the opening time of the meetings are simple enough to also be used for regathering (e.g., feelings charades, graffiti board, simple crafts). Choose ones your kids particularly enjoyed and repeat them.

GAMES FOR FAMILY NIGHT

Some of the favorite Family Night events are the games that all family members can play together. Any game that involves entire families will work. Below are a few that have been particularly enjoyable.

Wink 'Em

You will need an odd number of players for this game. Have half of the players sit in chairs arranged in a circle. Leave one chair empty. Have the rest of the players stand behind each chair, including the empty one. The person behind the empty chair is "it." The object is for the player standing behind the empty chair to call one of the others sitting around the circle to her chair by winking at that person. The player who was

winked at must then get up and move to the empty chair; however, the player standing behind him should try to stop him from moving to the empty chair by placing her hands on his shoulders. If the standing player can accomplish her goal before the seated person gets away, the seated person must remain in the chair and the person who is "it" must wink at someone else. If the person winked at gets away, his partner—whose chair is now empty—becomes the new "it."

Family Scavenger Hunt

This is a family cooperative game. Have the families sit together and be sure they have everything they brought with them, such as purses, wallets, or backpacks. Then call out a series of objects family members are likely to have brought and give each family who can produce that item a point. Be creative! Anticipate items you believe your participants will be carrying, but may be rare, such as:

- Red shoelaces
- A key ring with twelve or more keys
- A homework assignment
- Purple socks
- Hand lotion
- A watch with a cartoon character on it

You can also call out characteristics that only one family will win, such as the oldest person in the group, or the person with the longest hair, the most freckles, or widest smile.

Relay Races

Families enjoy all kinds of races. Examples include:

- Three-legged race
- Crab race
- Wheelbarrow race
- Passing an orange from chin to chin
- Pushing a peanut with their noses

Try to group families into teams so the families can stay together, but try to keep the teams even. If this is not possible, divide the group into even mixtures of adults and kids.

OTHER RESOURCES

Music

Music is an important part of the Confident Kids program. Music can provide high-stress families with two needed elements—a fun experience, and reinforcement of God's care and presence.

Music Tape. An audio cassette containing seven short songs written specifically for each Confident Kids curriculum topic is available. Side A of the tape contains music and words; side B is music only. You can order this resource from the Confident Kids office. (See order form on pages 383 and 385 for contact information.)

Children's Praise Tapes. Your local Christian bookstore will have many excellent children's music tapes. Look for ones that put the Psalms and other Scriptures to music.

Secular Tapes of Children's Classics. You can include some of the old favorites, such as the Disney music collections or the Wee Sing™ cassette series. Look in the children's sections of any bookstore, toy store, or discount store, such as Wal-Mart, Target, or Costco.

Badge-a-Minit™

Badge-a-Minit manufactures a high-quality badge maker, which will enable you to make your own 2" or 4" pin-back badges. These badges can be used in several ways:

- To make permanent name tags for group participants
- To have kids design their own badges and assemble them immediately
- To make attractive award ribbons for special events

Write or call for a complete catalogue, which lists various sizes of assembly machines, badge parts, and other ideas for using the badges. We recommend the Badge-a-Minit over every other brand of badge maker.

Badge-a-Minit
Box 800
LaSalle, IL 61301
800/223-4103
815/883-9696 (FAX)

"How Do You Feel Today?" Feelings Faces Materials

Use feelings faces posters, mugs, stickers, and buttons to help kids learn to identify and express their feelings. The Confident Kids office offers a variety of these items in several fun formats. Contact the office directly. (See pages 383 and 385 for more information.)

Training Resources

Seminars and Training Tapes. The Confident Kids organization offers a variety of training formats to equip you to administer a successful Confident Kids program and train your program leaders. One-, two-, or three-day training seminars are held throughout the country each year. Audio or video training tapes with six hours of training, a participant's workbook, and additional process activities for use in group settings are also available. Contact the Confident Kids office for more information.

Books. We recommend the following printed resources (listed by topic):

- **Family Systems**
  —Bradshaw, John. *Bradshaw On the Family*. Health Communication, Inc., Deerfield Beach, FL, 1988. This resource reads like a textbook, but has excellent material on how dysfunctional family behavior develops and is passed from generation to generation.
  —Satir, Virginia. *The New People Making*. Science and Behavior Books, Inc., Mountain View, CA, 1988 (revised). Satir was a pioneer in the field of family systems theory and family therapy. Her book is an excellent introduction to the complexities of family relationships, family

communication, and the development of self esteem in the family.

- **Legal Issues**
    - Hammar, Klipowicz, and Cobble. *Reducing the Risk of Child Sexual Abuse in Your Church.* **Church Law and Tax Report, 1993. (Order from Christian Ministry Resources, Mathews, NC, 704/841-8066; FAX 704/871-8039)** This is an excellent work that describes how to set policy, screen volunteers, train leaders, and keep appropriate records to reduce both the incidents of and your church or organization's legal liability for sexual abuse. A book, cassette tape, and workbook for church leaders are available.

- **Leading Parents Groups**
    - Curran, Dolores. *Working With Parents.* **American Guidance Service, Circle Pines, MN, 1989. (To order, call 800/328-2560.)** This excellent hand-book covers topics such as listening to identify parents' needs, conducting groups that empower parents, and dealing with problem parents.
    - Cynaumon, Dr. Greg. *Helping Single Parents With Troubled Kids.* **David C. Cook Publishers, Colorado Springs, CO, 1992.** This book is an excellent resource for helping parents and kids understand divorce and related issues. I highly recommend this one!

- **Resources for Parents**
    - Curran, Dolores. *Traits of a Healthy Family.* **Ballantine Books, New York, 1983.** This text gives an overview of what makes a family healthy, and describes how to begin developing these characteristics in families. (One of the handouts in the Confident Kids unit, *Living in My Family*, is taken from this book.)
    - Curran, Dolores. *Stress and the Healthy Family.* **Harper Collins, New York, 1989.** This book is a follow-up to her previous work, *Traits of a Healthy Family.*

- Faber, Adele and Elaine Mazlish. *How to Talk So Kids Will Listen, And Listen So Kids Will Talk.* **Avon Books, New York, 1980.** This small, practical book was written by two parent group leaders. It addresses common parenting problems and how to deal with them. There are easy-to-understand steps, and interesting cartoons illustrate the authors' points. This book is extremely helpful.
- Sanford, Doris and Graci Evans. **Heart to Heart Series. Multnomah Press, Portland, OR.** This series of books deals with the difficult issues children face, such as living with an alcoholic parent, sexual abuse, death, divorce, and more. Well written and illustrated, this book will teach adults how to help children deal with these issues. It clearly presents how God's love and presence help us through painful circumstances.
- Kondracki, Linda. *Going Through Changes Together.* **Fleming H. Revell (a division of Baker Book House), Grand Rapids, MI, 1996.** I wrote this book to help families grieve losses associated with major life changes. The text coordinates with the Confident Kids unit, *Growing Through Changes.* Each chapter is divided into three sections: Getting Ready (for parents), Read Along (for kids), and Family Activities.
- Sanford, Doris. *Helping Kids Through Tough Times.* **Standard Publishing, Cincinnati, OH, 1995.** This text contains reproducible "help" sheets adults can use to guide children through stressful times. Each sheet addresses a tough issue kids face and contains practical help and Scripture support to help kids understand and cope with that issue. Parents groups will find this resource particularly helpful.
- Smalley, Gary and John Trent. *The Blessing.* **Thomas Nelson Publishers, Nashville, TN, 1986.** Smalley and Trent give parents an easy-to-understand, five-part program to help them bond emotionally to their kids. The biblical practice of

parents blessing their children provides the foundation for this text.

—Wright, H. Norman. *Helping Your Kids Handle Stress.* Here's Life Publishers, San Bernardino, CA, 1989. Material on causes of stress in children, symptoms of childhood stress, and methods for dealing with specific stressors is included.

- **Secular Life Skills Resources You Should Know About**

All of the following publishers offer free catalogues.

—**American Guidance Service.** This company produces and publishes excellent educational materials in many areas, including self-esteem building, social skills development, chemical dependency prevention, and parenting. Materials are activity centered and include excellent teaching aids such as puppets, activity cards, and discussion starters.

AGS
Publisher's Building
P.O. Box 99
Circle Pines, MN 55014-1796
800/328-2560
800/247-5053 (Minnesota only)

—**Contemporary Health Series. Produced by ETR Associates.** This series of curriculum modules was developed for classroom use. The Into Adolescence series contains a number of modules for grades five through eight on subjects such as: communication, emotions, living in a family, enhancing self-esteem, and more.

Network Publications/ETR Associates
P.O. Box 1830
Santa Cruz, CA 95061-1830
408/438-4080 (order department)

—**STAGES: Education for Children in Transition. Developed by the Irvine, CA school district as a supplementary classroom curriculum for public schools.** STAGES teaches children how to cope with significant change in their lives, particularly divorce. Complete curriculum components for both elementary children and adolescents are included. Also available are student workbooks, a video, and parent materials. One-day training seminars are held in Irvine periodically.

Guidance Projects Office
5050 Barranca Parkway
Irvine, CA 92714
714/552-4882

—**Sunburst Communications.** Sunburst produces videos and filmstrips with accompanying study guides for classroom use on subjects such as self-esteem, skills for living, decision making, drug and sex education, and more. Materials are available for grades five through nine, and high schoolers. They are expensive, but well done.

Sunburst Communications
101 Castleton Street
Pleasantville, NY 10570-3498
800/431-1934

From the Directors of Confident Kids

Who Are We?

Confident Kids is more than the title of this curriculum series. Confident Kids is a national organization that has been promoting Christian support groups for children and families since 1989. From our headquarters on the central coast of California, we equip churches and other Christian organizations to effectively minister to today's hurting kids and struggling parents.

Confident Kids can be of service to you in one or more of the following areas:

- Getting support-group programs up and running in your community
- Providing in-depth training through videotapes and/or live seminars
- Supplying additional resources for ministry to families
- Putting you in touch with other churches or organizations using Confident Kids in your area

We're Here to Help!

Return the Confident Kids Response Form by letter or FAX or contact us by phone or e-mail. We are always happy to hear from you and welcome the chance to answer your questions. Let us be of service to you as you seek to bring God's love, hope, and healing to hurting kids in your church and community!

David L. Sibley
Executive Director
Linda Kondracki Sibley
Resource Development & Training
Confident Kids **Support Groups**
330 Stanton Street
Arroyo Grande, CA 93420
805/473-7945   FAX 805/473-7948
confidentkids@juno.com

Confident Kids

Response Form

I would like help and support with my ministry to hurting kids and their parents.

_____ Place me on your mailing list.

_____ Send me a product list of additional resources.

_____ Send me a schedule of training seminars.

Return form to:
Confident Kids **Support Groups**
330 Stanton Street
Arroyo Grande, CA 93420
805/473-7945; FAX 805/473-7948;
confidentkids@juno.com

Name _____

Church or organization _____

Address _____

City/State/Zip _____

Phone _____

This is my _____ *home address* _____ *organization address*

Describe your organization if other than a church.

Church or organization _____

Denominational affiliation _____

Size of church or organization _____

How do you plan to use Confident Kids? (for example, as part of a weekly church support-group program)

Confident Kids

Response Form

I would like help and support with my ministry to hurting kids and their parents.

_____ Place me on your mailing list.

_____ Send me a product list of additional resources.

_____ Send me a schedule of training seminars.

Return form to:
Confident Kids **Support Groups**
330 Stanton Street
Arroyo Grande, CA 93420
805/473-7945; FAX 805/473-7948;
confidentkids@juno.com

Name _____

Church or organization _____

Address _____

City/State/Zip _____

Phone _____

This is my _____ *home address* _____ *organization address*

Describe your organization if other than a church.

Church or organization _____

Denominational affiliation _____

Size of church or organization _____

How do you plan to use Confident Kids? (for example, as part of a weekly church support-group program)

Confident Kids

Response Form

I would like help and support with my ministry to hurting kids and their parents.

_____ Place me on your mailing list.

_____ Send me a product list of additional resources.

_____ Send me a schedule of training seminars.

Return form to:
Confident Kids **Support Groups**
330 Stanton Street
Arroyo Grande, CA 93420
805/473-7945; FAX 805/473-7948;
confidentkids@juno.com

Name _____

Church or organization _____

Address _____

City/State/Zip _____

Phone _____

This is my _____ *home address* _____ *organization address*

Describe your organization if other than a church.

Church or organization _____

Denominational affiliation _____

Size of church or organization _____

How do you plan to use Confident Kids? (for example, as part of a weekly church support-group program)